LEGENDARY LOCALS

OF

MERIDIAN

MISSISSIPPI

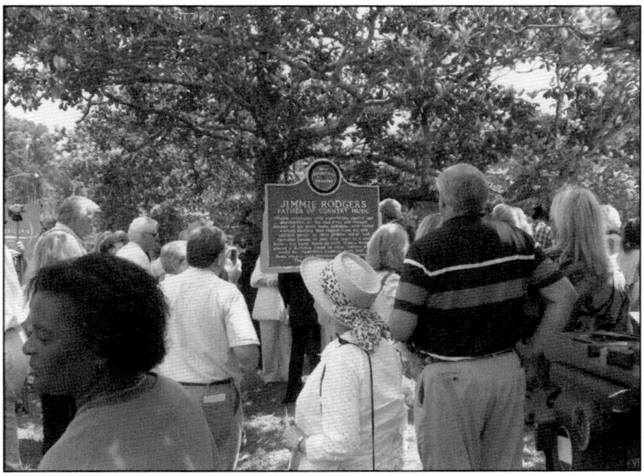

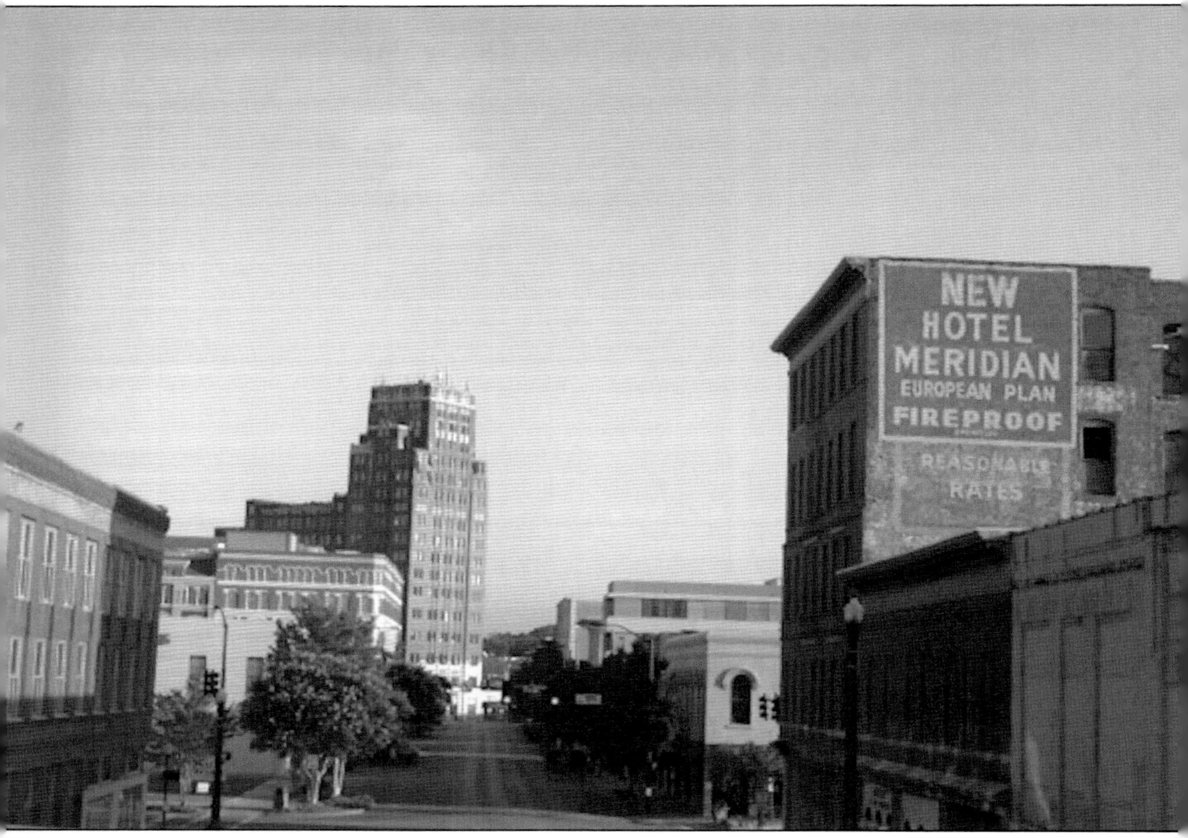

Meridian: A Place to Call Home
Meridian has been a place to call home for the people of Lauderdale County for over 150 years. Meridian's early growth was spurred by cotton and timber after the arrival of the railroad, and its merchants and entrepreneurs grew the city into the largest in the state from 1890 to 1930, a period of time considered Meridian's golden age. (Courtesy of June Davis Davidson.)

Page 1: Historical Marker
The first Country Music Trail marker is placed in honor of the father of country music, Jimmy Rodgers, at Oak Grove Cemetery in 2010. The burial location is also the site of the annual wreath-laying ceremony during the Jimmy Rodgers festivities. (Courtesy of Richelle Putnam.)

LEGENDARY LOCALS

OF

MERIDIAN

MISSISSIPPI

JUNE DAVIS DAVIDSON AND
RICHELLE PUTNAM

LEGENDARY LOCALS

ISBN 978-1-4671-0079-3

Legendary Locals is an imprint of Arcadia Publishing
Charleston, South Carolina

Printed in the United States of America

Library of Congress Control Number: 2013930900

For all general information, please contact Arcadia Publishing:
Telephone 843-853-2070
Fax 843-853-0044
E-mail sales@arcadiapublishing.com
For customer service and orders:
Toll-Free 1-888-313-2665

Visit us on the Internet at www.arcadiapublishing.com

Dedication

Without the cooperation of the people of Lauderdale County, this book would not be possible. We regret that we could not include all those who have given so much to our communities, city, and county.

On the Front Cover: Clockwise from bottom left:
Jimmy Rodgers, father of country music (Author's collection; see page 32), Camie Heard, educator (Courtesy of Debbie Fant; see page 83), Joe Norwood, supervisor (Author's collection; see page 117), Hartley Peavey, Peavey Sounds Systems and musical instruments (Courtesy of Hartley Peavey; see page 52), Chris Ethridge, musician (Courtesy of Eleanor Ethridge; see pages 20, 21).

On the Back Cover: From left to right:
Bill Gordon (Courtesy of Bill Gordon; see page 58), William Myles and Young People of Praise (Courtesy of Richelle Putnam; see page 26).

CONTENTS

ACKNOWLEDGMENTS

There are so many family members and friends whose patience, support, and love carried me through hours of photography and interviews and the many pages of writing and rewriting. Without the support of my husband, Tim, and my grandsons Lance and Brett, I would not have been given the hours after working hours to labor on this project. I look forward to paying their generosity forward.

My mother and my sister Robyn have always been behind every project I've taken on, even when they thought I was biting off more than I could chew. There were times I did, but they never said, "I told you so." Thank you for believing I could it.

Others in my family may have played a smaller role, but their support and love is no less appreciated. Thank you to Jeff, Kathy, Bill, Brittany, and Brianne. You are blessings to me.

Each of my children, John, Bailey, Eric and Erin, claims a piece of my heart. Without their love and support I simply wouldn't have had the heart to write anything. Thank you!

To my community, I thank you for making Meridian a place I love writing about and for allowing readers a glimpse of your hometown from the inside out.

—Richelle Putnam

My thanks to my husband, Bobby, for his love, support, patience, and the many meals he brought to my desk and said, "Eat."

To my daughters Susan and April, my sons Brent and Grey, and my grandchildren, thank you for your encouragement and believing that I am like the little engine that could, and to my dear friends who knew I would. To my brother Wayman Nason, with whom I share a close bond of sibling love.

In memory of my sister Marilyn, my mother Lillian Nason Davis, and my aunt Lena Nason Moody, who were much-loved members of my family that influenced my life.

—June Davis Davidson

INTRODUCTION

Choctaws villages including Alamucha (Old Town), Chunky-Chitto (Chunkey-Chitto), Toomsuba, Kewanee, and the Koosa (Koonsha) Towns existed throughout the future Lauderdale County in the Mississippi Territory. A village of 1,200 Choctaws, Koonsha extended for 2.5 miles along a bluff over little Lost Horse Creek—a favorite hiding place for horse thieves, according to legend.

When Meridian's first-known white settler, Richard McLemore, built his home of hewed logs on the road leading from Lauderdale to Enterprise, he most likely had no idea that in less than a century the 2,000 acres he received as a Federal Land Grant in 1831 would prosper into the largest city in Mississippi and be labeled as the Eastern city of the South.

Established December 23, 1833, Lauderdale County included an area of approximately 19 townships. It was named for Colonel James Lauderdale, a Tennessean of John Coffee's mounted brigade who was killed on December 23, 1814 in New Orleans during the night attack on the British.

In East Central Mississippi, Lauderdale County is surrounded by Kemper, Neshoba, Newton, and Clarke counties, and borders the Alabama line. The gentle climate and rich sedimentary soils supported the lifestyle of farming that lasted for over a century. Small streams trickle off the Chickasawhay and the Tombigbee Rivers, and other waterways like the Alamucha, Chunky, Tallahatta, Okatibbee, Chickasawhay, Sowashee, and Ponta Creeks. Artesian wells and minerals springs also feed the land. This diverse soil and water supply made the land very tempting to prospective settlers.

Settlers usually arrived in groups, herding in their cattle and sheep. Horse, mule, or oxen driven plows pulled up tree roots and rocks to loosen the soil for planting the fields. Families worked together to form a patron school near a spring or creek so daily water would be provided to the teacher and the students. Old Indian trails crisscrossing the county evolved into the county's first roads. Original surveys reveal a road running southwest to northeast between Lauderdale and Enterprise that is probably the early route of US Highway 11.

The Jewish culture flourished first in the town of Marion in as early as 1837. Records reveal that David Rosenbaum purchased land in Marion and joined Isaac Rosenbaum in the business partnership of D. & I. Rosenbaum. Also in the early years, the families of Isaac Rosenbaum and Leopold Rosenbaum lived in Marion.

In the 1800s, more and more forests were sacrificed to create more fields. Corn was the principal staple throughout the antebellum period and the long growing season allowed for two crops of corn to be planted each year, one in early March and the other in late May or June. Sawmills and gristmills rapidly grew in number. Farming life was difficult and sometimes overwhelming, but life for the slaves was arduous and in vain because they had no rights to their lives, their families, or the land they worked. Lauderdale County had some sizable plantations, including a 675-acre plantation in Suqualena, which included out-buildings, slave quarters and a cotton gin; a 4,000 acre plantation in Alamucha, and a 400 acre plantation in Chunkeyville. In the Sageville-Arundel area there was a 3,500-acre plantation that also enlisted Irish immigrants who had fled the Potato Famine. Other plantations were in the Toomsuba and the Pine Springs areas. Later, these slaves would fight for their freedom and their ancestors would fight for their Civil Rights.

The Mobile & Ohio (M&O) Railroad penetrated Lauderdale County in the mid-1850s. Rumor had it that Southern Railroad would connect with the M&O at the Town of Enterprise in Clarke County. However, Enterprise turned down Southern Railroad. That decision forever changed Meridian's history.

The City of Meridian incorporated on February 10, 1860. That same year, with the election of President Abraham Lincoln, South Carolina seceded from the Union. Immediately Mississippi followed suit. Meridian was still a village when the first shot of the Civil War was fired on April 12, 1861 at 4:30 a.m. On May 29, 1861, the long anticipated Southern Railway locomotive, Mazeppa, pulled into the Meridian station with confederate soldiers on board.

What followed secession was the war above all wars. Sherman's total war mentality burned Meridian to the ground, but Meridian survived and prospered as a multi-cultured city. It became the county seat in 1870 and one of the South's major railroad towns and the state's largest yellow pine and hardwood market.

Immigrant families contributed greatly to the early economic success of Meridian, constructing many of the downtown buildings that remain standing today. Meridian enjoyed a Golden Era from the late 1800s through the early 1900s. Much of the land in the south fell under the control of speculators who profited from harvesting timber. Northern investors contributed to the expansion of the railroad in Meridian and Lauderdale County, but, after the land was stripped, speculators and investors moved out leaving Meridian to face the Great Depression. Still, Meridian persevered and survived, as did many of its businesses.

Alex Loeb had opened his fine men's clothing store in 1887 and today it remains a family owned operation through his grandson Robert Loeb. Weidmann's Restaurant opened its doors in 1870 and is still known throughout the country for its black-bottom and lemon icebox pies. George Wilberforce Soulé moved his Morton and Shubuta operations to Meridian in 1879. Much of the original machinery still works and runs by steam in the original building. To celebrate its history, the Soulé Live Steam Festival occurs every November.

Each year, the Jimmie Rodgers Festival celebrates the father of County Music, Jimmie Charles Rodgers, bringing in nationally acclaimed performers, but never forgetting to highlight its homegrown talent.

Meridian could boast of its many celebrities, like Sela Ward, Alvin Childress, Paul Davis, and Chris Ethridge or its numerous successful entrepreneurs, like Hartley Peavey, Henry Burns, and Tommy Dulaney. As you turn these pages, you'll see and understand that Meridian is first and foremost a hometown, a place for people to settle in and settle down, a place where heroes become heroes simply because they care.

CHAPTER ONE

Arts and Entertainment

As early as the 1800s, flutists, violinists, guitarists, and piano players were regular attractions around the town square, which sometimes included the Riley family performing on violin, cello and guitar. By the late nineteenth century, Meridian had the one of the South's largest conservatories of music. Music also became a tool to help raise money for the war effort. Perhaps, however, the depth of the musical roots in Lauderdale County was not realized until "The Father of Country Music," Jimmie Charles Rodgers transformed American music in the early 30s.

But arts and entertainment in Meridian hasn't only been about music. In the early years, traveling artists made Meridian a temporary residence, staying in the rustic rooms above saddle shops or barns, while they painted. Meridian Little Theatre became Mississippi's largest community theatre and one of the South's oldest subscription-based community theatres. One of Meridian's own, Lloyd Royal became the first producer to make full-length films in Mississippi.

It's no surprise that the Mississippi Legislature chose Meridian to be home to the Mississippi Arts and Entertainment Center and to receive the State's first entertainment district designation. From Jimmie Rodgers to Jimmy Ruffin, from Wilbur Higby and Alvin Childress to Sela Ward, the number of famous people whose roots dig into Lauderdale County soil is incredible. However, it's the local artists daily sharing their talents with their community that make Meridian a hometown you never want to leave.

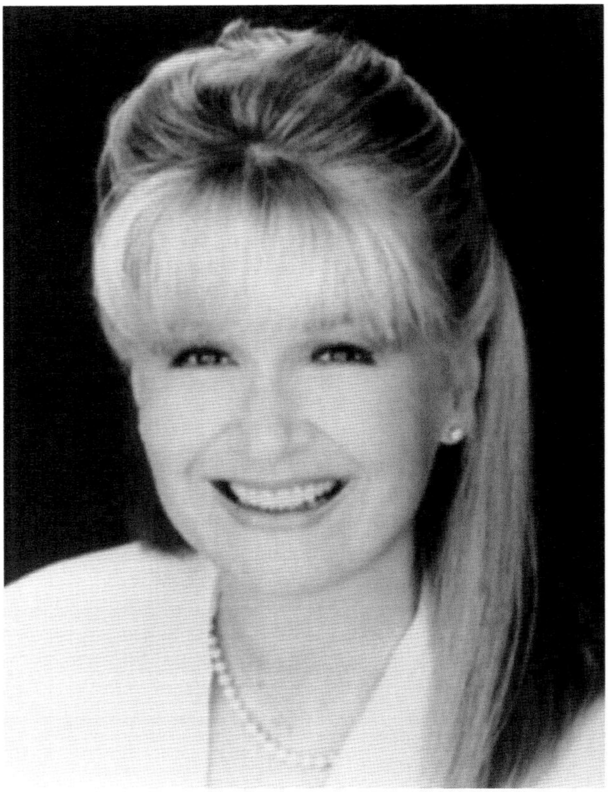

Southern Belle

Internationally acclaimed actress-writer-author-director Diane Ladd, winner of some 37 awards including the British Academy Award, is a three-time Oscar nominee and a three-time Emmy nominee. She is the daughter of Mississippi-born veterinarian Preston Paul (Lanier) Ladner and Bernadette Anderson Ladner from Mobile, Alabama. The Ladners were visiting family in Laurel on Thanksgiving Day, November 29, 1942, when Rose Diane Ladner (Diane Ladd) was born. Within a few weeks after her birth, they returned to their home in Meridian with their newborn infant. Diane grew up in Meridian and attended St. Joseph school and Meridian High School. She graduated at age 16.

Ladd made her theatrical debut in New York City at age 17 in her cousin Tennessee Williams's hit Off-Broadway revival *Orpheus Descending*. Diane was also a dancer at New York's famous Copacabana. After numerous stints as a stand-up comedian and singer, she appeared in summer stock and other productions.

Ladd portrayed Kitty Styles on the CBS soap opera *The Secret Storm* from 1971 to 1972. She won her first Oscar nomination for the role of Flo in Martin Scorsese's *Alice Doesn't Live Here Anymore* and played singer/songwriter waitress Belle on the sitcom *Alice*, for which she won a Golden Globe Award.

She and her daughter, actress Laura Dern, made show business history as the first mother-daughter tandem to both receive Oscar nominations for the same film in the same year, *Rambling Rose*. This film was chosen by the late Princess Diana as one of her all-time favorites and she had a royal premiere in London and a party in their honor.

Ladd also costarred with Albert Finney in London's hit miniseries *Cold Lazarus* and in Stephen King's miniseries *Kingdom Hospital*. She was recently seen the HBO series *Enlightened*. She has appeared in more than 300 television and feature films, including David Lynch's *Wild at Heart* (Cannes Film Festival Award winner and Oscar nomination), *Cemetery Club* with Olympia Dukakis, and *World's Fastest Indian* with Anthony Hopkins, among many others. She wrote and directed as well as costarred in the film *Mrs. Munck*, for which she received three Best Director Awards. She has enjoyed success on Broadway and authored two books: a spiritual healing and wellness book called *Spiraling through the School of Life* and a book of short stories called *A Bad Afternoon for a Piece of Cake*, which Rex Reed compared to the work of such great writers as Truman Capote, Eudora Welty, Flannery O'Connor, Carson McCullers, and Tennessee Williams. Reed wrote, "Ladd has the same gift they do—you can't just learn it in writing class."

After the tragic accidental death of her 18-month-old daughter Diane Elizabeth Dern, Diane was blessed with another daughter, Laura Elizabeth Dern, on February 10, 1967. However, her marriage to actor Bruce Dern ended in divorce in 1969. Her second marriage to William A. Shea Jr. ended in 1976. She has been happily married since 1999 to Robert Charles Hunter. Together they share 10 grandchildren. (Courtesy of Diane Ladd.)

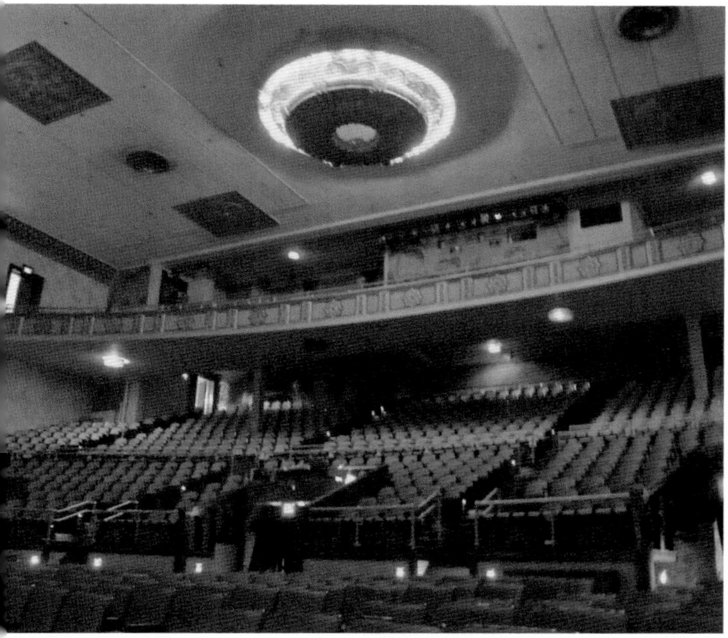

The Met

Opera tenor John Alexander was born in Meridian on October 21, 1923. He studied in New York City and made his debut with the Philadelphia Opera Company in 1957 as Lieutenant Pinkerton in *Madama Butterfly*. Alexander's distinguished 26-year career with the Metropolitan Opera began in 1961. He and his wife, Sue, lived in Cincinnati, Ohio. On December 8, 1990, Alexander attended a Temple Theater fundraiser and collapsed. He was rushed to Anderson Regional Medical Center and died. (Courtesy of Richelle Putnam.)

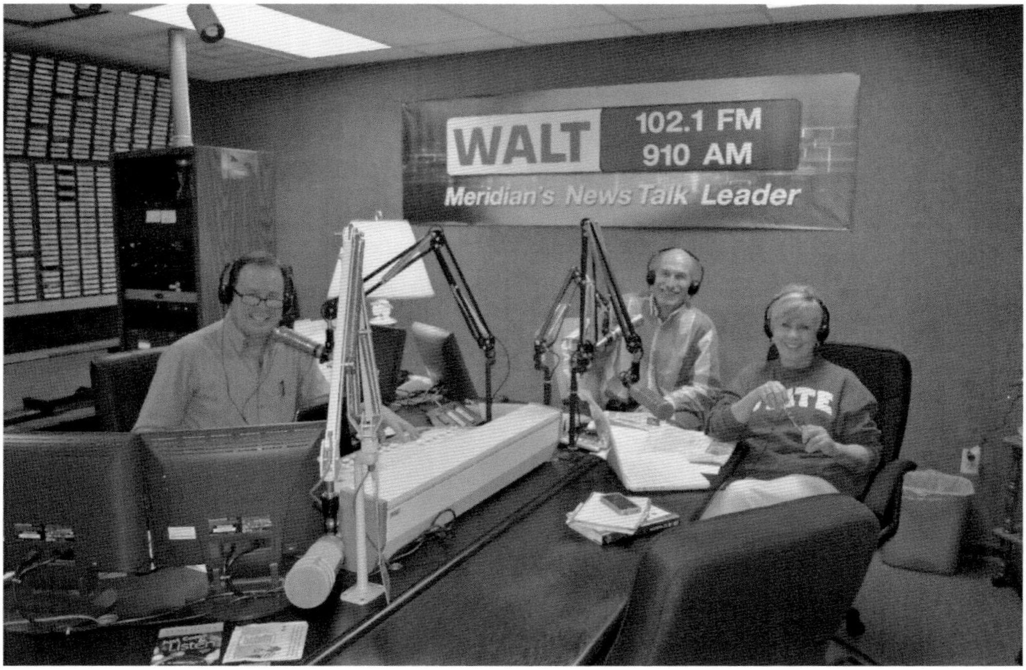

Morning Chatter

WALT's *Mornings in Meridian* airs each weekday from 6:00 a.m. to 9:00 a.m. The talk show is hosted by Roger Burk and Billy Jack Ethridge. On Friday mornings, Sidney Covington pops through the door and adds her brand of humor to the show. The team often interviews guests and highlights important local and national issues. Callers participate by voicing personal opinions. Burk is pictured on the left with Ethridge and Sidney Covington. (Courtesy of June Davis Davidson.)

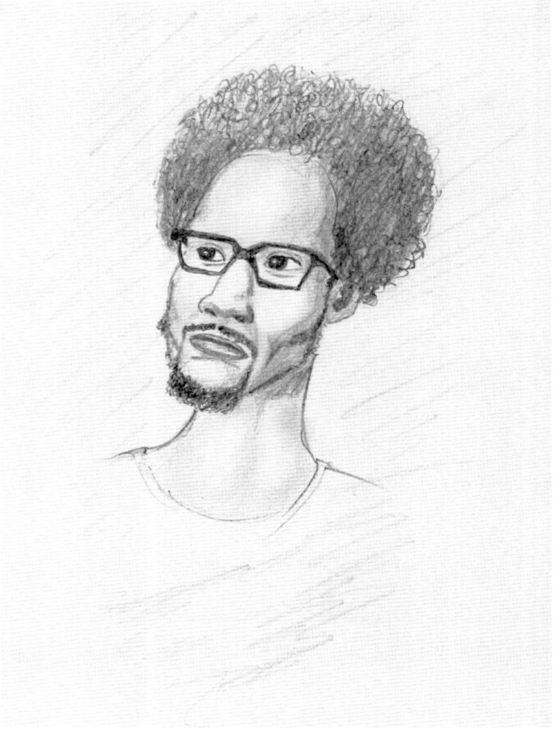

Temptation

Eli Ruffin, a black minister, was the father of David, Jimmy, Quincy, and Rita Mae. David's mother, Ophelia Davis Ruffin, died within a few months of his birth. David attended New Salem Church on the Whynot–Alamucha Road, where as a youth, he became seeped in black spiritual music. If you listen closely, you might hear the lingering echo of his tenor voice rise over Whynot. (Illustration courtesy of John Aycock.)

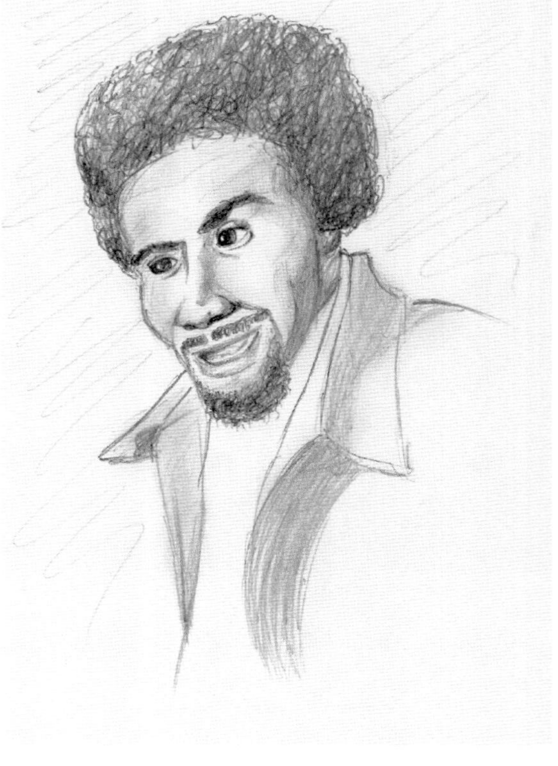

A Rise to Stardom

Brothers David and Jimmy Ruffin moved to Chicago and joined the vocal group The Temptations. David's success came when he performed as the group's lead singer. His first hit "My Girl," recorded in 1963, hit No. 1 on the pop chart. The brothers withdrew from The Temptations and recorded a spiritual, "My Brother's Keeper." In 1989, David was inducted into the Rock and Roll Hall of Fame. In 2009, he was named one of the top 100 vocalists by *Rolling Stone* magazine. (Illustration courtesy of John Aycock.)

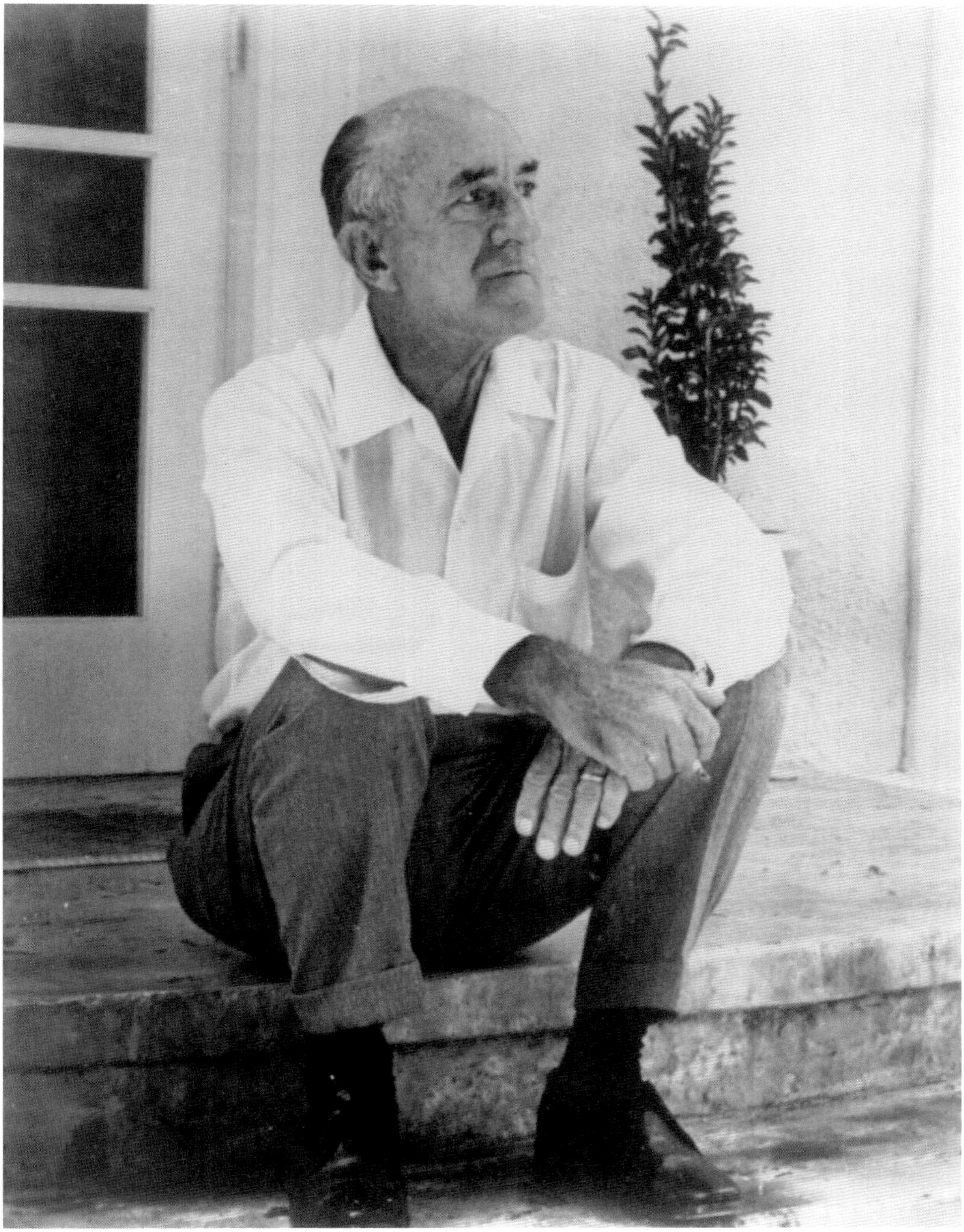

Imagination Time

World War II Marine veteran Edwin Phillips Granberry is most famous for his 30-year career as scriptwriter for Buzz Sawyer, a nationally syndicated comic strip illustrated by Roy Crane. Granberry, born in Meridian on April 18, 1897, is the winner of the 1932 O. Henry Award for his short story "A Trip to Czardis." Granberry penned three novels: *Ancient Hunger*, *The Earl King*, and *Strangers and Lovers*, published in the late 1920s and 1930. (Courtesy of the University of Mississippi Archives and Special Collections.)

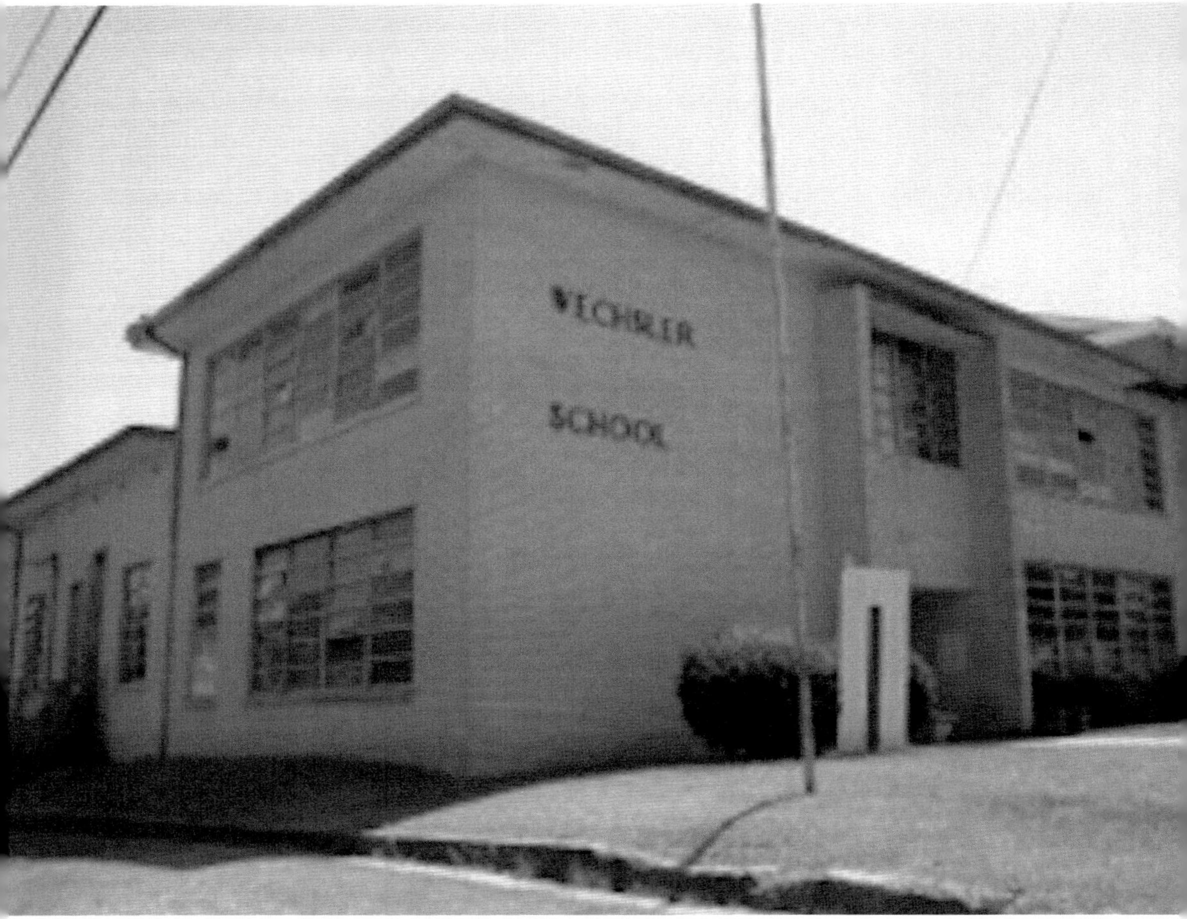

The Actor
Alvin Childress would have attended Meridian's Wechsler School, which is listed in the National Register of Historic Places, was built in 1894 for Negro children on Thirtieth Avenue.

Childress was born on September 10, 1907. He was the son of John L. and Beatrice Stokes Childress of Meridian. The 1923 city directory located the Childress home at 322 Twenty-eighth Avenue. Alvin graduated in 1931 with a bachelor of arts degree before moving to Harlem, New York. He was an actor with the Lafayette Players before he was employed as writer and drama coach at Columbia University as part of Roosevelt's Works Progress Administration. He became well known for his portrayal of Amos Jones in the1951 *Amos 'n' Andy* television series that aired until 1953 on CBS. Childress married Alice Herndon in New York. The couple had one child, Jean Rosa, born in 1936. Parkinson's disease and diabetes plagued Childress later in life. He died at the age of 79 in Englewood, California. (Courtesy of June Davis Davidson.)

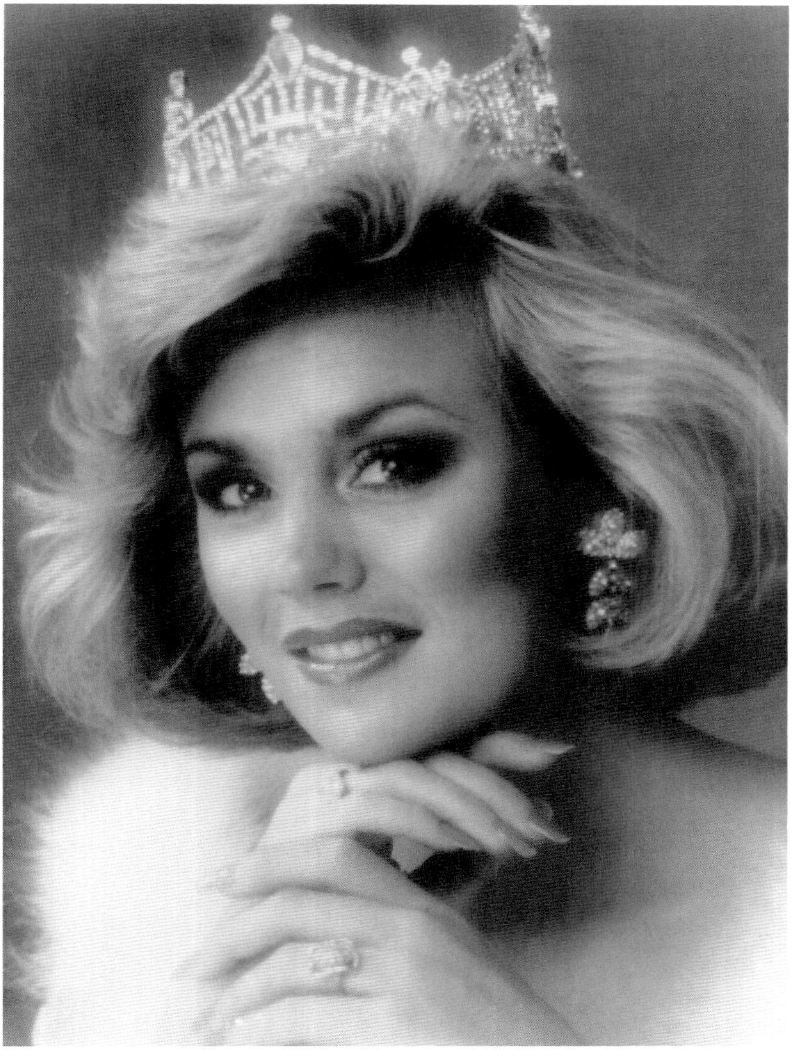

A Crowning Moment

The climb to the top may be difficult, but Meridian native Susan Akin enjoyed each step of her journey. The apex represented hard work and dedication to the dream of becoming Miss America. Susan is the daughter of Earl Akin and Dorothy Little. Dorothy, an entrepreneur in her own right, entered Susan in state and local beauty pageants, the training ground for future Miss Americas.

In 1986, when Miss America master of ceremonies Gary Collins introduced Miss Mississippi, Susan Akin, she stepped onto the stage and belted out an Italian love song, "You're My World," a ballad that brought rounds of applause from a packed audience.

As a contestant finalist, she wore a white, sleeveless beaded and tasseled form-fitting gown with fur-trimmed shoulders that dropped to a deep V in the back.

When Gary Collins announced Susan Akin as the winner of the 1986 Miss America Pageant, he sang "There she is, Miss America." The 5'9" blue-eyed blonde held her head high and waved as she walked down the aisle of dreams that former beauty queens had walked in Atlantic City since 1921.

Although Susan had worn many crowns during her pageant days, none wore as well as the Miss America crown. (Courtesy of Richelle Putnam.)

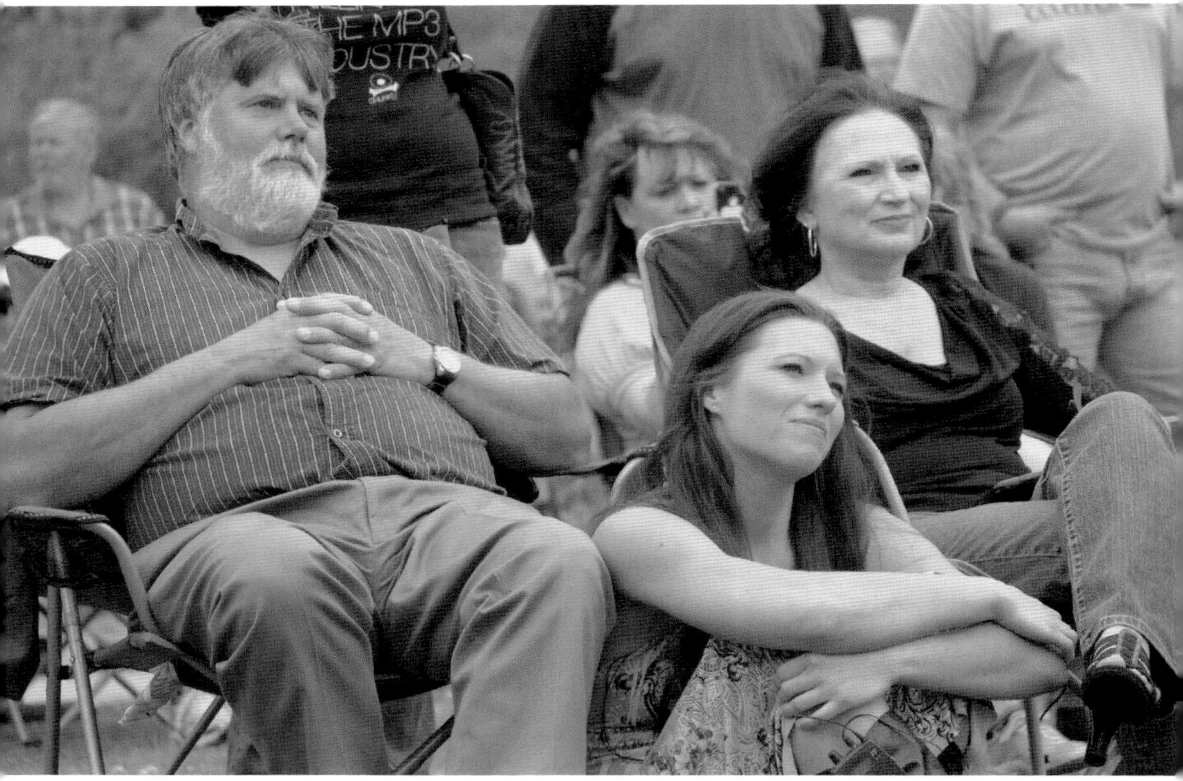

Miracle Child

"Amy's seizures started when she was 15 with no warning," said Terry Lott, Amy's mother. "The seizures were grand mal, and overwhelming. She would lose consciousness and have a seizure, then regain consciousness with extreme body cramps." It was very rare for her not to have an episode a day. The Lotts took Amy all over the country trying to get help, but the doctors could not diagnose her. Seizure medications did not help. The Lott family welcomes Princess, Amy's seizure dog, at the latter part of Amy's senior year in high school year. "It was quite a sight to see that big German shepherd walking down the halls of Meridian High," said Terry. "I never realized at the time that it would take 15 years for her to be healed. But God has his own plan."

Princess gave Amy the opportunity to gain some independence, and she was able to go to the University of Southern Mississippi. "That was very hard on me, but it was very important to Amy," said Terry. Princess sensed the seizures coming on, and she never left Amy's side. "Princess had a sense of humor too," said Terry. She "literally changed all of our lives for the better." When Princess got old, she lost the use of her hind legs, but even in that state she tried to take care of Amy. "I don't think most people understand the bond between a service dog and its owner. When Princess passed on, it was such a loss to Amy. . . . She was her companion, her friend, her liberator. And the grief was almost unbearable," said Terry.

Seeing Amy on stage singing and playing the many instruments she can play, hearing the songs she has written, gives Terry such joy. "The music that she has written comes from her life experiences." Amy plays piano, clarinet, flute, harmonica, and accordion. "If someone knows her life story, they can understand the depth of her songwriting." After Princess passed away, Amy had her cremated so that her faithful companion would remain always with Amy. (Courtesy of Amy Lott.)

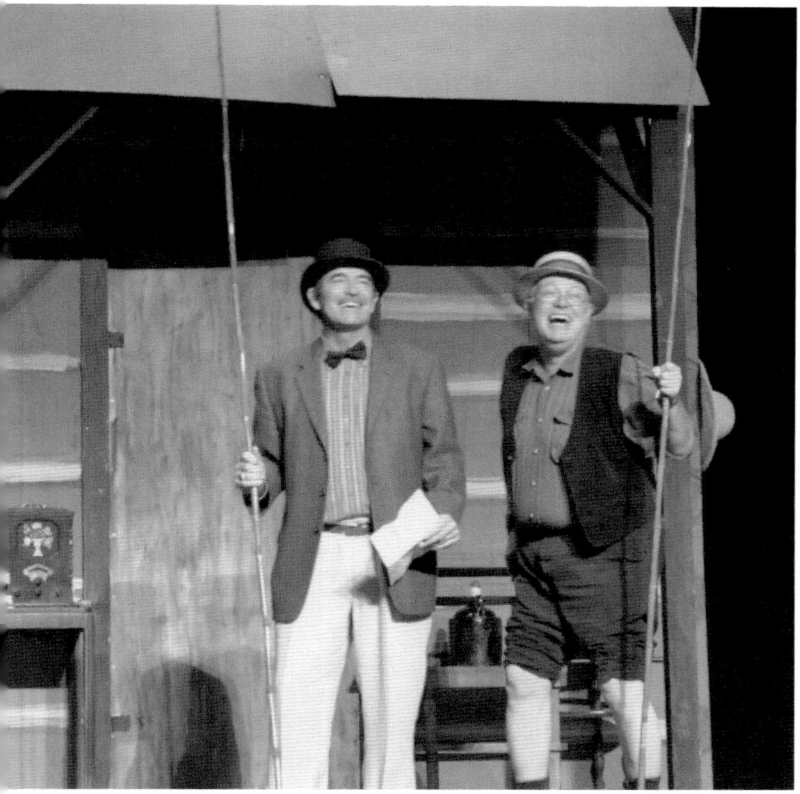

Acting Out
Earl Aycock Jr. and Steve Nabors perform *Boys of Autumn*, the winner of the 2013 Mississippi Theatre Association's Annual State Community Theatre Play Festival, which was a Company of Angels production. Earl was selected to the Festival All-Star Cast, and Steve won the award for the Best Actor in the festival. (Author's collection.)

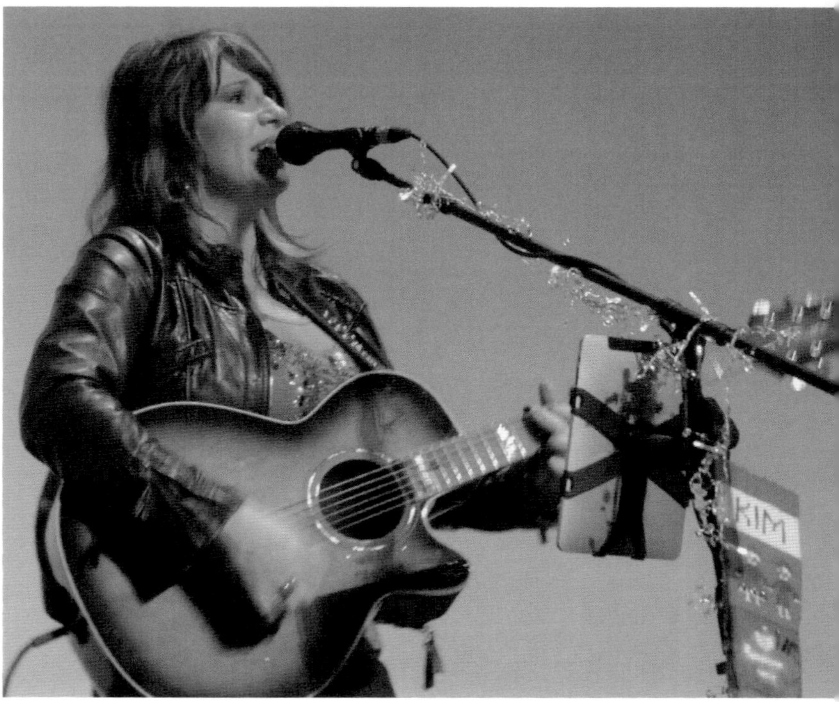

Sing Praises
Kim Hill's first album, "Brave Heart," earned a Grammy nomination for Best Rock/Contemporary Gospel Album. She received Dove Award nominations for her first two Christian market releases. In this photo, Kim returns to the historic Temple Theatre to share music with her hometown and to share a few stories from her life and the challenges she has faced in motherhood, career, marriage and the social and cultural pressures in being all things to all people. (Author's collection.)

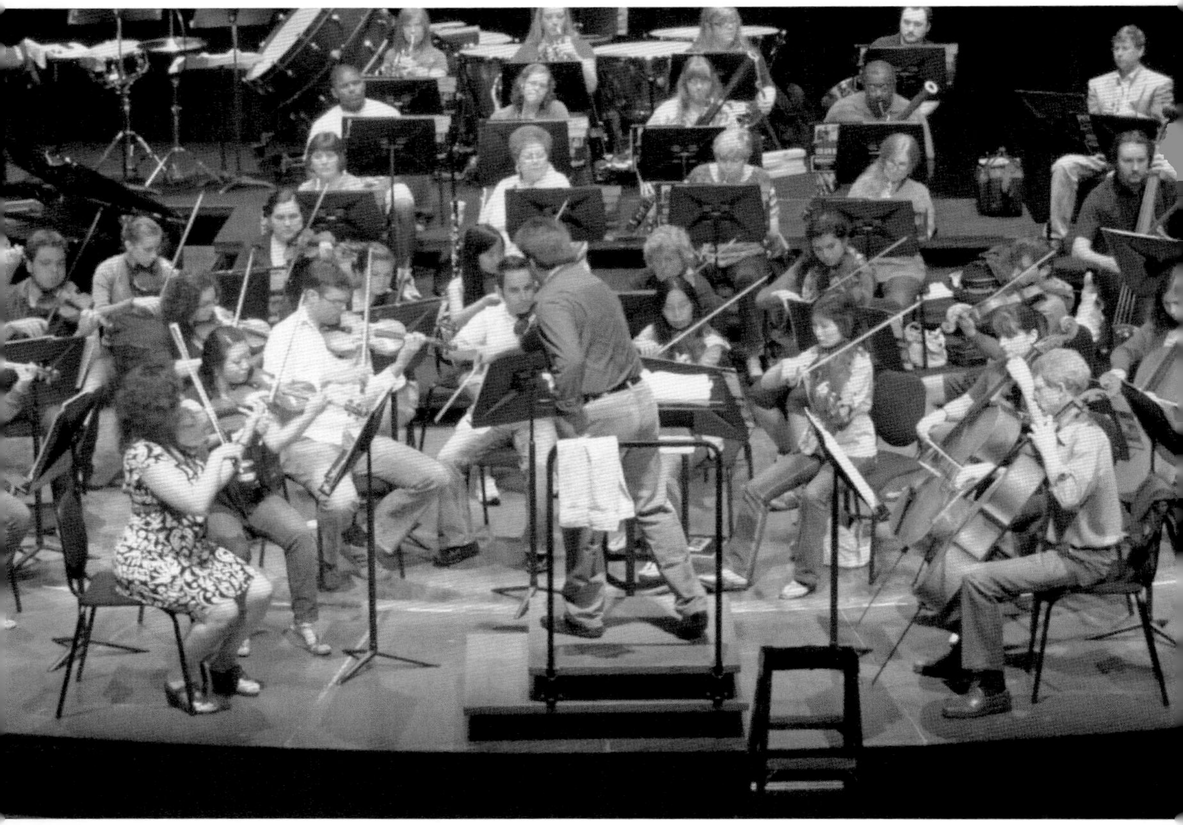

Meridian Symphony Orchestra
In 1961, a small group of Meridian citizens met to discuss forming a chamber music group. Dorothy Lerner, a founding member of the orchestra, approached Vernon Raines, then a professor at Livingston State College in Alabama, about leading the newly formed orchestra as its music director and conductor. Vernon Raines became Meridian Symphony Orchestra's first conductor and remained in the role for 30 years. The year 2011 marked MSO's 50th anniversary. (Courtesy of Meridian Symphony Orchestra.)

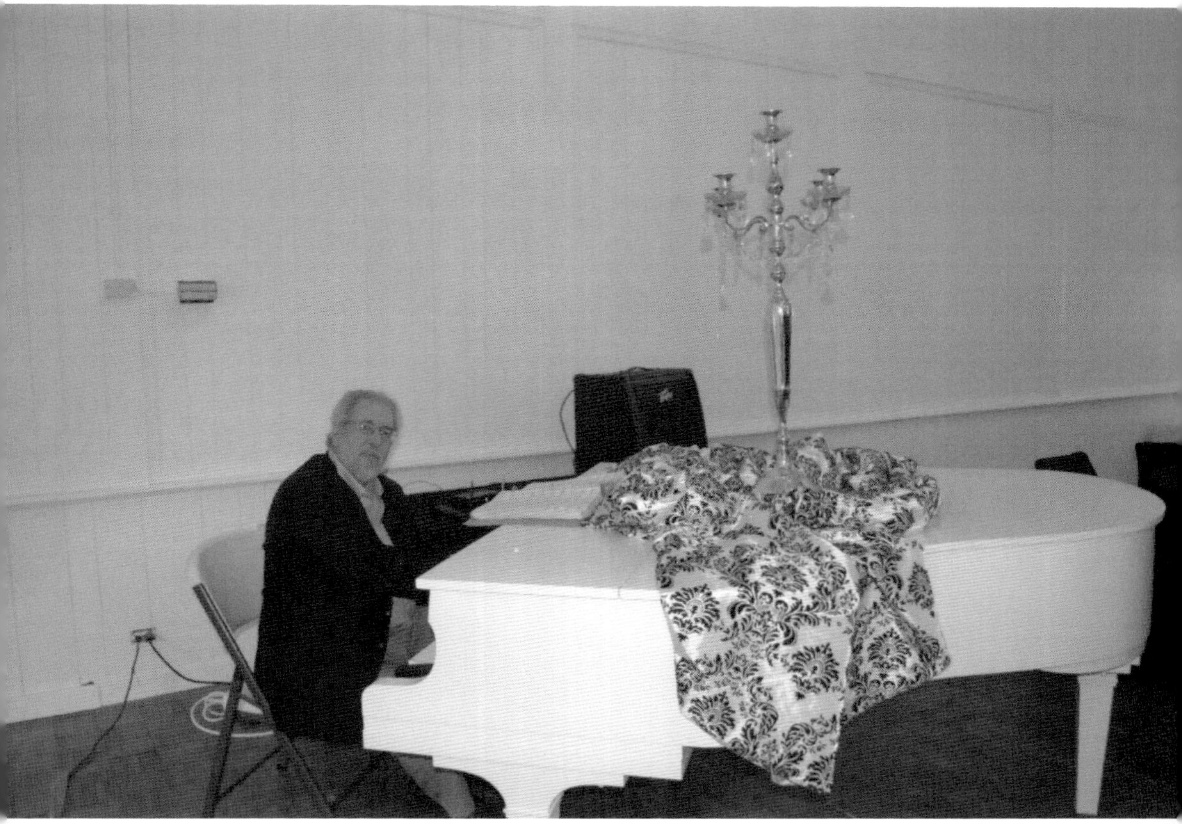

I Hear a Symphony
Professor of music at Meridian Community College (MCC), Carey's MCC bands have played for the world's fair, President Bush's arrival in Meridian, and at Carnegie Hall in New York. For the 50th anniversary of Meridian Symphony (MSO) in 2011, the orchestra performed Carey's original symphony, *Elements*, a symphonic portrait of four movements: air, water, fire and earth. Other compositions include *Meridian 150*, a musical montage celebrating the Queen City's 150th birthday. (Courtesy of Meridian Symphony Orchestra.)

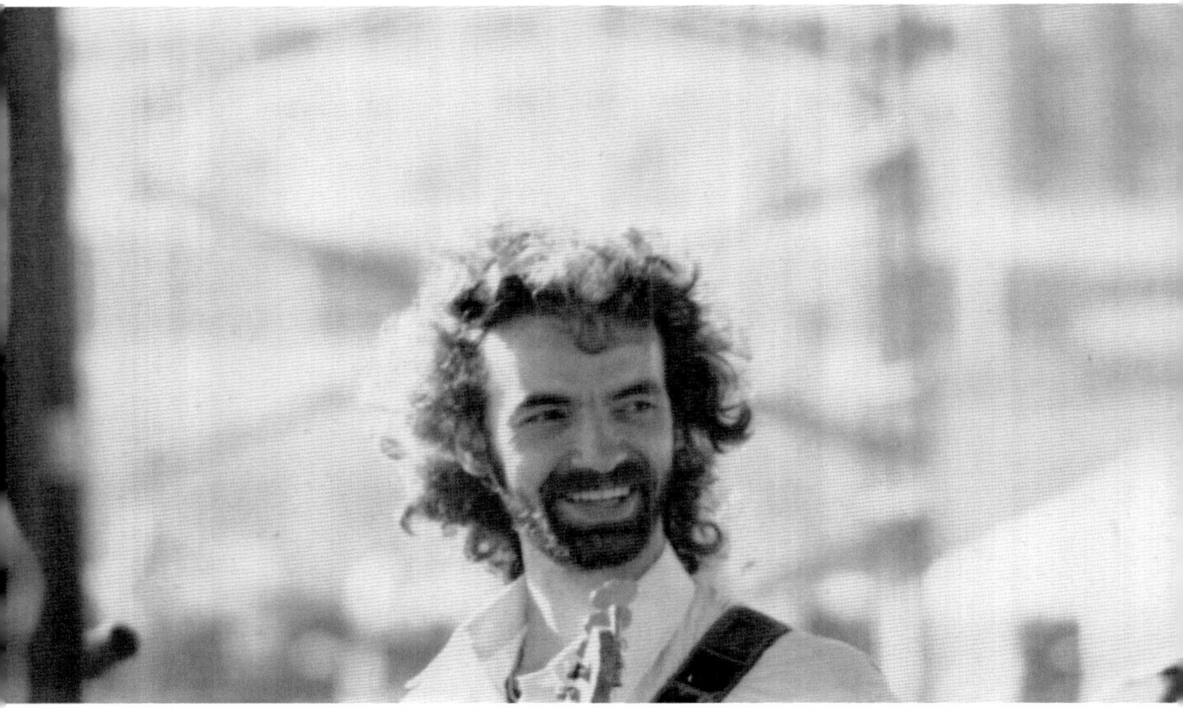

Songwriter and Musician
Chris Ethridge's first instrument was a little red toy guitar. "He would sit on the steps and pick and sing," said his mother, Eleanor Ethridge. "He loved to listen to the radio and would sit with his little toy guitar and sing and play along to songs like "My Hair's Still Curly and My Eyes Are Still Blue." Chris had his favorite radio shows and knew what time to listen to them.

But Chris Ethridge decided on the bass rather than the guitar and made history doing so. His band was playing on the Mississippi Gulf Coast when he met Johnny Rivers, who asked Chris to go back to California with him. "He got to know people at the recording studio and everything and then people started hiring him to play sessions in the studio," said brother Joey Ethridge. He ended up being the top bass recording player for about 8 to 10 years. He met Gram Parsons in that period of time. Three of Gram's greatest songs were cowritten by Chris: "Hot Burrito No. 1," "Hot Burrito No. 2," and "She." Ethridge also spent about eight years in Willie Nelson's touring band, a gig during which he recorded one of Nelson's most famous anthems, "Whiskey River."

"My dad bought him a bass," said Joey, "and he used that bass on all his early sessions with Johnny Rivers and all the recording sessions he did back in the 1970s. One time, the airline lost the bass. When they asked Chris how much it would be to replace it he said it was priceless. That bass has never been found. Though Chris Ethridge played with many musical legends, he played on many stages in Meridian with any and everyone. He died from complications due to pancreatic cancer on April 23, 2012. (Courtesy of Eleanor Ethridge.)

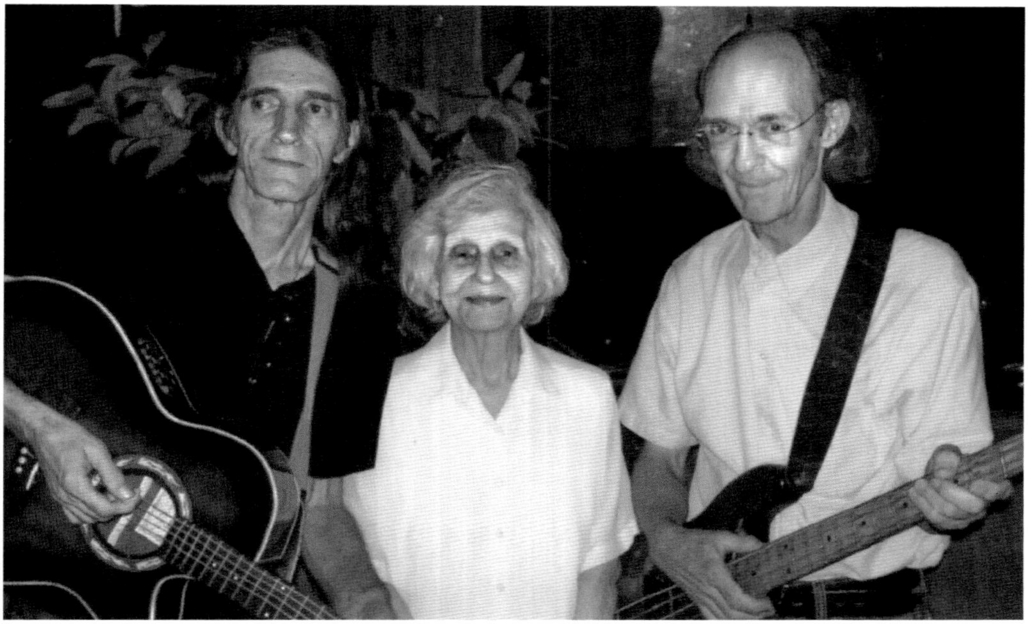

All in the Family
Eleanor and John Ethridge married on June 25, 1945, in Meridian. Their oldest son, renowned musician Chris Ethridge, was born in 1947. Eleanor's other two sons, Tommy (born in 1949) and Joey (born in 1952), are both acclaimed musicians. "Music was just a part of the family," she said. Son Joey accompanied Chris when Chris went on tour with Booker T. While Booker T opened for Santana, Joey hung out with Carlos Santana backstage. (Courtesy of Eleanor Ethridge.)

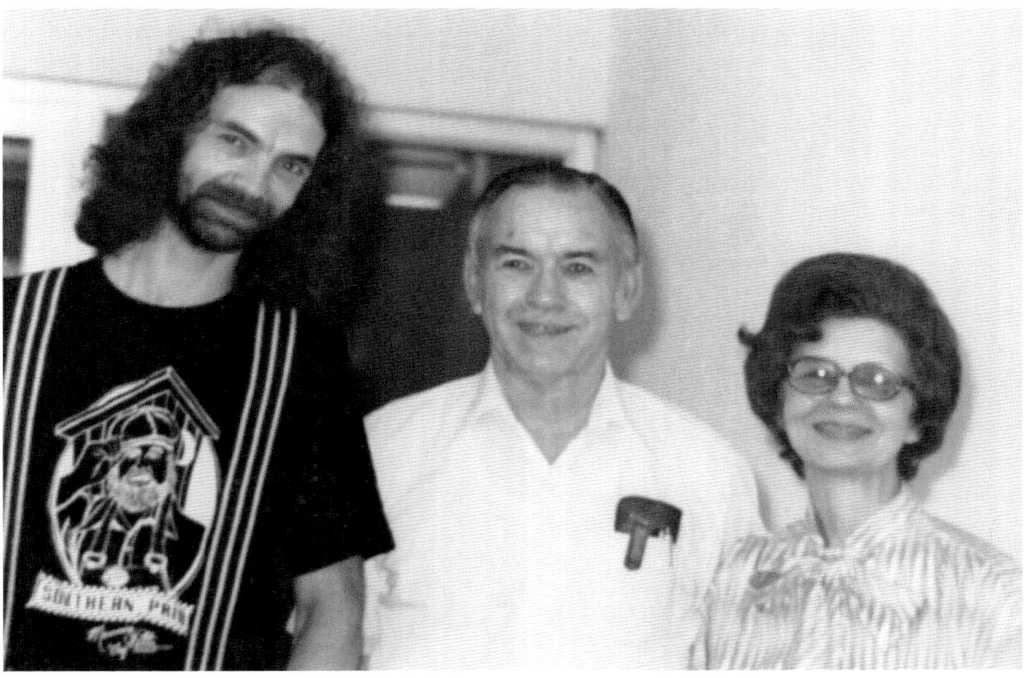

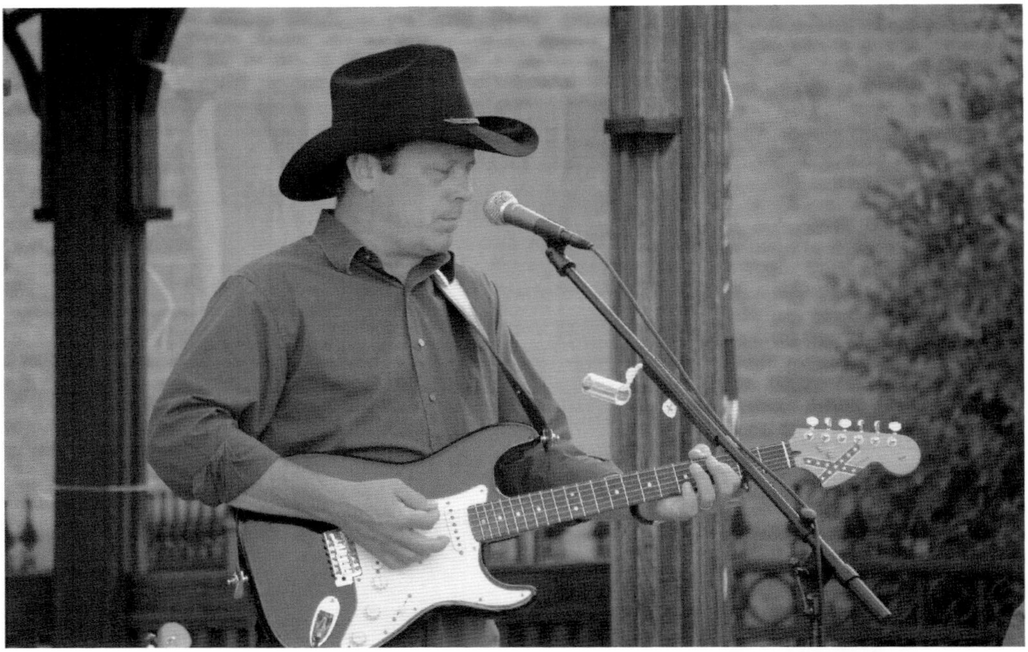

Local Tomcat

Scott McQuaig wrote his own music and performed for years before finally recording them. Meridian native Chris Ethridge, known for his work with The Flying Burrito Brothers, Willie Nelson, Ry Cooder, and countless others, encouraged Scott to share his songwriting. Scott teamed up with his band, The Tomcats, and Point Recording owner Clay Barnes, former guitarist for Steve Forbert, to record his latest album, *I'm Still Falling*. The Tomcats perform weekly at the Echo Lounge, one of Mississippi's oldest honky-tonks, soon to celebrate its 25th anniversary. (Author's collection.)

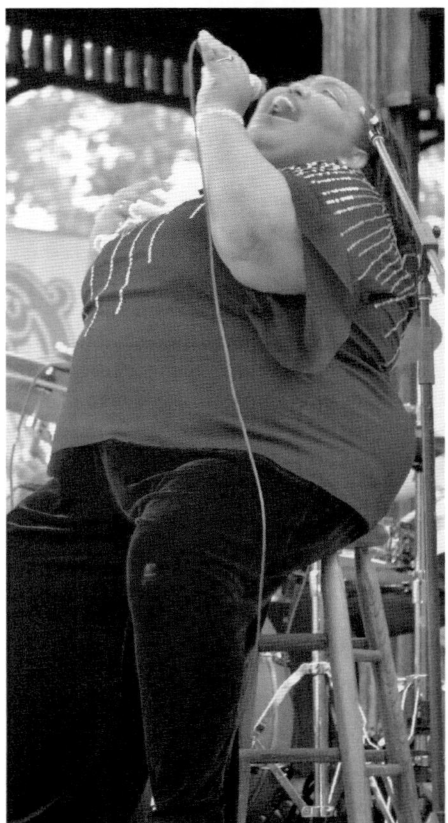

Voice of Meridian

Here at one of Meridian Main Street's Concert Series shows featuring the House Rockers, Patrice Moncell belts out a tune in her "Queen of the Blues" style. Opening for such greats as Little Richard, The Spinners, Gladys Knight, The Temptations, Cocoa Taylor, and Michael McDonald, Patrice has shared the stage with the great Etta James and performed before Pope John Paul II in Italy. (Author's collection.)

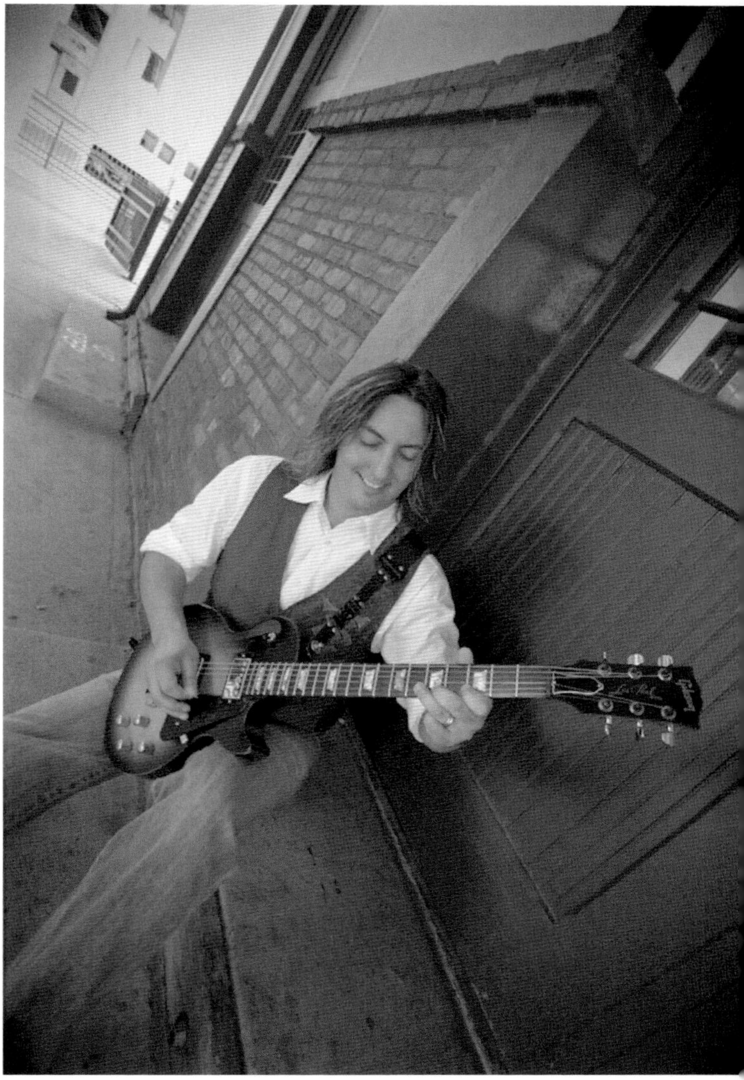

Reaping a Dynasty

In 2005, Tony Pasko relocated to Meridian to work as product manager for Peavey Electronics, running the guitar and amp division. After five years, Tony left to start his own business and offer his skills and knowledge to smaller companies, showing them how to write a business or marketing plan or helping with manufacturing problems and cutting down costs. He made connections with companies overseas and helped them build a customer base in the United States.

In 2012, Tony's life steered him into another direction when his record label asked him to send snippets of music for a production company that produces music for TV. They also told Pasko to look up a television show called *Duck Dynasty*, which Tony had never heard of nor seen. Using his skills on the guitar and his musical genius to learn banjo licks and percussion instruments, like shakers, sticks, and tambourines, Tony sent his music to the label, which forwarded it to the television producer. They wanted more.

Each episode of *Duck Dynasty* began to include more and more of Tony's music. Over 6.5 million people watched the Christmas episode of *Duck Dynasty*, and 75 percent of the music came from Pasko. The Christmas episode was the highest-rated television show on cable that night and the highest watched television show in the history of the A&E network.

"Before I left Chicago, I had a friend tell me that my career was over, that nobody leaves a major market area to move to Mississippi. Your career is done. One friend said, 'Go work with Peavey a couple of years and then come back.' Another friend was like, 'You are completely insane. You go to L.A., you go to New York. You don't go to Meridian, Mississippi.' But it just felt right for us. It was something about a feeling, and we just went with it."

To Tony's dad, who was also a musician, playing at church was no different than playing in a bar. As long as you are playing, you are a musician. "I wanted to be a rock star, but my dad said, 'Rock stars burn out, musicians have careers. Learn your instrument and be a musician.' "

Tony was 27 when his father passed away from leukemia. "I can still hear his voice. And that's focused me as a musician."

The Meridian community has been very special to Tony. At a time when Tony was at a crossroads, people stepped up and they were there. Tony said, "I would have never gone into business for myself without the encouragement and support of the Meridian community." (Courtesy of Tony Pasko.)

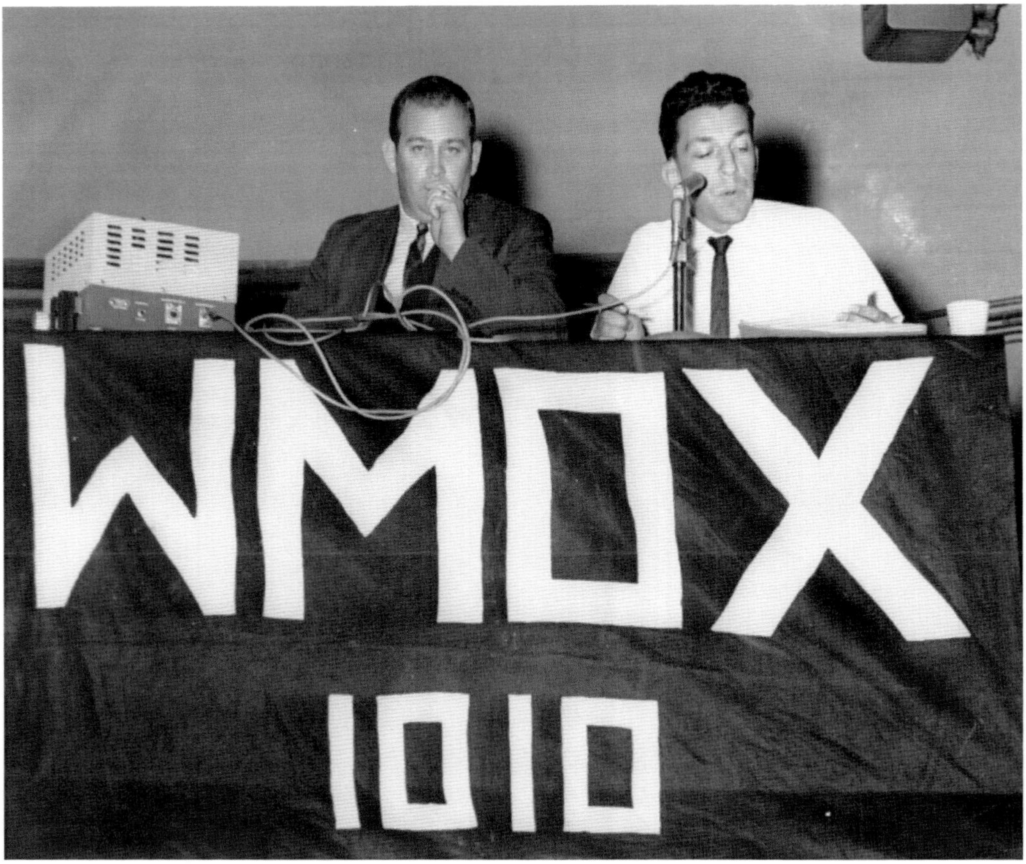

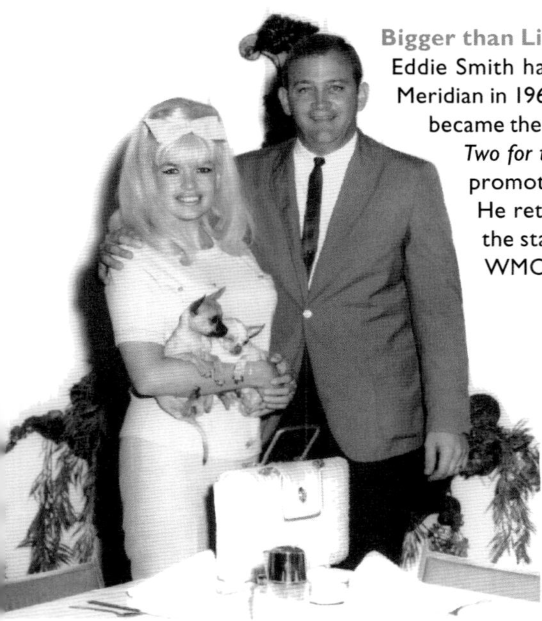

Bigger than Life

Eddie Smith had been in radio more than five years when he moved to Meridian in 1961 when he was hired as the sales manager of WMOX. Eddie became the station manager in the mid-1960s and started his radio show *Two for the Road*, which was later renamed *The Morning Show*. Eddie promoted the needs of the community, especially charity events. He retired in 2005, and his son Bill took over the management of the station. Eddie passed away on October 25, 2009. (Courtesy of WMOX and Jane Smith.)

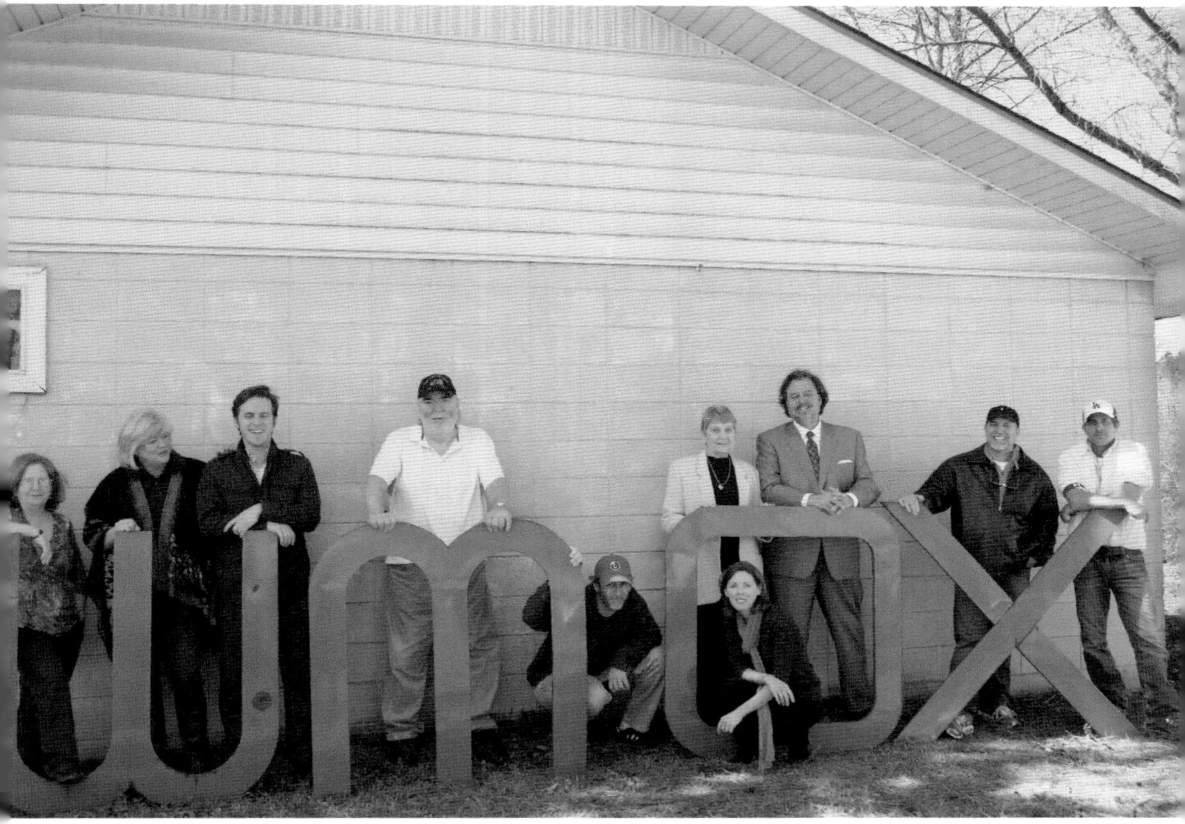

WMOX Radio

Off Highway 80 East outside of Meridian, across the railroad tracks in a big pasture, you'll find WMOX Radio Station. The building appears lost in time, but once you open the door, you feel the connection WMOX makes with their listeners. WMOX started in 1946 on the corner of Ninth Street and Twenty-third Avenue, broadcasting many live programs, such as hillbilly, country, and bluegrass music. The Morning Show includes Bill Smith, Cat Owen, and Kelly Corey. The Afternoon Show has Al Brown teaming with Ellie Massey and other cohosts like Elliott Street, and discussing what's going on in East Mississippi and West Alabama. "People may disagree with what I have to say, but they get to disagree on the air and have a place to voice that opinion," said Al. (Author's collection.)

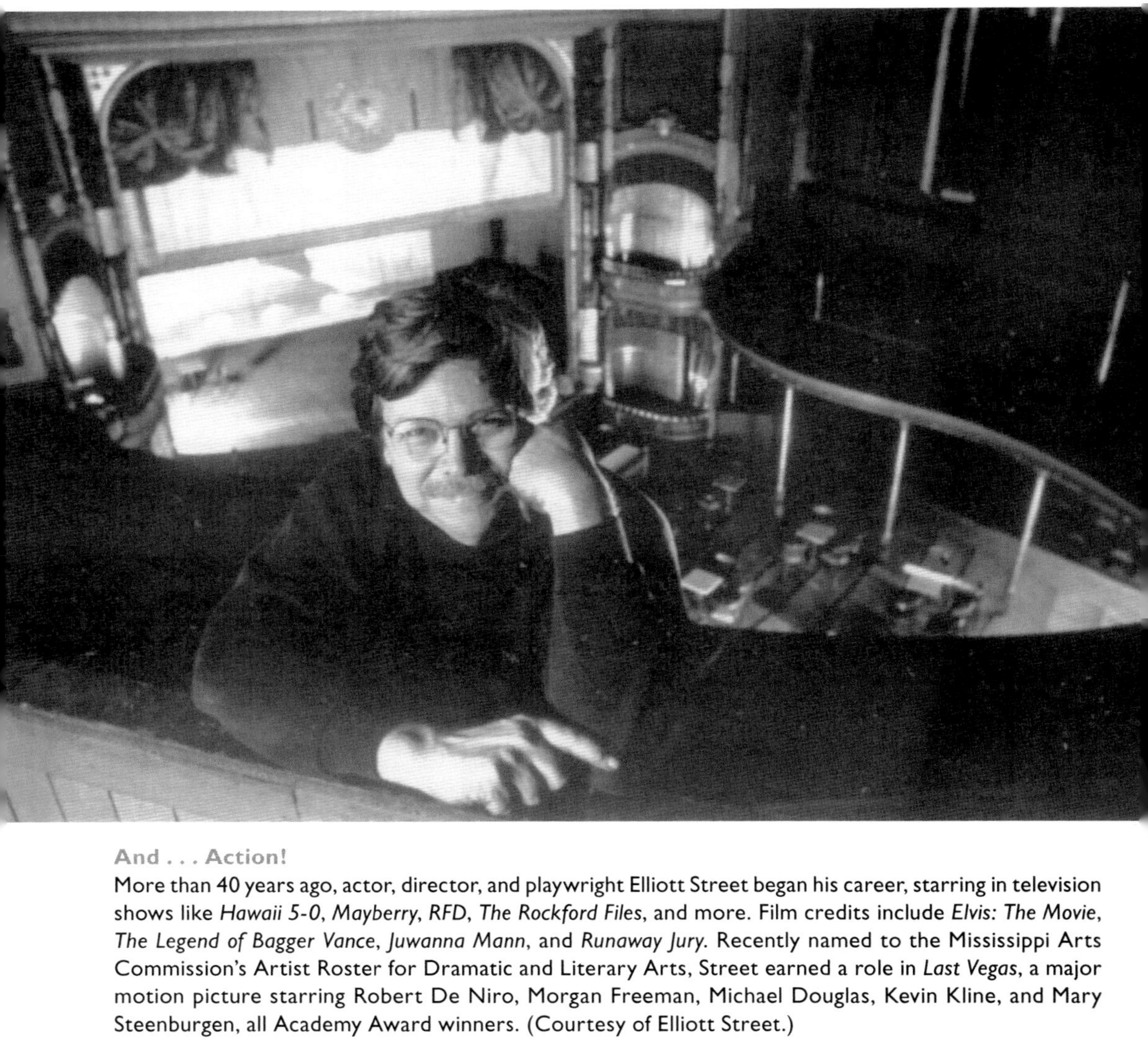

And . . . Action!

More than 40 years ago, actor, director, and playwright Elliott Street began his career, starring in television shows like *Hawaii 5-0*, *Mayberry, RFD*, *The Rockford Files*, and more. Film credits include *Elvis: The Movie*, *The Legend of Bagger Vance*, *Juwanna Mann*, and *Runaway Jury*. Recently named to the Mississippi Arts Commission's Artist Roster for Dramatic and Literary Arts, Street earned a role in *Last Vegas*, a major motion picture starring Robert De Niro, Morgan Freeman, Michael Douglas, Kevin Kline, and Mary Steenburgen, all Academy Award winners. (Courtesy of Elliott Street.)

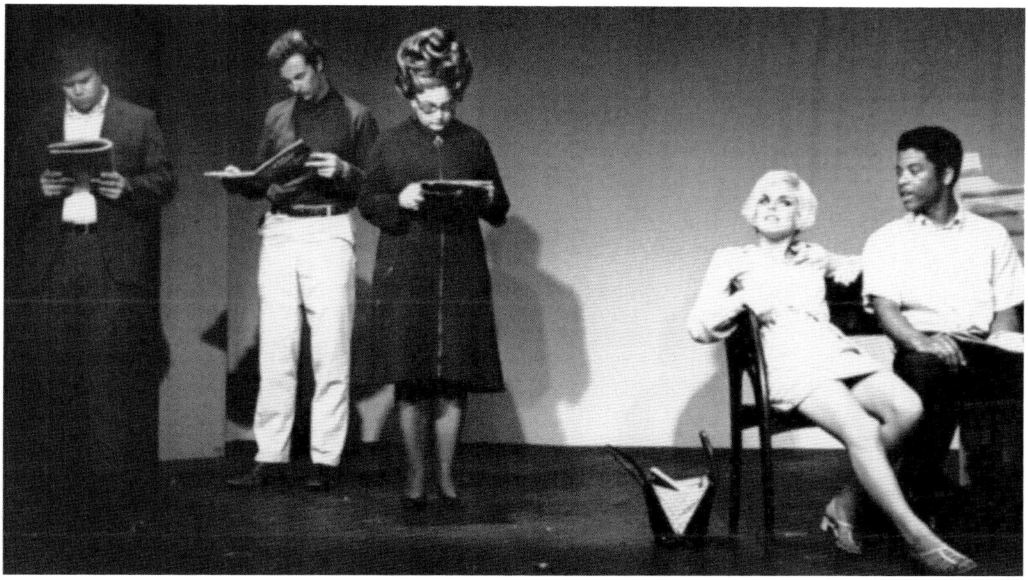

On Stage
Past producer and artistic director with Company of Angels, the oldest professional theater company in Los Angeles, Elliott Street named the Meridian Company of Angels after the California company. Elliott served as the first executive director of the Merry Street Theatre, which was Elliott's first nonprofit, and he was on the first board that saved the Grand Opera House. (Courtesy of Elliott Street.)

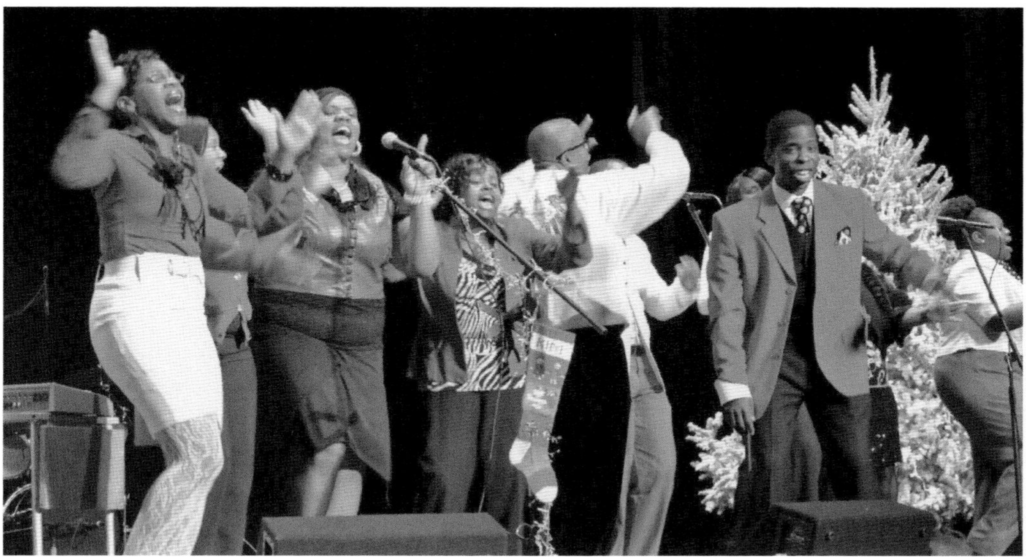

Praise Him
William Myles is founder-director of Young People of Praise (YPOP), based out of Meridian. Having performed together for 11 years, YPOP was a Gospel Search of America 2008 finalist and a Mississippi Gospel Music Award nominee. YPOP has shared the stage with Maurette-Brown Clark, John P. Kee, Donald Lawrence, Martha Munizzi, Dottie Peoples, and the Mississippi Mass Choir. Myles & YPOP positively impact young people through their music. (Author's collection.)

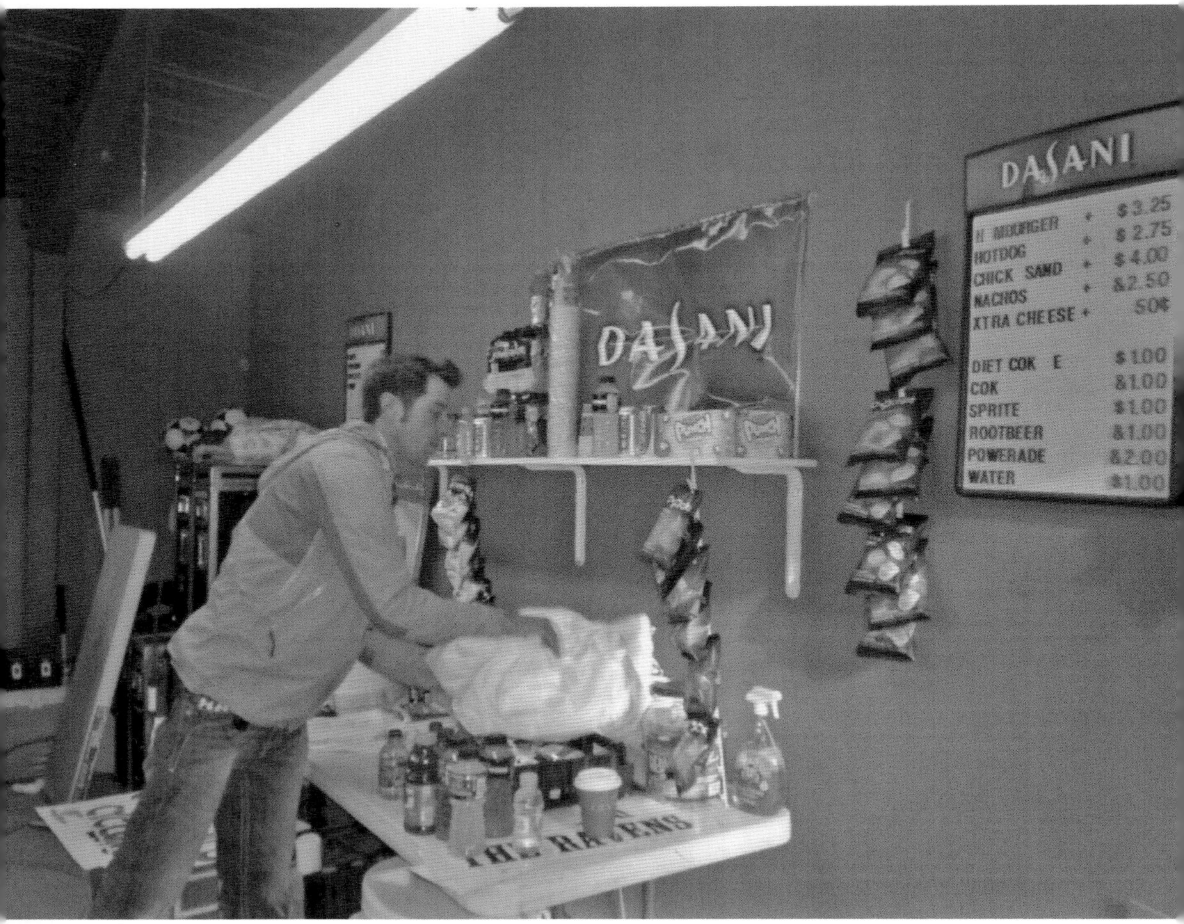

Set Dressing
As a child, Eric Aycock often dressed up and performed before or with his family. His short skits included John Wayne's "What's It to You, Pilgrim?" and his song performance of LL Cool J's "Going Back to Cali," with his mom and sister as backup singers. His dream of going "to Cali" became reality when he headed to Los Angeles at the turn of the millennium. As a set dresser, he has worked with Warner Bros., Millennium Studios, MGM, Oliver Stone, Paramount Pictures, Fox Studio, and Sony Pictures on such films as *Iceman*, *Leatherface*, *The Curious Case of Benjamin Button*. He is pictured here working on the set of *Playing for Keeps*. With too many credits to name, his television, print, and commercial credits include *Fergalicious*, *Kid Magician*, *Monk*, *Lincoln Heights*, *TV Guide*, *Vogue*, *GQ*, *Nike*, *Mazda*, *Toyota*, and *Sprint*. Now a resident of New Orleans, he continues to work in the film industry. (Courtesy of Eric Aycock.)

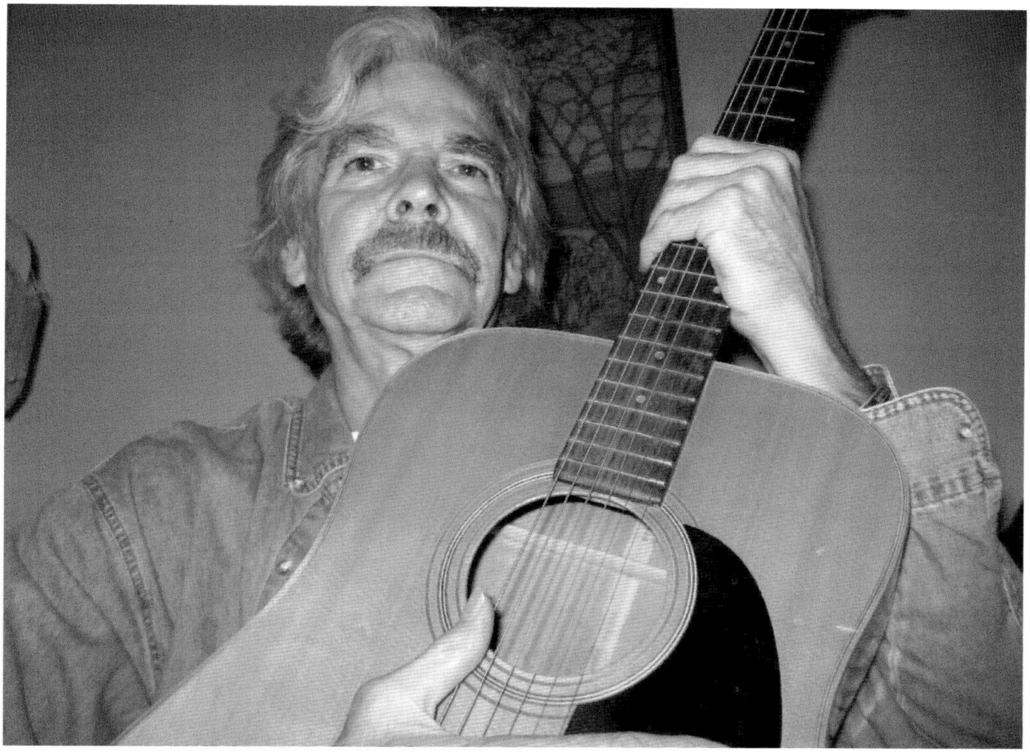

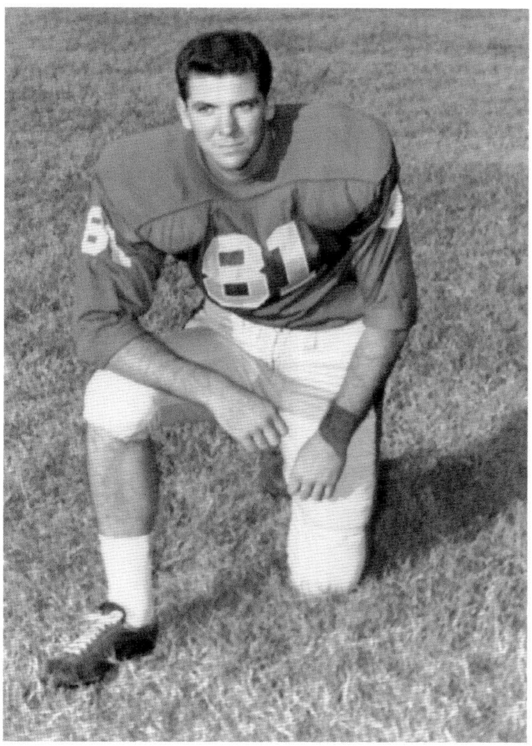

On the Cover of the Rolling Stone
George Cummings loved sports and played football and baseball at Meridian High, East Mississippi Community College, and the University of West Alabama. When he couldn't go pro, George chose the next best thing: music. He founded the acclaimed group Dr. Hook and the Medicine Show during the turbulent 1960s. Their big break came when Hollywood music director Ron Haffkine had Dr. Hook perform "Last Morning" for the 1969 Dustin Hoffman film *Who Is Harry Kellerman and Why Is He Saying Those Terrible Things About Me?* The group performed on the soundtrack written by songwriter-poet-musician Shel Silverstein and later signed on with CBS. Silverstein went on to write all of the songs on their 1971 debut album, *Dr. Hook*, which included "Sylvia's Mother." Silverstein would later write "Cover of the Rollin' Stone," a satire on the rock celebrity that got Dr. Hook on the cover of *Rolling Stone*. (Courtesy of George Cummings.)

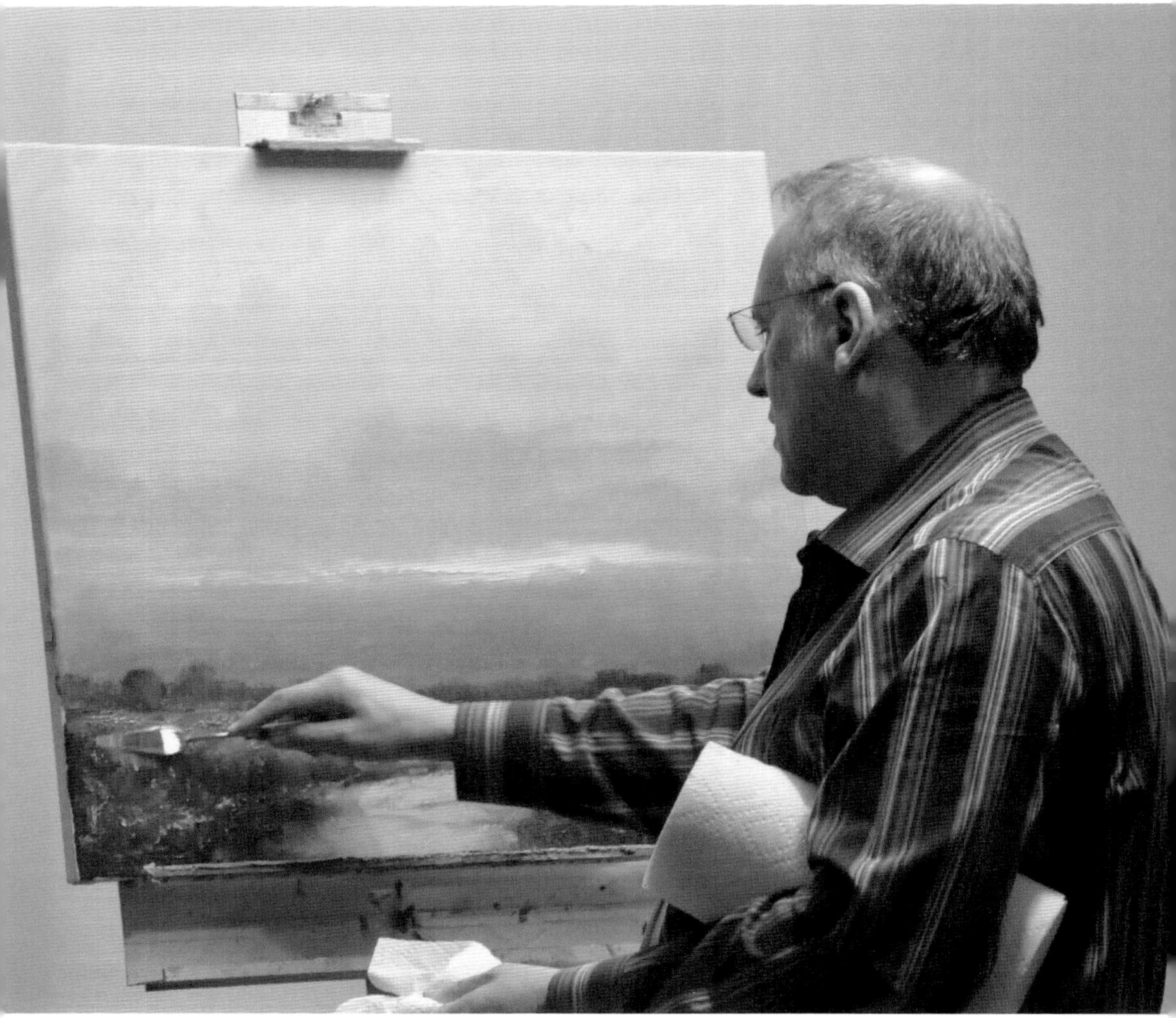

With the Stroke of a Brush

For more than 30 years, artist Greg Cartmell, of Plymouth, Massachusetts, has made Meridian his home. His portraits include First Lady Barbara Bush, Rep. G.V. "Sonny" Montgomery, musician Ray Charles, and television journalist Mike Wallace. In his recently commissioned portrait of former Mississippi governor Haley Barbour, Cartmell included two images in the background: a portrait of Barbour's ancestor, Walter Leake, who served as Mississippi's third governor (1822–1825) and the Biloxi lighthouse, symbolizing Barbour's impact on the state after Hurricane Katrina. Cartmell teaches art classes to adults at his studio and is also a skilled musician. (Author's collection.)

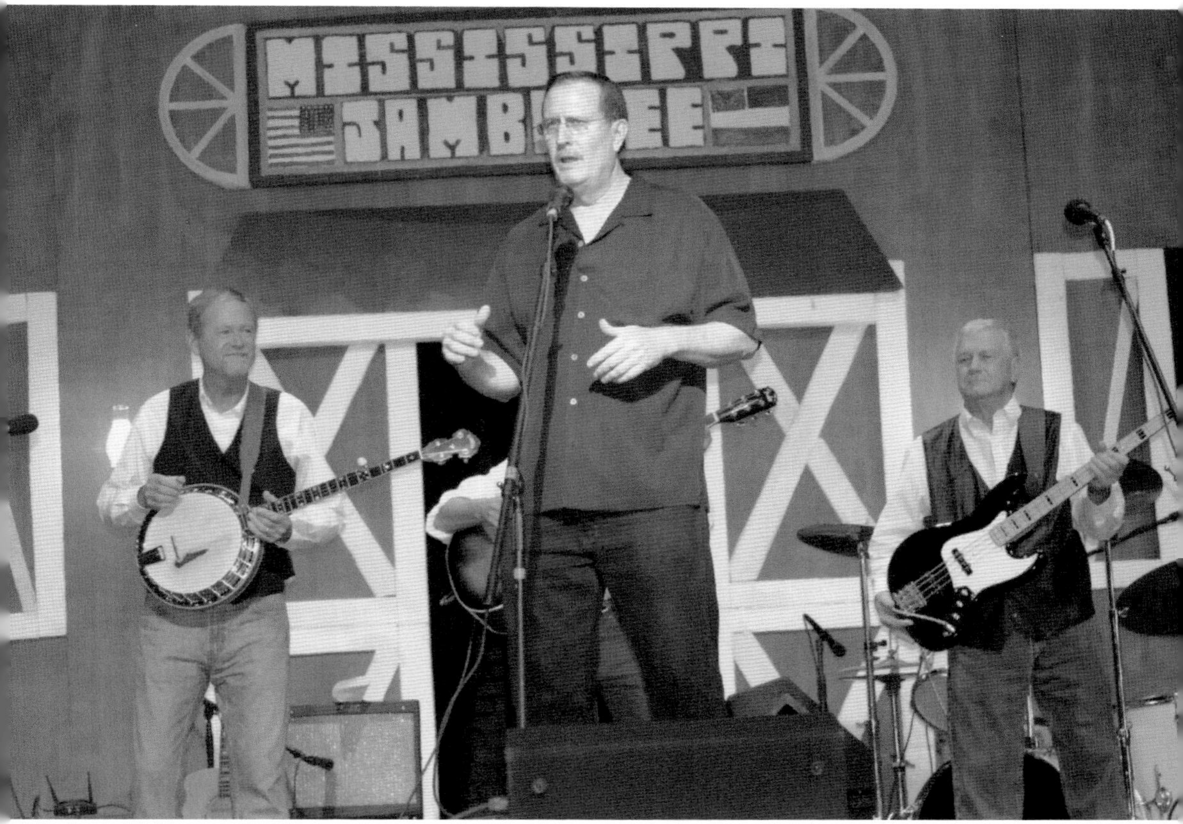

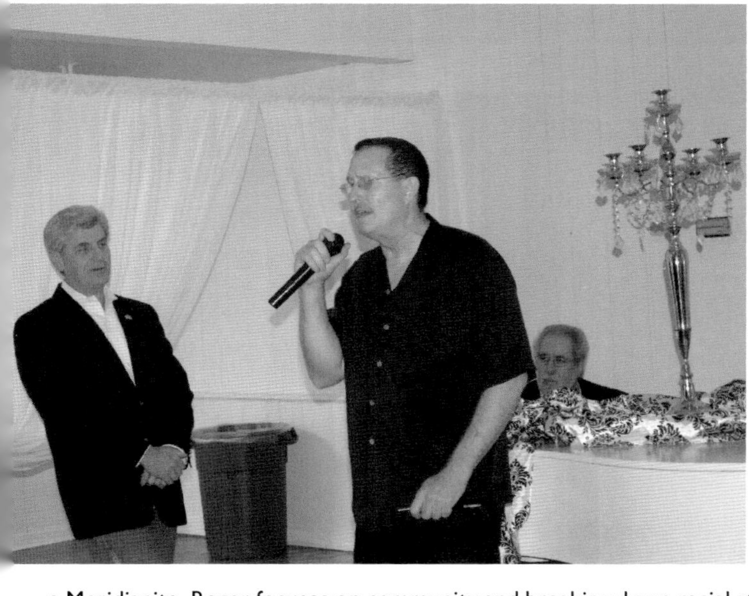

The Man in the Temple

To pay for flight school, Roger Smith produced a commercial for the flight school from still pictures and a voice-over that he showed on a slide projector at drive-in theaters. After completing flight school at the age of 25, he flew for a Dallas television station for 21 years. "But all the time I was flying I was thinking about preparing for the eventuality of not flying," said Roger. He found the historic Temple Theater, which had been built by the Shriners in the late 1920s. Roger thought it was a perfect fit because he is a Shriner and a Mason. Now a Meridianite, Roger focuses on community and breaking down racial stereotypes. "We are all different and we have to embrace diversity in our differences and not be afraid of it." Smith is pictured at left introducing Gov. Phil Bryant, with Carey Smith at the piano. (Author's collection.)

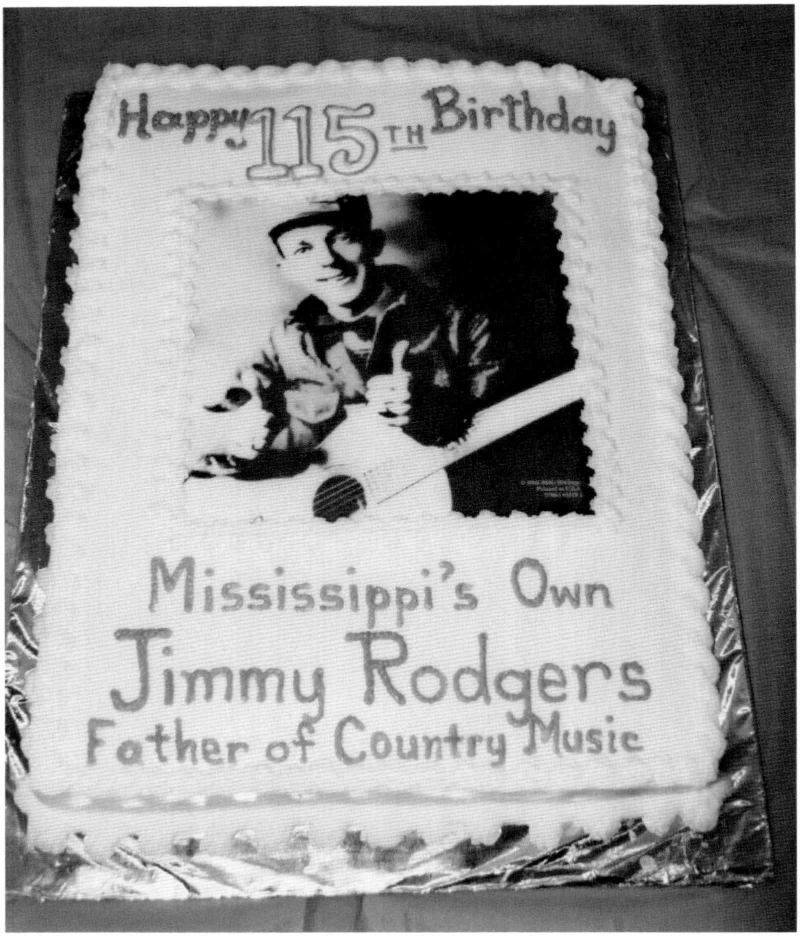

Father of Country Music
Mississippi has always been known for its music, from the Delta Blues to Elvis Presley, the country's first rock and roll star. But Mississippi also birthed "The Father of Country Music," Jimmie Rodgers, known as "The Singing Brakeman" and "America's Blue Yodeler."

In the *Journal of the American Academy for the Preservation of Old-Time Country Music*, Charlie Seemann wrote, "The father of country music inspired a generation of young singers, some of whom became legends themselves. Country music historian Bill Malone's book, *Country Music, U.S.A.*, added, "In assessing Jimmie Rodgers' influence on American folk music and on a later generation of commercial performers, one can safely use the adjective 'phenomenal.' " Seemann also said that over 75 percent of modern country performers were directly or indirectly influenced by Jimmie Rodgers.

In 1924, tuberculosis halted Jimmie's life as a railroad brakeman, but he was finally able to concentrate on his music. Jimmie's decision to travel to Asheville, North Carolina, in 1927 changed American music forever. In February of that year, Jimmie Rodgers and Otis Kuykendall performed on Ashville's WWNC. Jimmie recruited a group from Bristol, Tennessee, called The Tenneya Ramblers, and they later performed on WWNC again. Renamed The Jimmie Rodgers Entertainers, the group took a weekly slot on WWNC.

Including the 15 years after his death, Rodgers sold approximately 12 million records. He was the first person inducted into the Country Music Hall of Fame when it was created in 1961. Between 1927 and his death from tuberculosis on May 26, 1933, Rodgers recorded more than 100 songs. A 13¢ US postage stamp was issued on May 24, 1978. (Author's collection.)

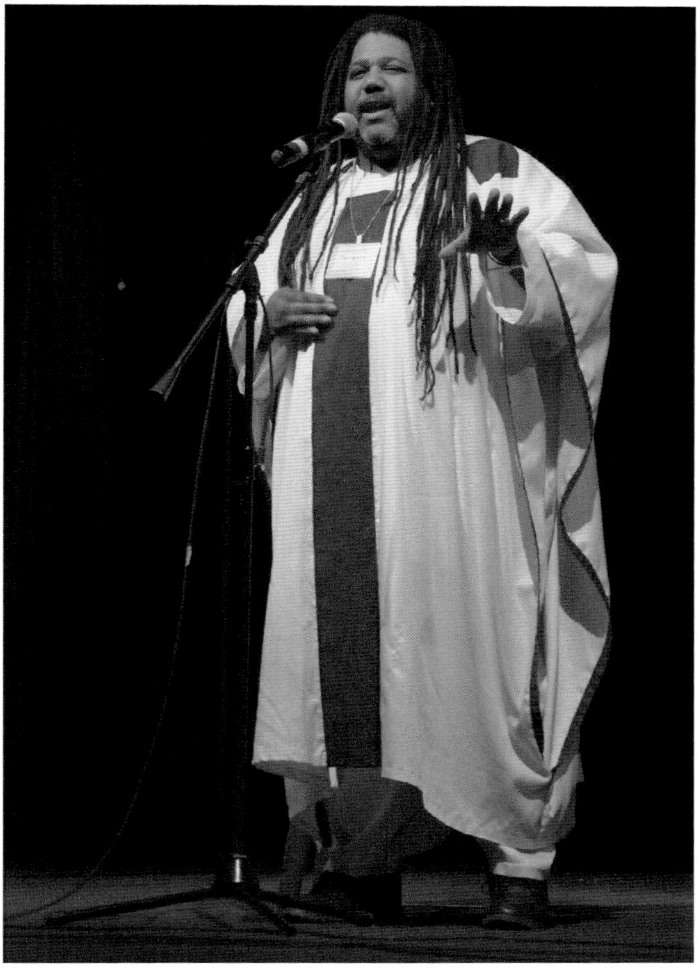

Storyteller
"I've always had the desire to tell a good story and to inform people. My storytelling happened with parenting," said professional storyteller Terrence Roberts. "When I got married, my wife had a young daughter. I knew the importance of reading to your children and helping them have a strong foundation for education. I remembered as a kid, every so often a storyteller might come to the school and share a story. I don't know if they were professional or not." Terrence started finding folk tales, specifically African tales: "I would memorize the stories and then tell the stories." Terrence became an active parent and told stories instead of reading the story to the preschool children. Other teachers wanted Terrence to come into their classrooms. For 12 years, he did that in the schools. "In the process I met some local storytellers who were professionals, and they shared with me that you could pursue storytelling as a profession." Terrence applied and was accepted to the Mississippi Arts Commission's Artist and Teaching Artist Roster.

"History is important because if you don't know your history you're destined to repeat it. It gives you the sense that you belong to something greater, that you just didn't end up on this rock. You are tied to something; there is a legacy. Because of slavery, that link is broken for the African American. When you have a sense of being connected you view the world differently. When we have the sense that we belong to something greater, it shifts the way we think about the world and the way we interact." Terrence believes that stories provide healing and hope through perspective. (Author's collection.)

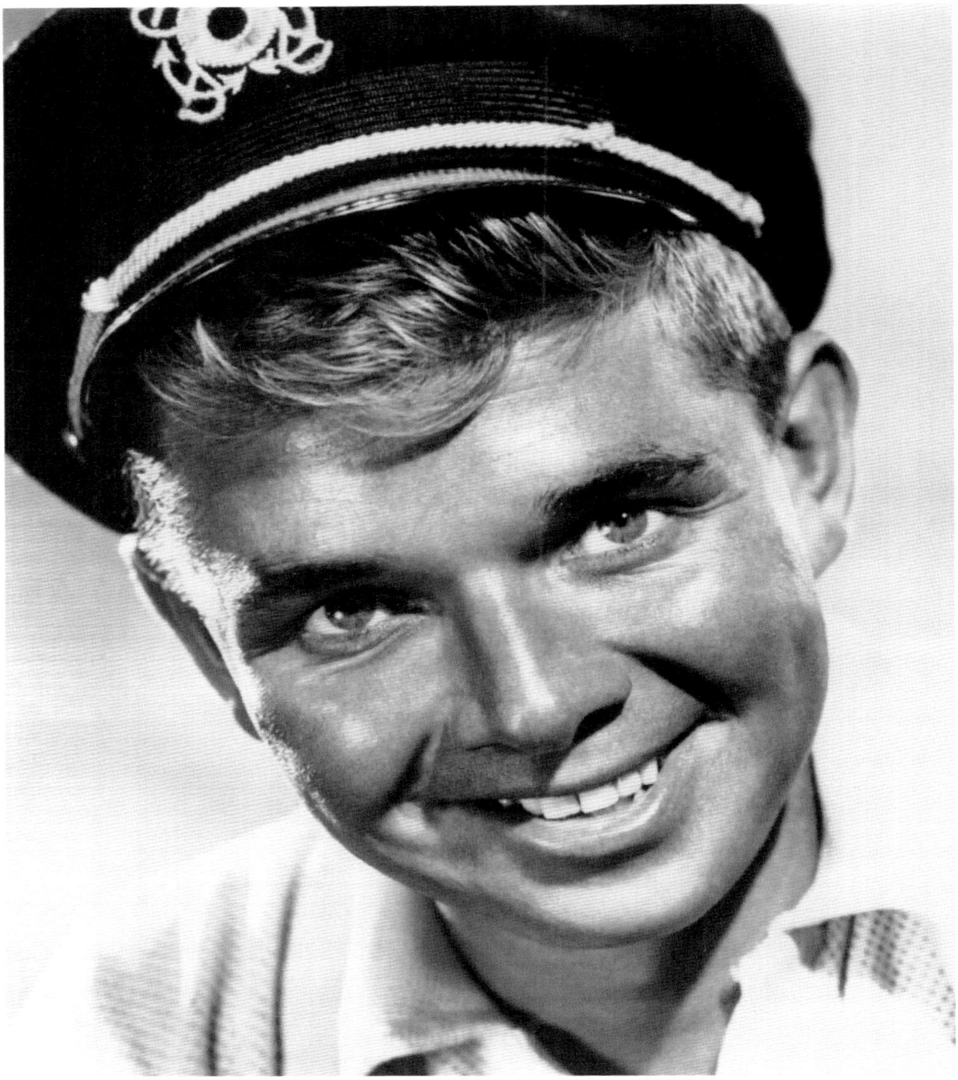

Off-Broadway

A 1956 graduate of Ole Miss, Jimmy Pigford began his stage and screen career after college, appearing in 30 television shows and several movies. He returned to Meridian and organized the Theatre Guild in 1968, the MLT Youth Division in 1969, and the Summer Youth Workshop in 1996. Pigford was voted The Meridian Star Readers' Choice Man of the Year in 2012. At that time, he said one of his proudest achievements with MLT was the number of young people who had participated in Youth Division productions. Over the years, Pigford brought professional performers to his hometown for productions on the MLT stage, including Mercedes McCambridge, Russ Tamblyn, Virginia Mayo, Cyd Charisse, and Barbara Rush. Pigford has received the Meridian Council for the Arts Excellence in Arts Award and the Daughters of the American Revolution Award for Community Involvement for Outstanding Contributions in the World of Art and Entertainment. He was a past president of the Mississippi Community Theatre Association and served as chairman of the Mississippi State Theatre Convention. Born on September 2, 1923, he died on February 4, 2013. The Meridian Little Theatre cherishes the many memories he made possible, and they work to keep his spirit alive. (Courtesy of Meridian Little Theatre.)

Remembering Jimmy

"To say that Jimmy Pigford was just a director is to say that the Pacific Ocean is just a body of water," said Sidney Covington. "He was a visionary, an artist, an educator, a mentor. He could see a diamond in the rough, and through his mastery directing and encouragement, the diamond sparkled center stage! Anyone who had the great privilege of being 'tutored' by Jimmy, is forever molded and changed . . . they continue to sparkle. No, he wasn't just a director . . . he was, and always will be, a legend!" (Courtesy of the Meridian Little Theatre.)

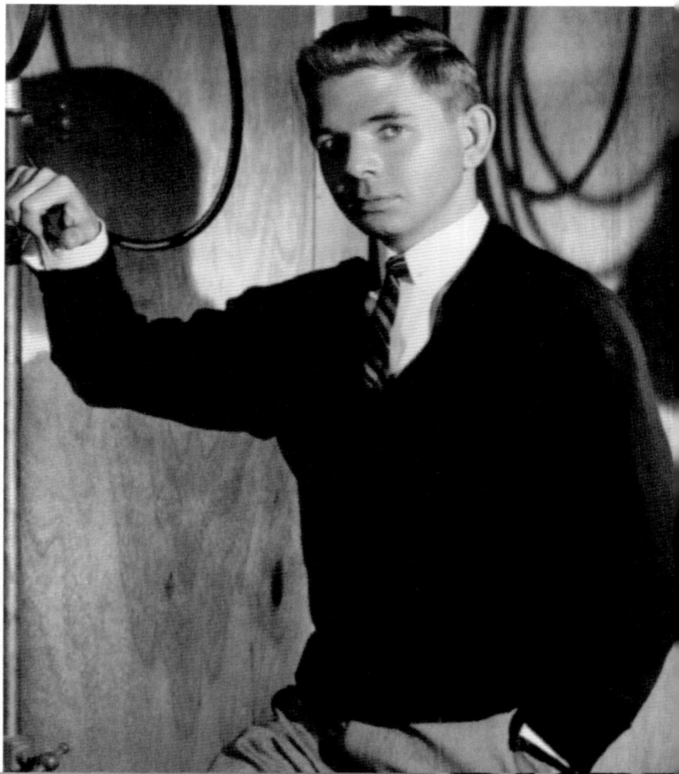

Steel Magnolias

The cast of Meridian Little Theatre's 2013 production of *Steel Magnolias* by Robert Harling featured, from left to right, Millie Robinson as Clairee, Sidney Covington as M'Lynn, Bennie Jean Fortenberry as Ouiser, Donna P. Colburn as Truvy, Katie Coleman as Shelby, and Tiffany Brooks as Annelle. (Author's collection.)

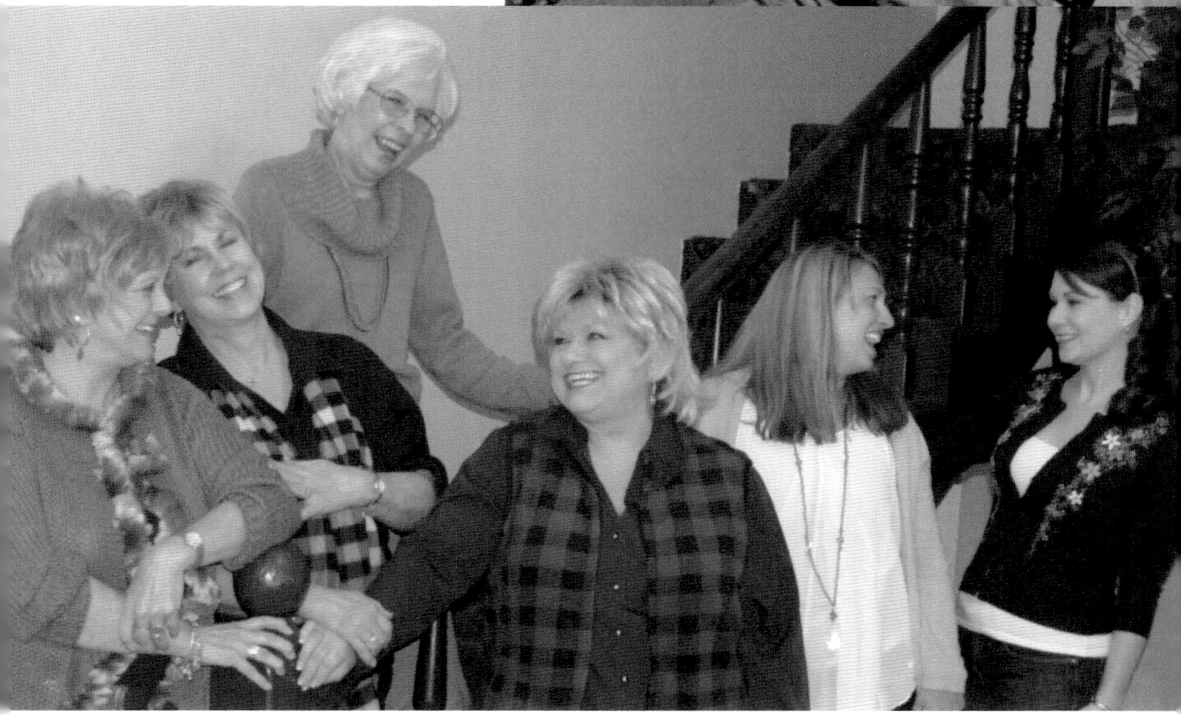

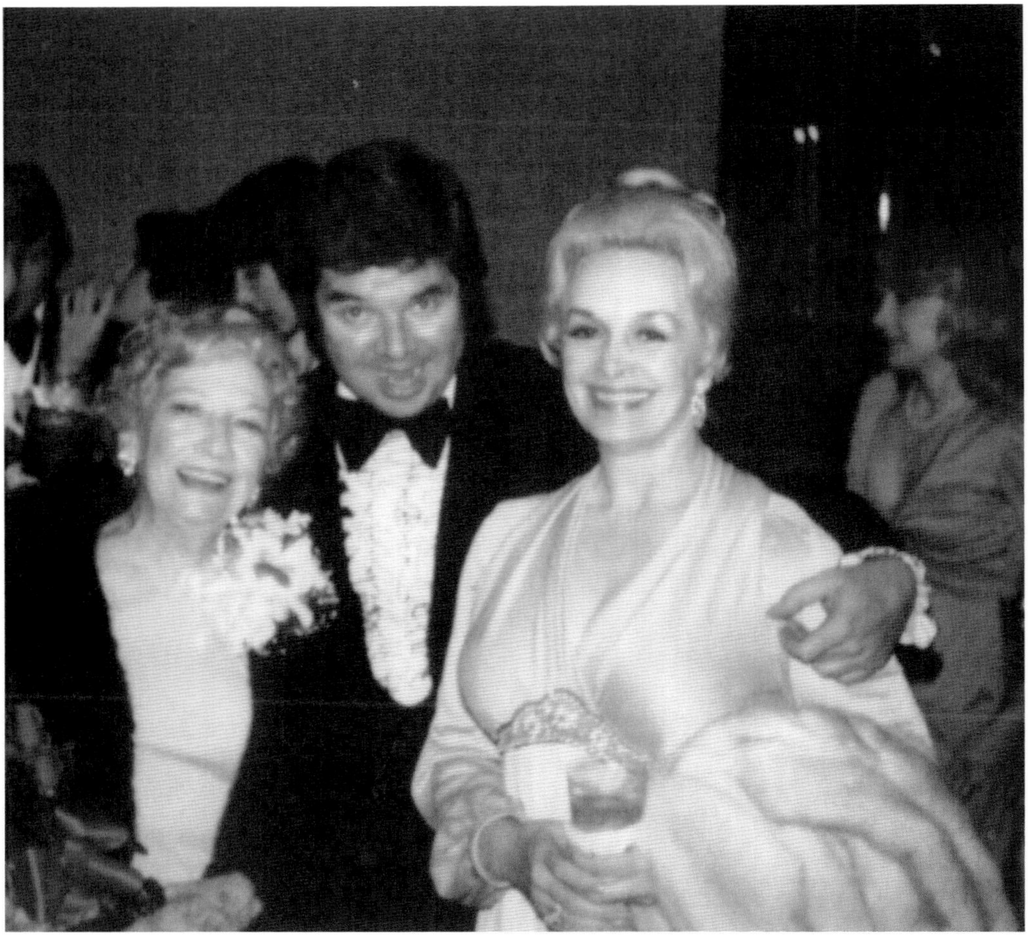

Dancing Queen
At 19, Mary Alpha (pictured here with Jimmy Pigford) opened the Alpha School of Dance. She taught dance for over 65 years. She won the First Place National Award for State Production several times as choreographer of the State Junior Miss Pageant of Mississippi, and she received the Amblin Award for Best in Choreography by the Mississippi Fashion Women in 1983. In 2003, Mary Alpha was awarded the MLT Austin Award for Lifetime Artistic Achievement. Mary Alpha created a teaching tool for young dancers called the Alphamat and authored a dance encyclopedia, *The Magical Kingdom of Dance*, which is still used today. Mary Alpha died on October 15, 2012. (Courtesy of Meridian Little Theatre.)

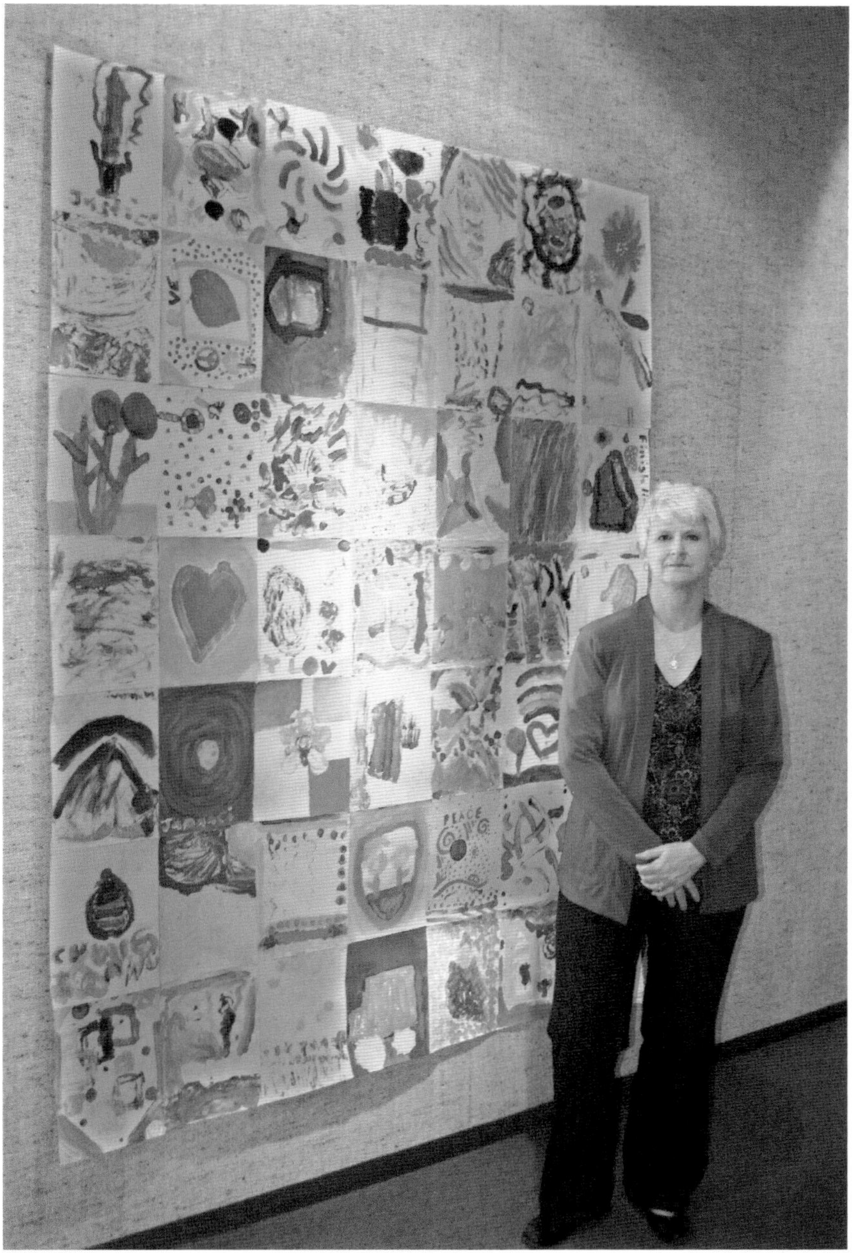

The Whole Brain

Kate Cherry uses both sides of her brain, and Lauderdale County is so glad she does. "We use the right side of the brain in creating art," said Kate. "We keep track of time and balance our checkbook with the left side of the brain. When we begin to engage both halves of our brain, magnificent things can happen." In the early 2000s, she established and instructed after-school art programs at Kemper Academy. In September 2008, Kate became executive director of the Meridian Museum of Art. "The reason art is important is because it allows us to use the whole brain," said Kate. "Many people do not realize that. Art gives us the freedom of expression, and allows us to pursue that expression." (Author's collection.)

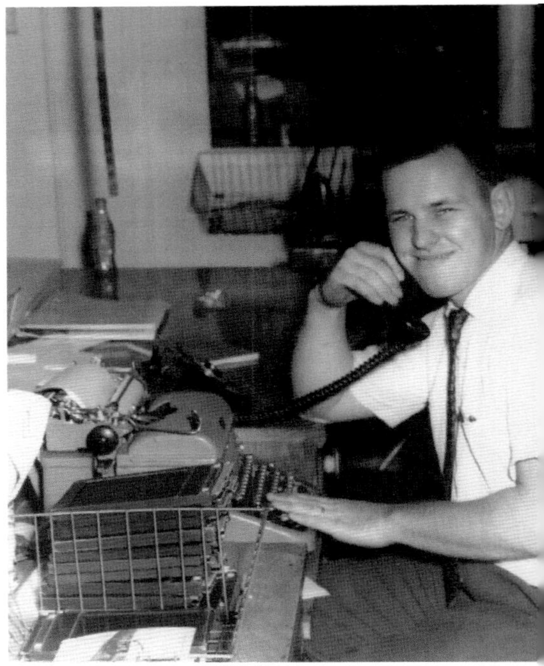

Turn Your Radio On

In 1965, Ken Rainey went to work for a radio station in the Threefoot Building. In 1969, the station moved up the hill off Highway 45 South, where WOKK was born. In 1981, at Kenny's suggestion, WOKK became an all-country station. Kenny left the radio show and formed Z 95.1 and the 14.50 AM Southern Gospel station, both of which he later sold and bought the frequency 97.9, a Newton station that is still on the air. In 1972, Ken was instrumental in revitalizing the Jimmie Rodgers Festival, and for over 30 years he booked the talent for the event. He is the past president of Mississippi Broadcasters and served on the Meridian City Council for four years. He helped Scott McQuaig get a recording contract in the early 1990s and later took Randy Houser to Nashville. "His next big project is our granddaughter, who lives in Nashville," said Cheryl Rainey, Ken's wife and the daughter of the late Rod Goodling. (Courtesy of the Rainey family.)

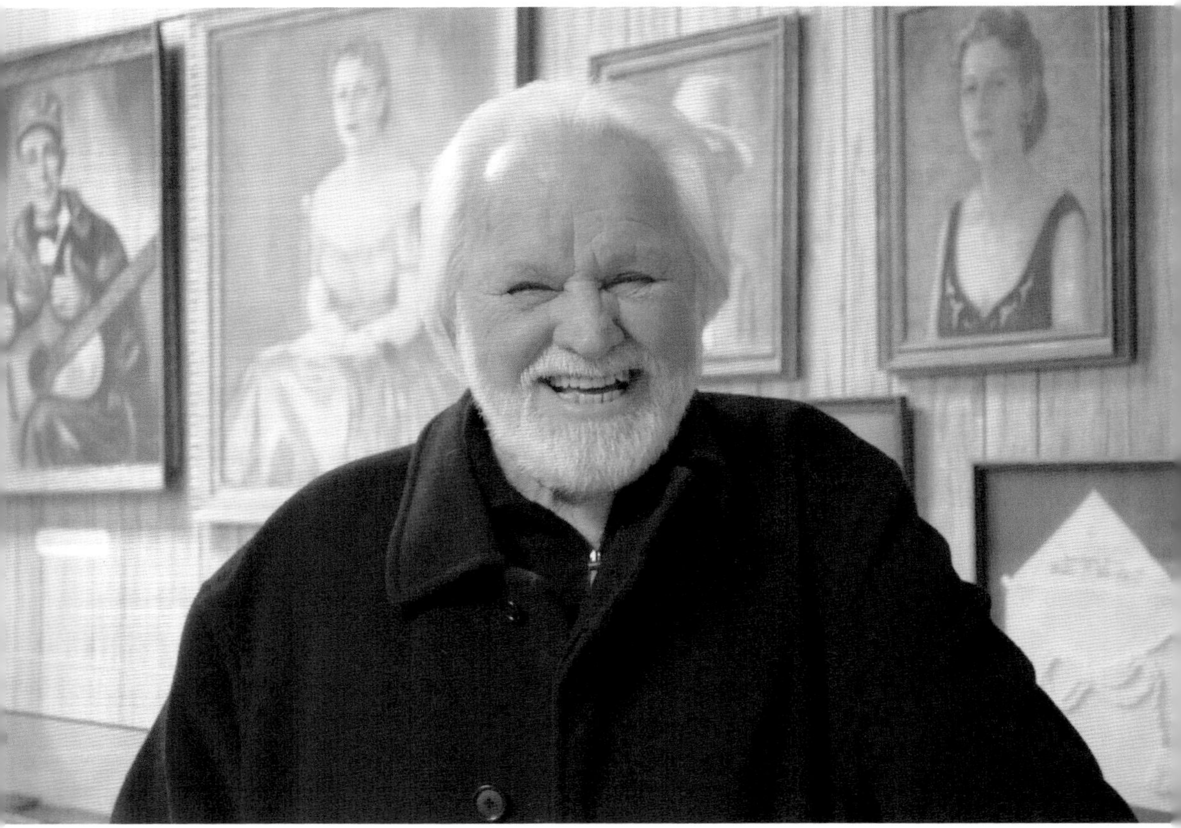

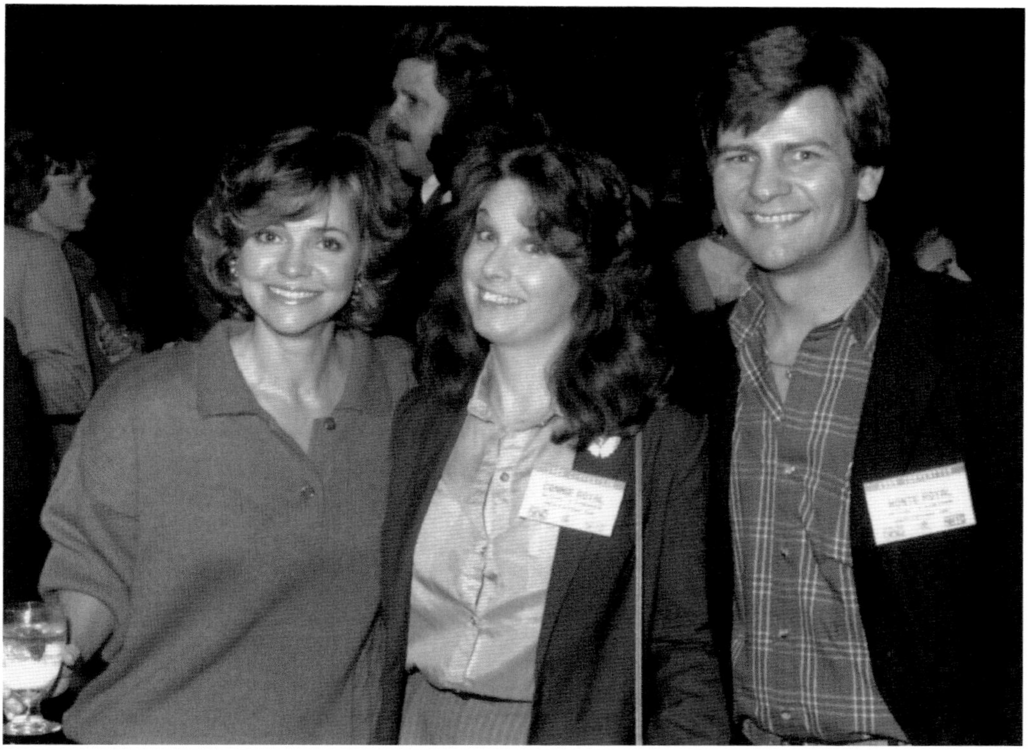

Picture This!

At a National Association of Theatre Owners (NATO) Convention in Los Angeles, Monte and Connie Royal chat with actress Sally Field. "The photographer was getting ready to take the picture but ran out of film and had to go get another roll," said Monte. "Sally would not let us leave until the picture was taken, so we got to hang with her for quite a while." (Courtesy of Monte and Connie Royal.)

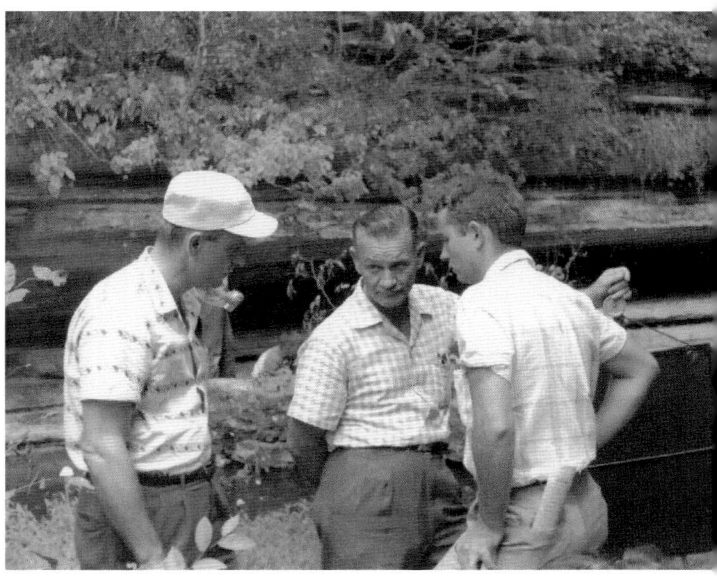

Lloyd Royal

On January 6, 1941, Lloyd Royal (pictured in the center) opened the Royal Theater across from Paragon Book Store in Meridian. During the 1950s, he became the first producer to make full-length films in Mississippi. *Jesse James' Women* (1954) starred Don "Red" Barry and Peggie Castle. *Frontier Woman* (1956) starred Ann Kelly (Royal's wife), Cindy Carson, and Lance Fuller. Award-winning actor and producer Ron Howard made his film debut as the baby in *Frontier Woman*. *Natchez Trace* starred Zachary Taylor, William Campbell, Irene James, and Ann Kelly. (Courtesy of Monte and Connie Royal.)

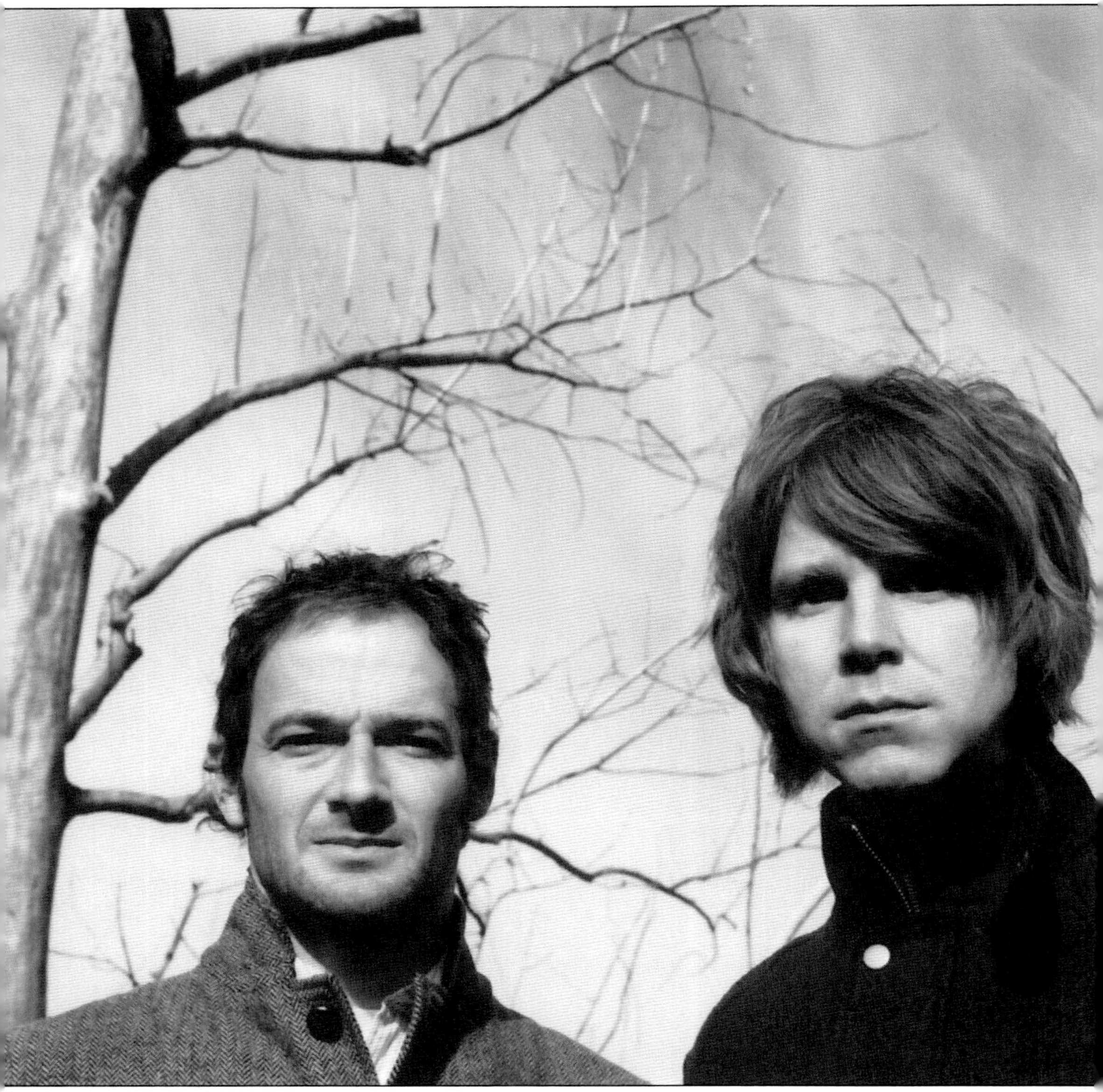

Family Ties

Patrick Sansone grew up in a musical family. Music and show business were as much a part of life as breakfast, lunch, and dinner. Patrick's paternal grandmother had been a performing singer in the 1930s and 1940s. Years later, a young Patrick listened to her play the piano and sing. Both Patrick's parents, Karen and Tony (see page 77), filled his world with entertainment, through his mother's glorious singing and his promoter father who loved to perform vaudeville acts on The Temple Theatre stage, where Patrick literally grew up. "When he was just a baby and I directed Junior Miss programs," said Tony in an interview, "I carried him around like a football." A multi-instrumentalist, Patrick joined Wilco in 2004. He also performs with Wilco bassist John Stirratt in their band The Autumn Defense. With Wilco, Patrick is more of an instrumentalist and band member. In The Autumn Defense, he's out front, performing his own songs. He admits having the best of both worlds. (Courtesy of Patrick Sansone.)

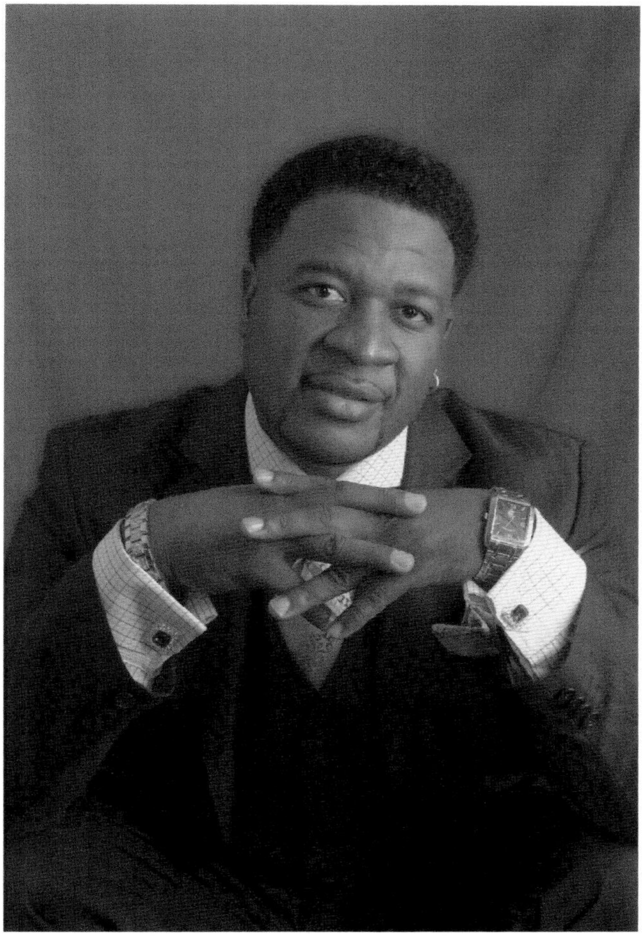

Rap on!
"My father's uncle is the late Al Wilson, so my father sang because his uncle sang. Hearing my dad sing, of course I wanted to sing as well," said Terrence Davis.

Terrence's partner in the early days was Treasure Shields Redmond. During high school, they formed their group One Cause, One Effect. After graduation, they moved to California and recorded their first album.

Terrence began doing backup rap for MC Hammer's stage show. From 1990 to 1993, Terrence toured the country with Hammer on a Boeing 757. During the last leg of the MC Hammer tour, Terrence concentrated on promoting the One Cause, One Effect CD.

"Everything became redundant and habitual. I had started coming back home and spending more time at home," said Terrence, adding that he was able to spend a good deal of time with his mother before her passing in 2001.

Today, Terrence reads water meters for the city of Meridian, but in his spare time he is still producing, writing songs and spending time with his childhood sweetheart and wife, Yolanda. He educates those who want to go into the music industry and prepares them for the reality of the music world.

Terrence has brought the Williams Brothers, Rance Allen, and Pamela Mann to the Temple Theatre. "Now it's like Meridian has a name for Gospel music. Gospel music is a really good market because people treat you really well." Terrence works closely with Temple owner Roger Smith in bringing more acts to Meridian. (Courtesy of Terrence Davis.)

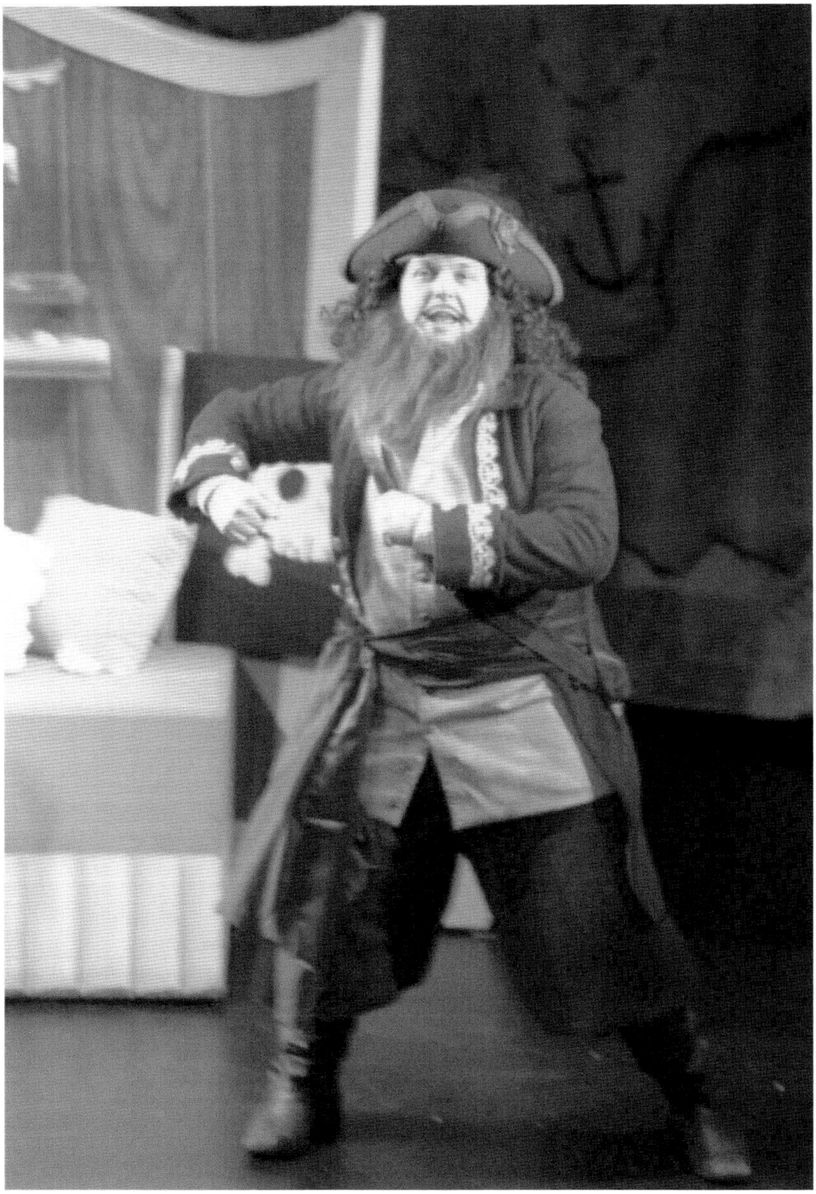

I Love New York!

Theatre flows in Pep Speed's blood, thanks to his mother, Susan Speed, the past president and stage manager of the Meridian Little Theatre. "[Pep] first really remembers seeing MLT's Showboat and being totally involved with the music and how it came together," said Susan. When Pep was five, director Jimmie Pigford suggested to Susan that Pep play the mouse that drives the Cinderella carriage in the youth play. Pep then played Oliver in the MLT production of *Oliver*, and in his senior year he played Mordred in *Camelot*. Pep earned a bachelor of fine arts degree in musical theatre from the University of Mississippi. For the past four years, he has been in New York, where he was cast as Uncle Pirate in an Off-Broadway play with the same title. Pep has sung at Lincoln Center and sang in the choir for the Marvin Hamlisch memorial service. (Courtesy of Susan Speed.)

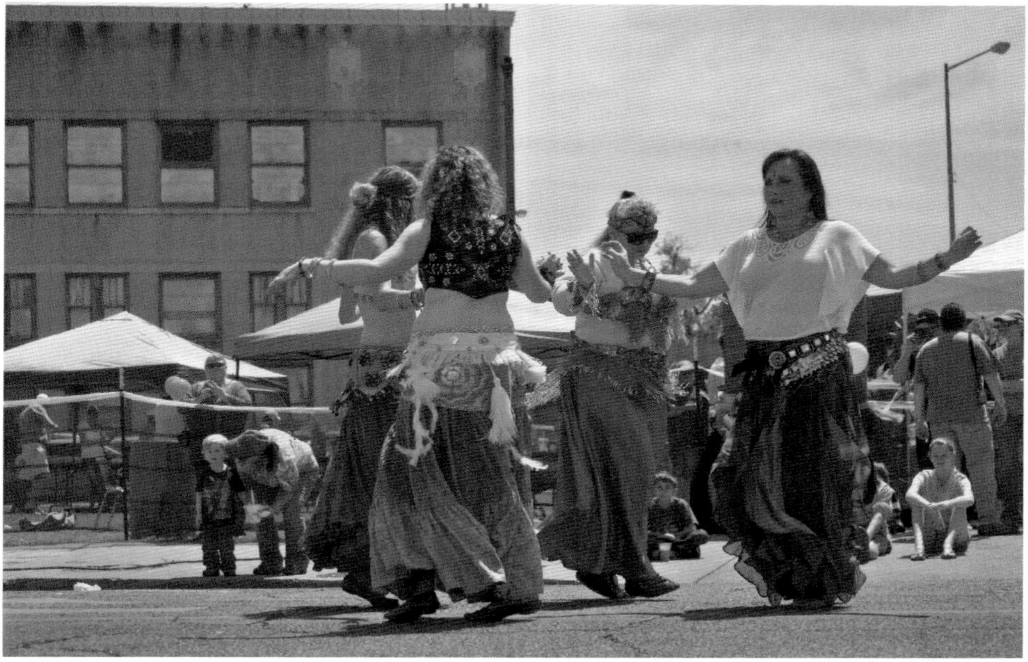

I Could Have Danced All Night

Named in honor of Gypsy Queen Kelly Mitchell, who is buried in Meridian's Rosehill Cemetery, the Queen City Gypsies were formed in 2002 by "Gypsy" Williams. Michelle Griffith Joyner of the Queen City Gypsies said, "I bellydance to relieve stress. Many of us refer to it as 'bellydance therapy.' " The group performs at festivals and at various events and other venues throughout the state. "I love the control of the isolations and the flow of the sweeping moves. Bellydance celebrates our femininity," said Michelle. (Author's collection.)

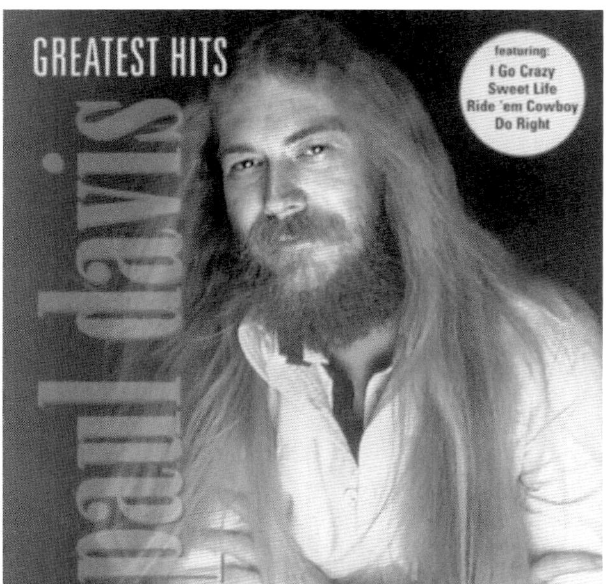

I Go Crazy!

Paul Davis once said, "I try to be very sincere with my music and have fun doing it and hope that it comes off on record that way." A singer-songwriter from Meridian, Paul's 1978 single "I Go Crazy" was in the Billboard Hot 100 chart for 40 weeks. In 1986, his duet with Marie Osmond, "You're Still New to Me," which he cowrote with Paul Overstreet, was his first No. 1 hit on the country chart. The next year, he had another No. 1 country hit, "I Won't Take Less than Your Love" with cowriter Don Schlitz. Paul died on April 22, 2008, in Meridian at the age of 60. (Authors collection.)

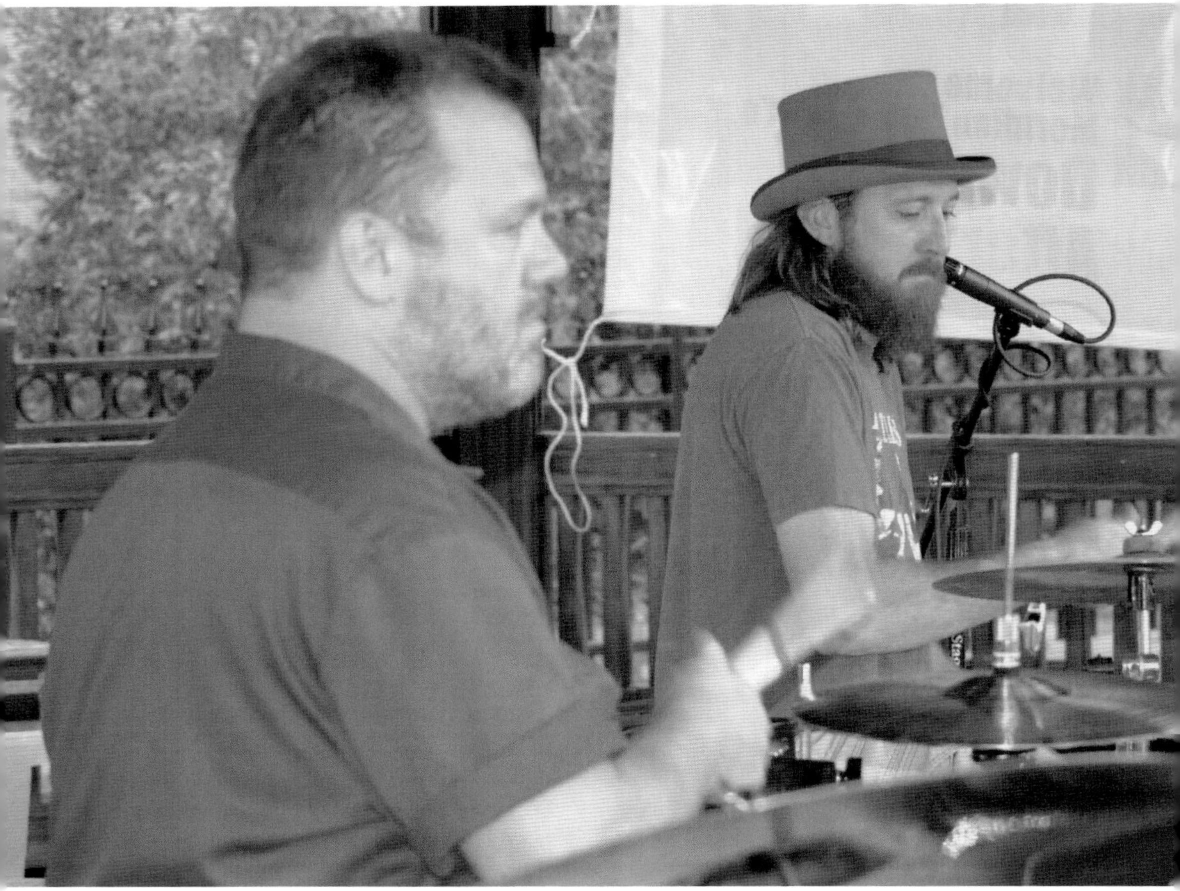

They're All Stars
At the Al Brown All Star Band concert series, drummer Fred LeBlanc (who also performs with Cowboy Mouth) and drummer David Zettler keep perfect time to "Roadhouse Blues" by The Doors. (Author's collection.)

Meridian's Sweetheart (OPPOSITE PAGE)
On June 23, 2010, actress Sela Ward was honored with a bronze star in the Mississippi Arts and Entertainment Center's Walk of Fame in front of the MSU Riley Center. A native daughter of Meridian, Ward has won Emmy Awards for her starring roles in the television series *Sisters* and *Once and Again*. In 2010, Sela Ward accepted a role in *CSI: NY* as Jo Danville, a former FBI agent from Washington, DC, driven by her empathy for crime victims. Possibly her greatest feat was in 2000 when she and her husband, Howard Sherman, founded Hope Village for Children, a Meridian shelter and residence for children. Her dream is to expand the residence to include a home for seniors. "They can be grandparents to the children and the children can be grandchildren," she said. Though Sela travels back and forth from Los Angeles to Meridian, her heart is and has always remained in the South and her hometown. "I miss family around the dinner table time," she said. (Author's collection.)

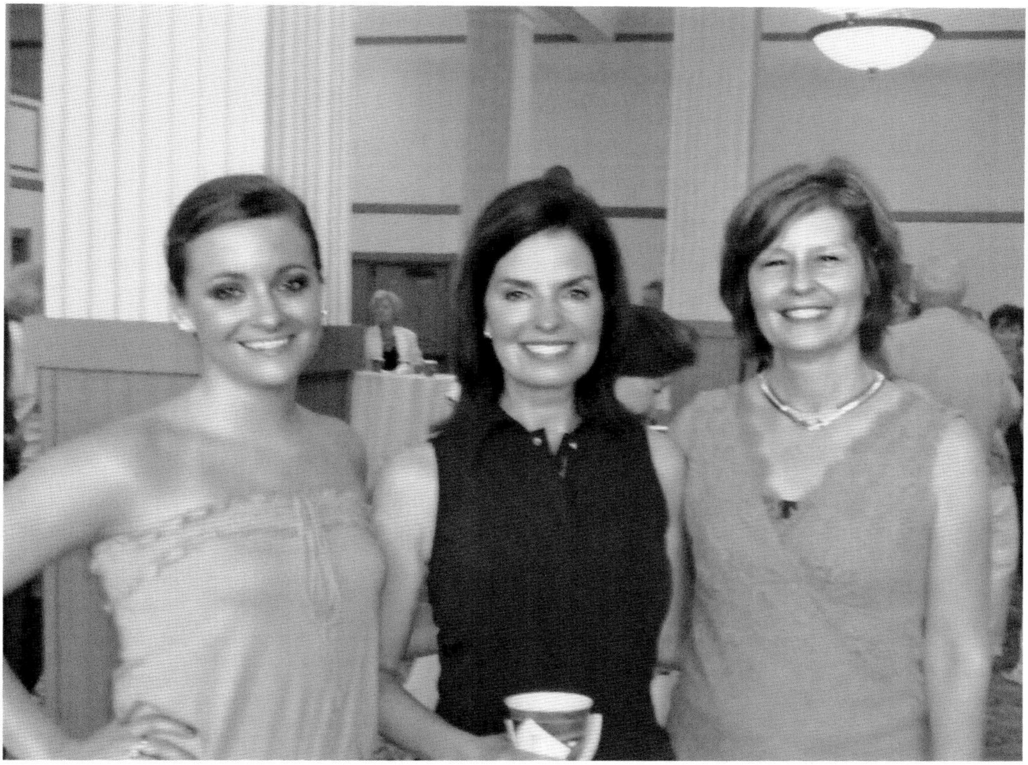

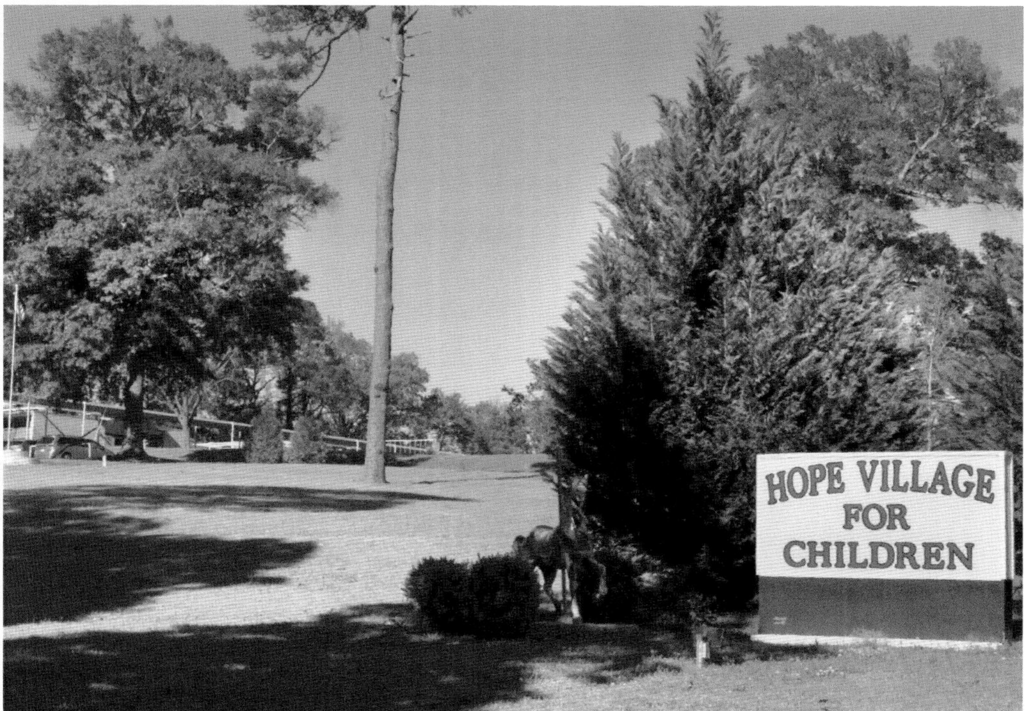
HOPE VILLAGE
FOR
CHILDREN

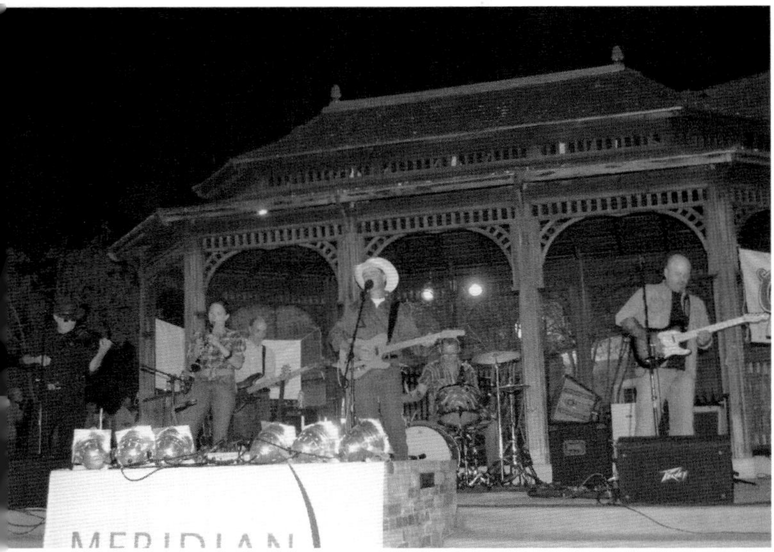

Meridian Main Street Concert Series

At the microphone, Britt Gully sings in his signature country voice. He is one of the top interpreters of Jimmie Rodgers music in the world and performs at many major city events and most all Jimmie Rodgers events. Currently a nursing student, Amy Lott is also a multitalented musician who plays clarinet, piano, flute, accordion, and harmonica. Tommy Ethridge, brother of the late Chris Ethridge, plays bass. Terry Lee Baker is on fiddle, and Steve Wilkerson is on keyboard. (Author's collection.)

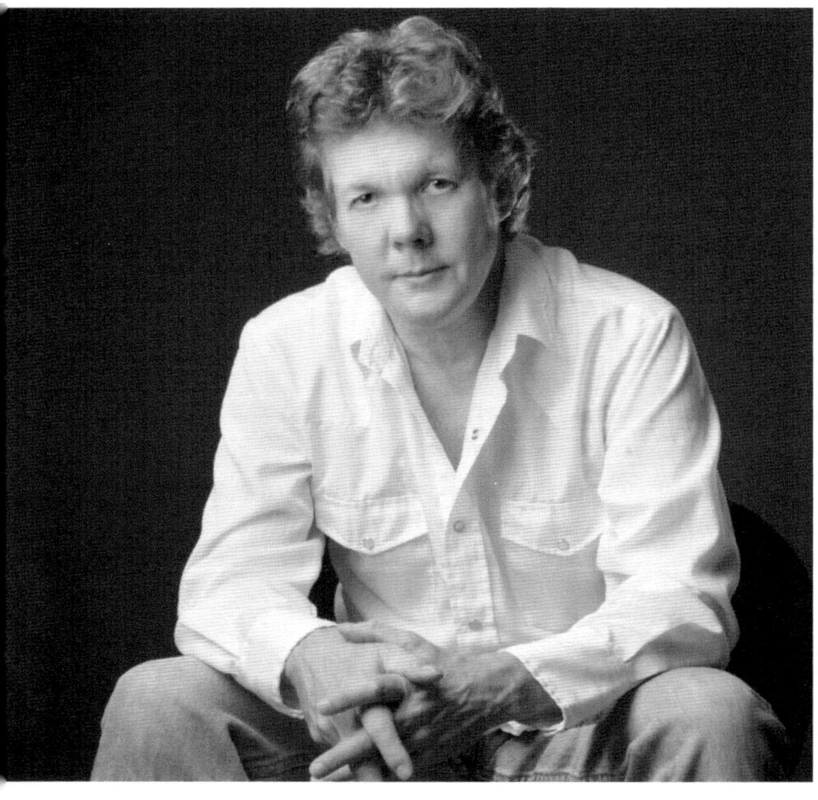

Romeo

Born in 1955, singer-songwriter Steve Forbert picked up a guitar at the age of 10. In his hometown of Meridian, he played in several bands before heading to New York City in 1976 where he performed in Grand Central Station for spare change. By 1978, Forbert had made his recording debut with *Alive on Arrival* and was referred to as "the new Dylan." Forbert's biggest single was his folk-rock hit, "Romeo's Tune." He was inducted into the Mississippi Musicians Hall of Fame in 2006. Grammy winner Keith Urban covered "Romeo's Tune" on his Greatest Hits set. (Courtesy of Steve Forbert.)

CHAPTER TWO

Economic Development

Meridian owes its early prosperity to the men who built its railroads, sawmills and gristmills, general mercantile stores, hotels, and factories. Not to be forgotten are the farmers picking cotton and the teachers dedicated to providing quality education. The vision and investment of early Meridians, still evident in many of the buildings and businesses standing today, paid off when the city came into its own among the finest places in the South—even after Sherman's torch burned through much of the area. Although much of the flourishing manufacturing and lumber industry declined during the Great Depression, many local businesses persevered. Meridian has sent soldiers off to war and wept for them when they fell on the distant shores. Surviving much adversity, the people of Meridian continue to dream of what is still to come.

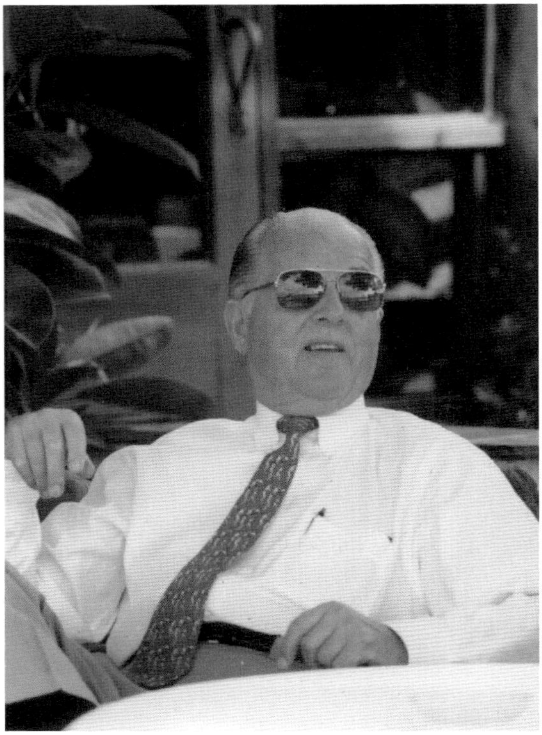

If You Plant It, It Will Grow
Van Zyverden, Inc., founded in Holland by Jack Van Zyverden, has grown into one of the world's largest wholesale flower bulb distributors. In 1966, Jack retired and left the family business to sons Dirk and Paul. When the company divided, Dirk acquired the Flower Bulbs, Inc., facilities in Edison, New Jersey. Paul took over the wholesale bulb business, Van Zyverden Bros., and built a warehouse in Meridian. In the 1980s, he purchased Flower Bulbs, Inc., from Dirk and Brown Bulb Ranch from a West Coast supplier. Paul retired in 1996, but Van Zyverden, Inc., remains a family business. (Courtesy of Van Zyverden Inc.)

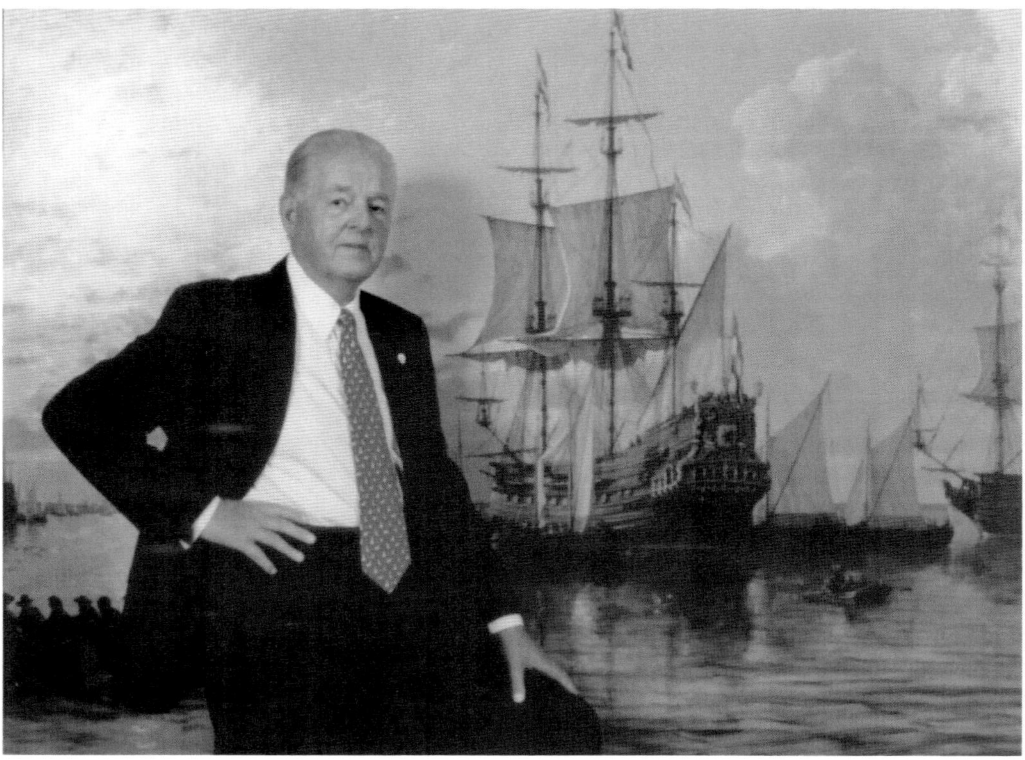

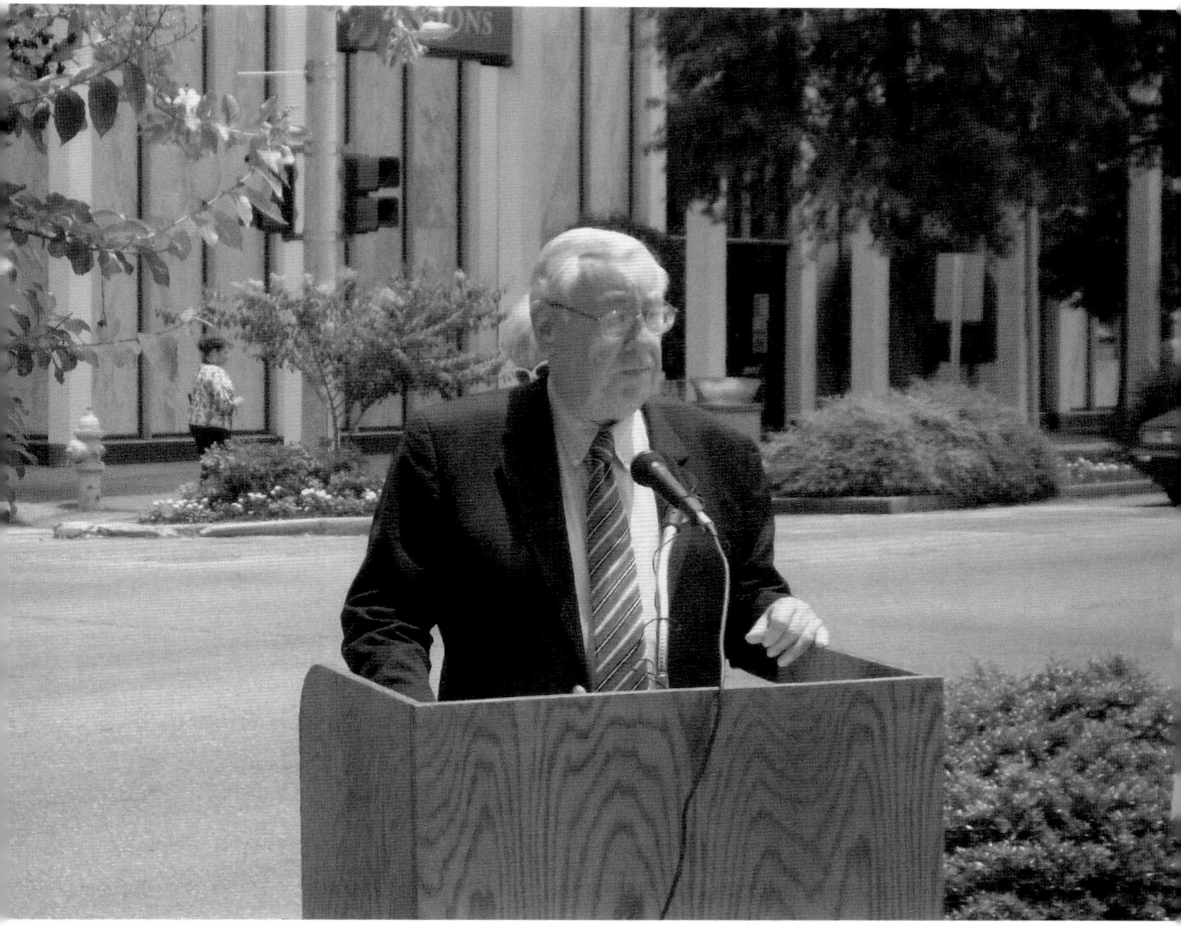

Man of Steel
In March 1967, when Tommy Dulaney went to work for Bates Steel, he had no idea that in 1975 he would start his own steel business, Structural Steel Services, Inc., with the help of a few backers. "I wouldn't be here today if it wasn't for Sammy Davidson," said Dulaney. "My success is due to my employees and those who helped me get started. I feel like you owe back to the community." He has paid forward many times the generosity he received. In this photograph, as president of Mississippi Arts & Entertainment Center (MAEC), Dulaney addresses the crowd at a MAEC Walk of Fame Star presentation. (Author's collection.)

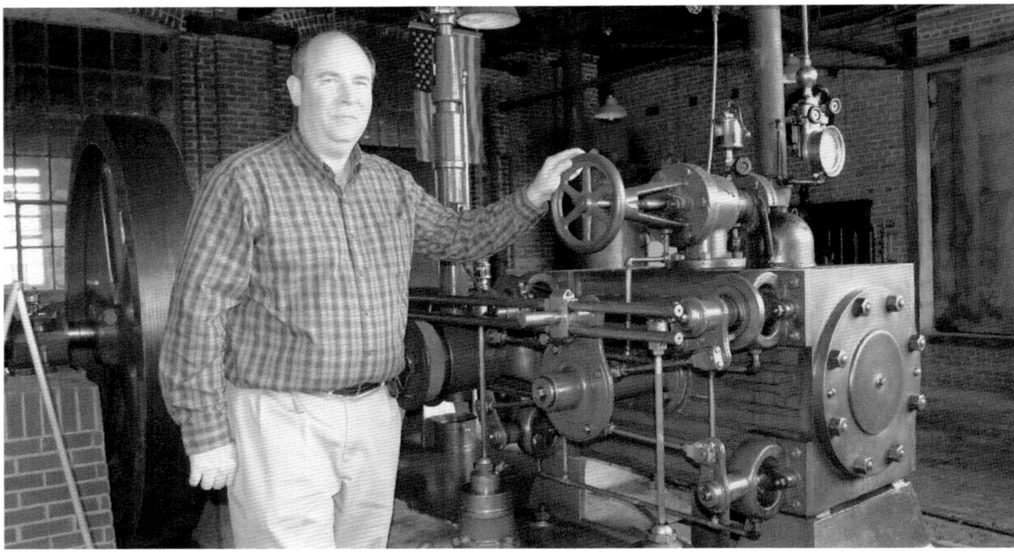

Blowing Off Steam

George Soulé, one of Meridian's early entrepreneurs, arrived in Meridian in 1879. He founded the Southern Cotton Standard Press, which manufactured and sold his invention of an innovative cotton press. Before 1894, he invented the Ideal Hay-Press and founded Progress Manufacturing Company between Twenty-sixth and Twenty-seventh Avenues and Forth and Fifth Streets, the same location as Soulé Steam Feed Works. Greg Hatcher stands beside Soulé machinery. Photograph courtesy of June Davis Davidson.)

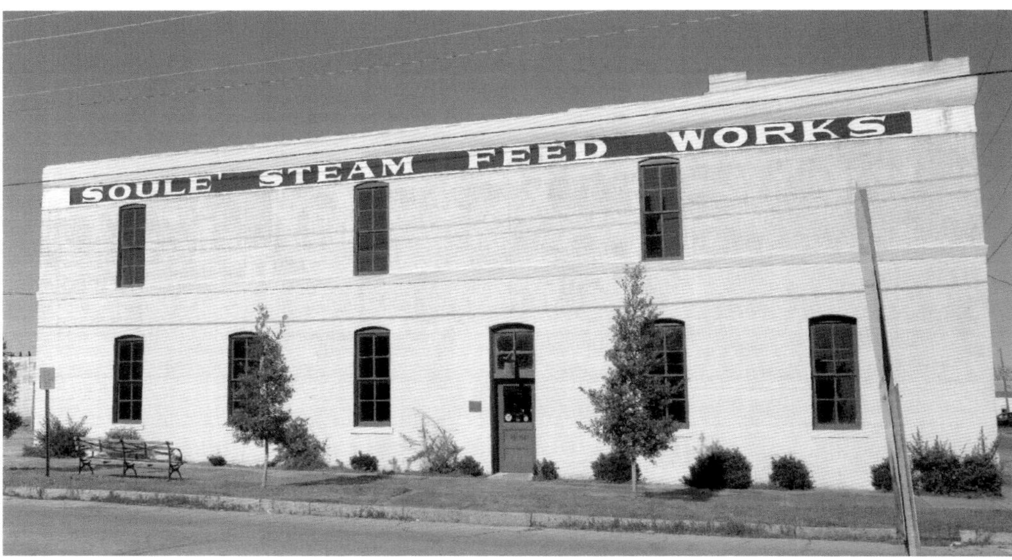

Patents

A progressive inventor, and businessman, Soulé saw the need for steam-powered engines in the thriving timber industry. He formed Soulé Steam Feed Works, which remained open from 1893 to 2003. George Soulé acquired over 40 patents before his death in 1922. Soulé Steam Feed Works is listed on the National Register of Historic Places. The Soulé Live Steam Festival is held each fall. (Courtesy of June Davis Davidson.)

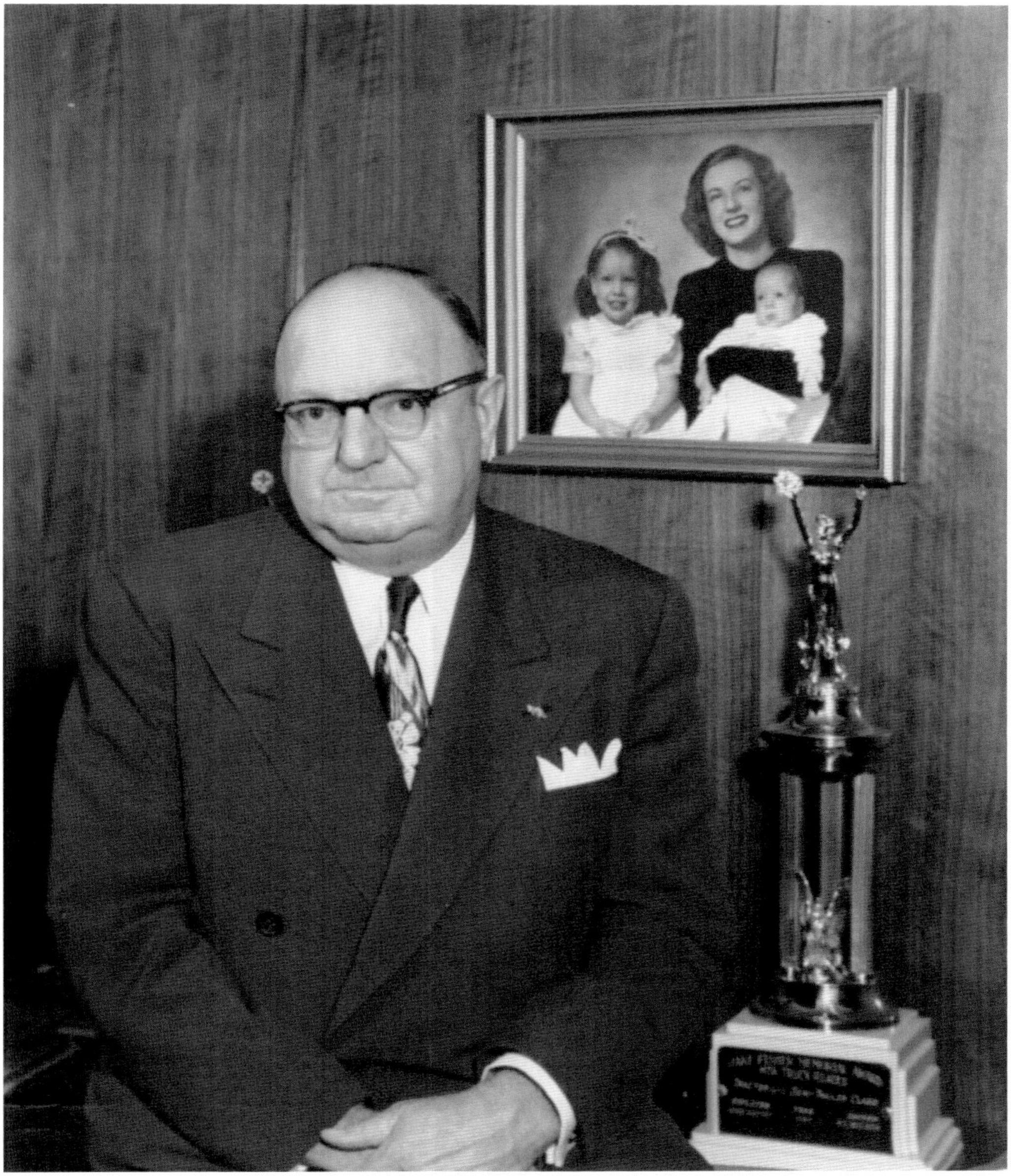

Entrepreneur
Rodney (Rod) Anthony Goodling was born in New York. "His initials were RAG, and he was always kidded about that," said his daughter Cheryl Goodling Rainey. Rod joined the military when war broke out and married his sweetheart before going overseas. When he returned to the states, according to Cheryl, he worked with his father-in-law, L.L. Major, who owned Sinclair Oil, L.L. Major Transport, and Dixie Highway Express. Rod served as president of the Mississippi Trucking Association but got out of the trucking business because of the unions. He built the Downtowner Motor Inn in Meridian, as well as inns in Vicksburg and on the Mississippi Gulf Coast. He built the first cable system in Meridian and at the Navy base. He sold the Meridian cable system to Comcast, which was their first cable system. (Courtesy of Cheryl Goodling Rainey.)

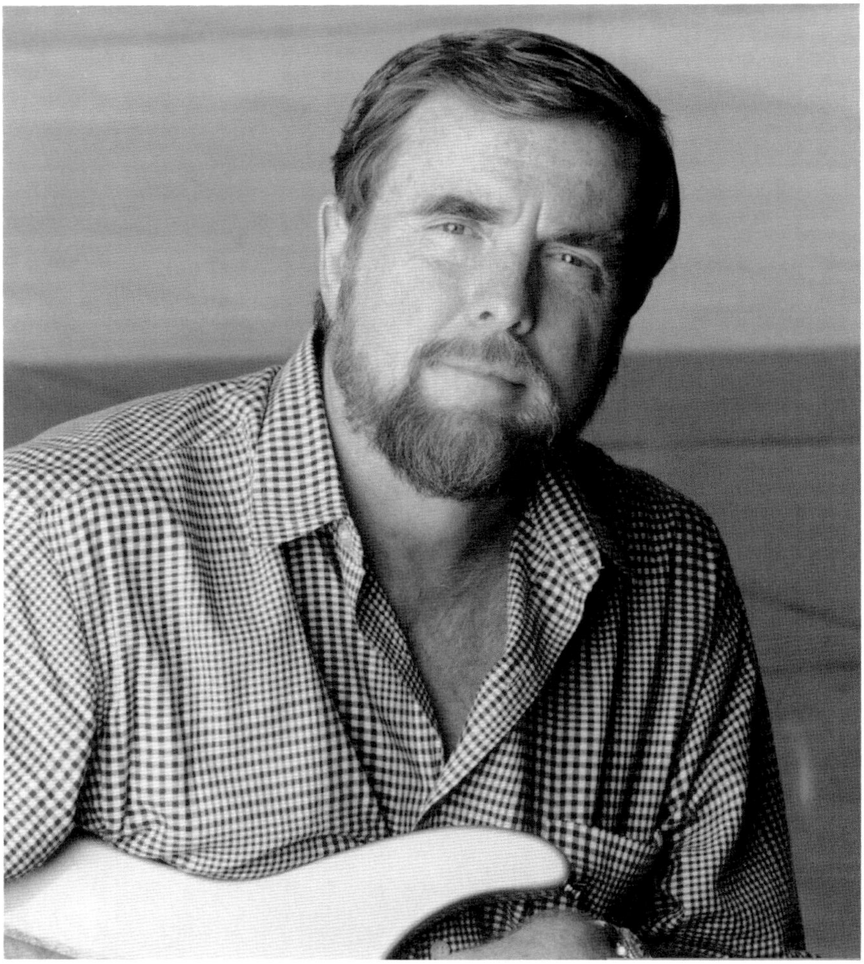

Ramp Up the Sound

Hartley Peavey did not inherit his father's musical ability. He realized he lacked the skills of a professional guitarist during his college days at Mississippi State University. Upon graduating in 1965, he set his sights on something he knew best: amplifiers.

A young and budding entrepreneur, Hartley built his first amplifier out of spare parts in his father's store, Peavey's Melody Music. His growing business relied on quality that was affordable to both the amateur and professional musician.

Almost 50 years later, with a hands-on approach, Hartley Peavey is known worldwide as a manufacturer of amplifiers and musical and audio equipment.

An innovator of musical and sound products, Peavey created a successful, privately held company with over 1,000 employees scattered around the globe. Today, he holds over 170 patents in sound and music equipment.

His words, "It comes from within," are quoted from an interview with KVR Audio. To most Mississippians, like Hartley, "within" means to be the best you can be—with the talent God provided.

Peavey is hailed as one of Meridian's great success stories. Today, Peavey products are manufactured worldwide and sold in over 130 countries. His company's equipment logo, Peavey, is recognizable as a leader in the sound and music industry. (Courtesy of Hartley Peavey.)

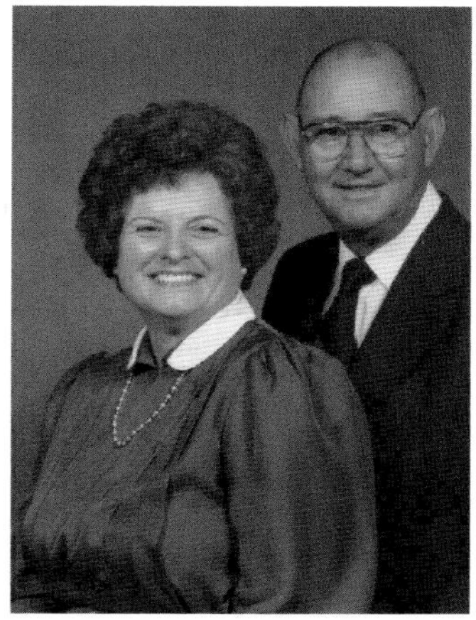

Heart of Gold
When David W. (D.W.) Carr received his discharge from the Navy, he returned to what many locals consider the garden spot of Mississippi. Meridian. Before church services began on a Sunday morning in 1949, he married Ruth Carolyn Tedder in the parsonage of Poplar Springs Baptist Church. He joined his father, Evan Carr, who had leased the Sinclair Service Station on Twenty-second Avenue near his mother's restaurant. D.W. is pictured here with Ruth Carolyn Carr. (Courtesy of Ruth Carolyn Carr.)

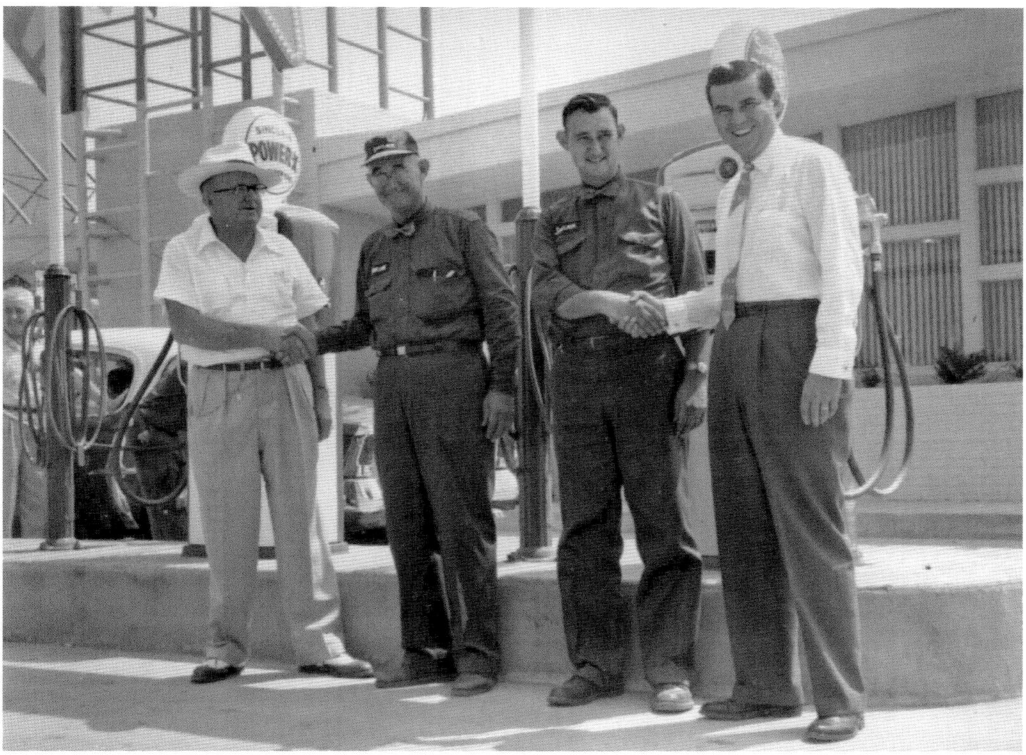

Red Hot
Carr leased the Texaco Station a block south of the Sinclair Station, but when Lon Majors asked D.W. to lease the recently constructed Red Hot Truck Stop, he accepted. His mother, Thelma, and his wife, Ruth Carolyn, joined him and managed the restaurant. His father grew the vegetables and raised the chickens that were prepared daily at the restaurant. "We would shell peas and cut corn off the cob early in the mornings for lunch," Ruth Carolyn said. "We worked three shifts with three waitresses each shift. We had other help, cashiers, dishwashers, and busboys. Our sons, Russell and David, worked outdoors caring for the Red Hot's Filling Station. We closed each night at 10:00 p.m., and we were open every day except Christmas." Carr and Lon Majors pose for a photograph during the Red Hot Truck Stop grand opening. (Courtesy of Ruth Carolyn Carr.)

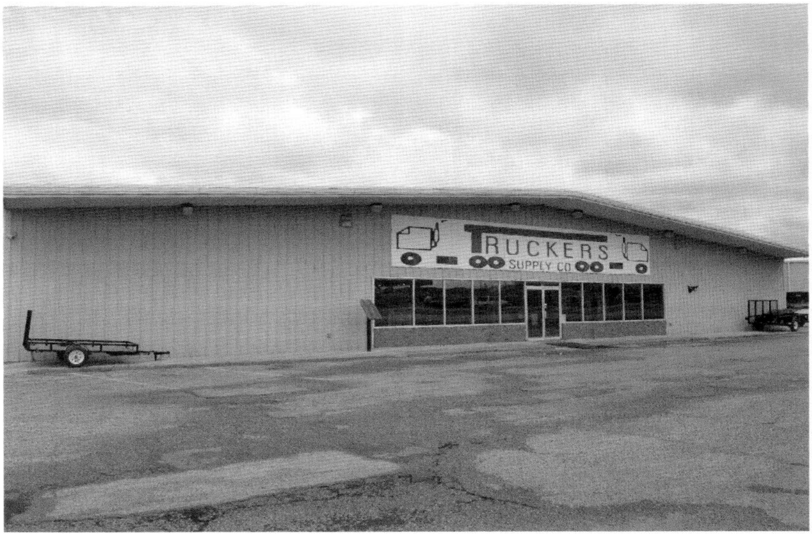

A Good Heart

Helping came as naturally as breathing to D.W. Carr. His caring heart and wallet opened to many who walked through the doors of the Red Hot, hungry and stranded in need of food for their families. D.W. saw that their need was filled. According to Ruth Carolyn, "Once when we were reading about gifts in the Bible, I asked D.W. what he thought his gift was. He said, 'I guess it would be the ability to make money so I can help others,' " Helping others would be D.W.'s motto throughout his life. He also opened Roll Your Own Tires on Front Street. When he outgrew that, he bought the corner lot and opened Trucker's Supply in 1967. (Courtesy of June Davis Davidson.)

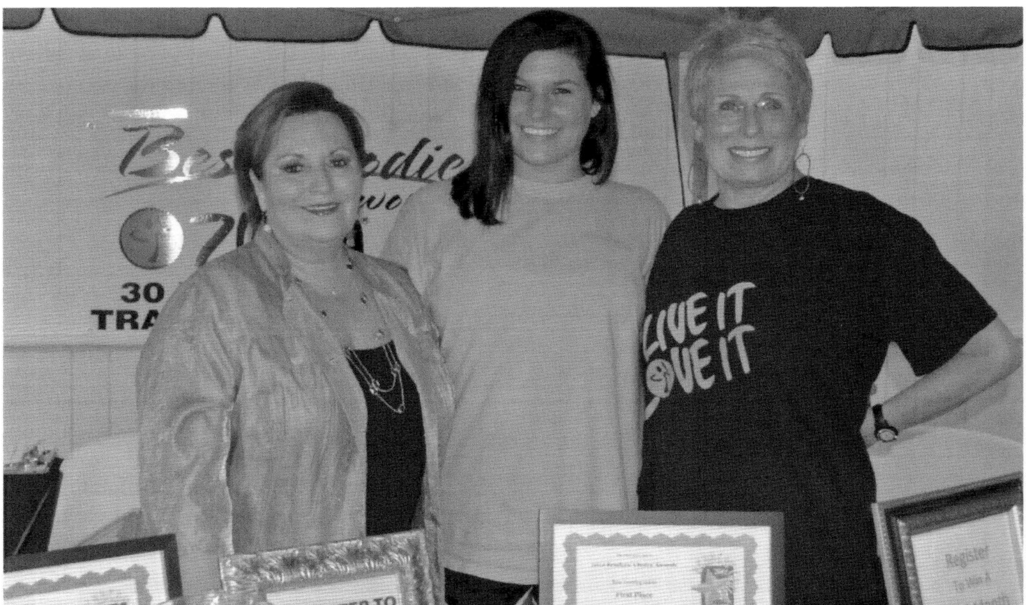

Staying in Shape

Friends for almost a lifetime, Becky Sims and Linda Holloway have been the co-owners of Best Bodies for five years. The business is more like a ministry to them, because they guide and encourage their members and help them discover good health and fitness habits. "I do a lot of counseling with the women," said Becky. "We've all been there, so we relate to the individual." (Author's collection.)

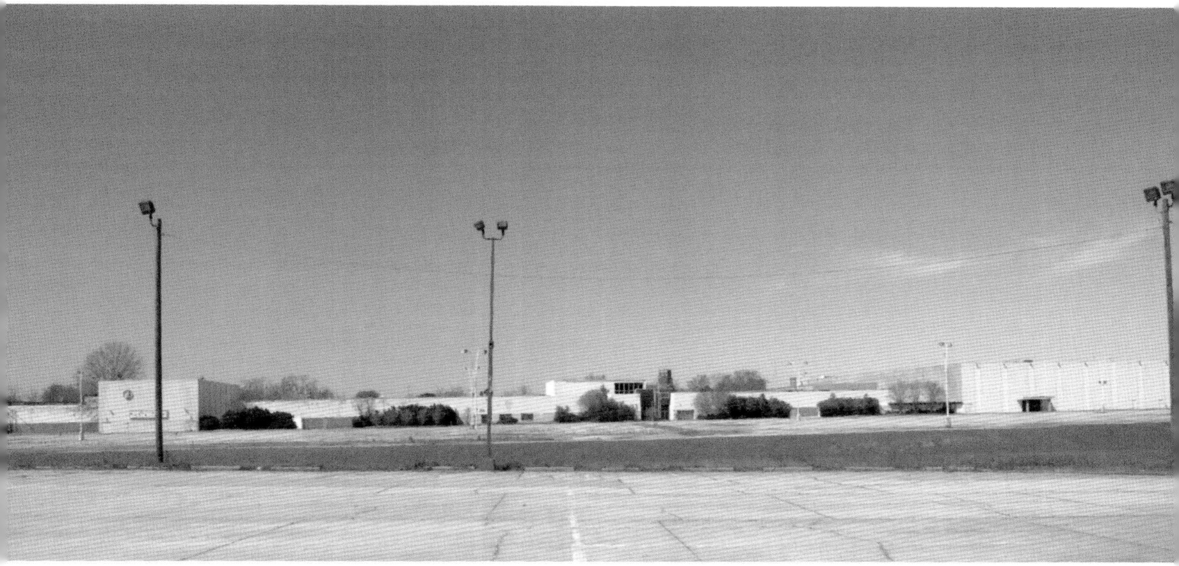

Family Clan

Paul Broadhead came from Needham, Alabama, to Meridian with his mother, Verdie; father, Sam (a sawmill operator); and siblings Paul, Norris, Carline, and Sadie. At the time, Paul Elzie Broadhead was nine years old.

A graduate of Meridian High, Paul attended the University of Mississippi and graduated with a liberal arts degree. A developer, he constructed Meridian's first mall, Village Fair Mall. Although real estate and banking was Broadhead's livelihood, he also believed in the natural preservation of Mississippi's natural resource: land. His company developed a muscadine processing plant and urged farmers to plant vineyards as an alternative to cotton and corn crops.

As his success grew, so did his compassion, and his unsung contributions to community and civic organizations in Meridian were many.

In later years, he developed a heart condition that required a heart transplant. He died on August 5, 2009, in Boynton Beach, Florida, at the age of 70. Pictured in 2013 is the former Village Fair Mall, Village Fair Mall, once a vibrant shopping center for east Mississippi and West Alabama residents. (Courtesy of June Davis Davidson.)

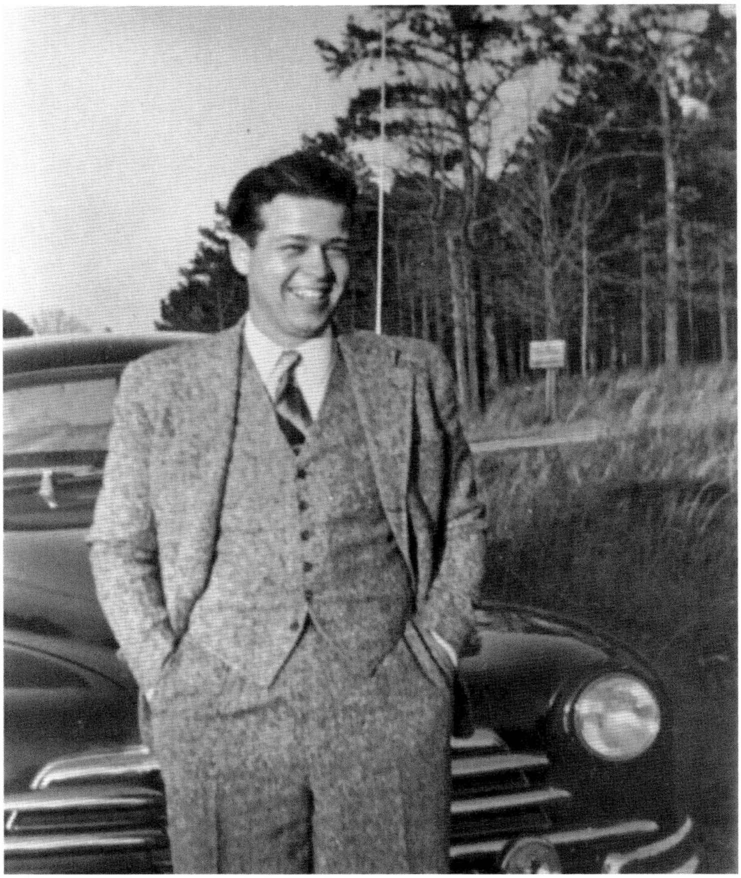

A Penny Earned
Henry David Burns, born on September 28, 1927, in Pushmataha, Alabama, was the son of Heidelberg merchant Beaury C. Burns and his wife, Grace. A veteran of World War II, Henry began his career in 1956 with his brother B.C. as the owners of a Pan-Am gas station on Highway 80 in Meridian. By the 1960s, he became one of, if not the most influential men in the state. (Courtesy of David Burns.)

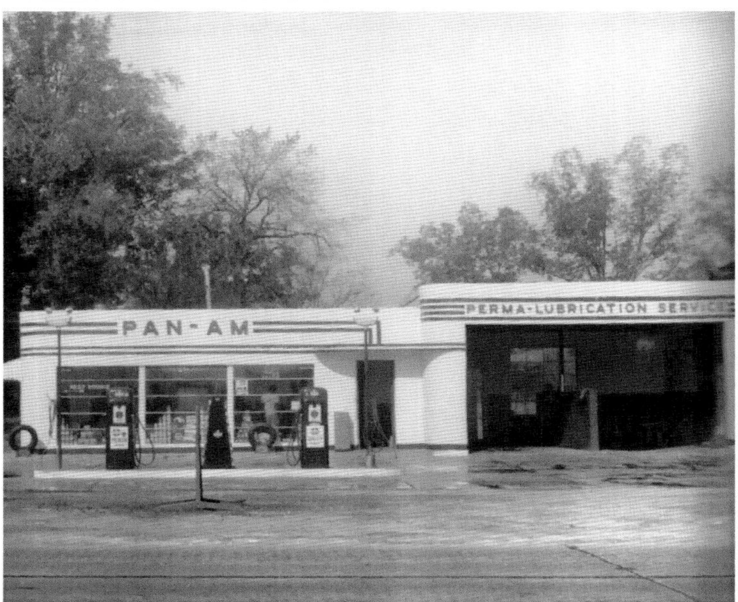

A Penny Saved
Burns was a charismatic and brilliant man known for his successful business ventures, He earned the respect and friendship of governors, presidents, and businessmen. He served as president of the Mississippi-Alabama Oil Jobbers Association. Active in community service, Burns was an astute businessman who held the belief that "if you take care of pennies, the dollars will take care of themselves." (Courtesy of David Burns.)

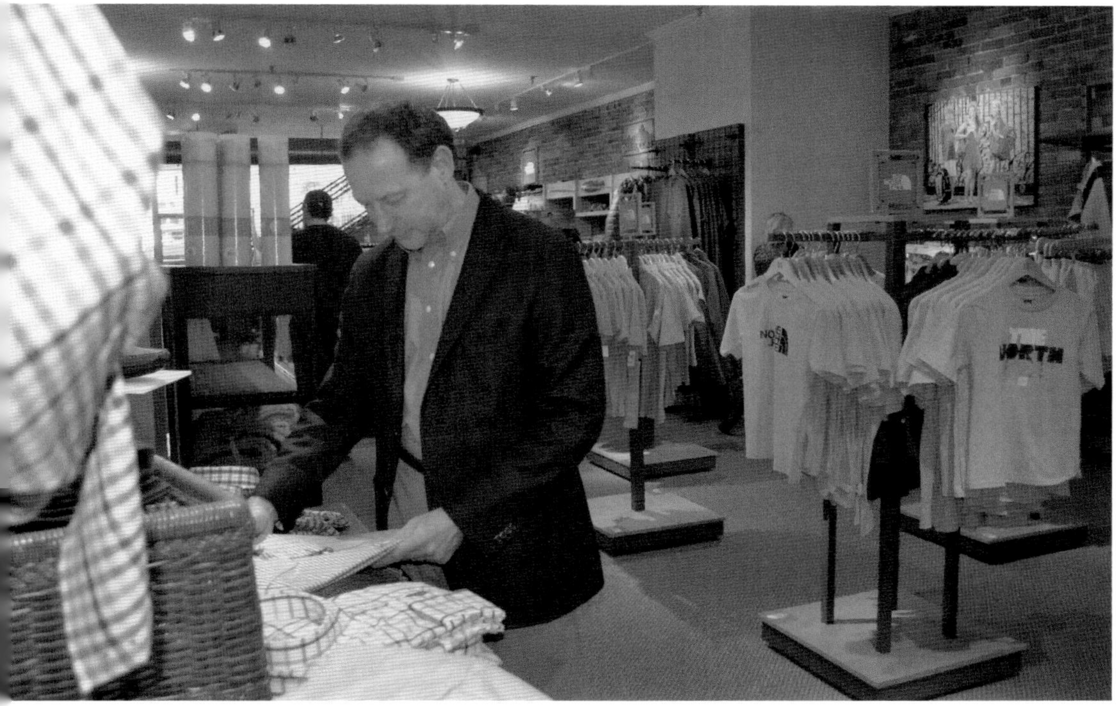

Family Business
In 1988, Robert Loeb, great-grandson of Alexander Loeb, opened his Loeb's store on Twelfth Street and Twenty-second Avenue as a men's only store. Ten years later, Robert moved Loeb's, which now carries women's apparel, into the current building on Front Street. "We love being downtown, in the heart of the city, where the character is," said Robert. "I hope to keep Loeb's a family business." (Author's collection.)

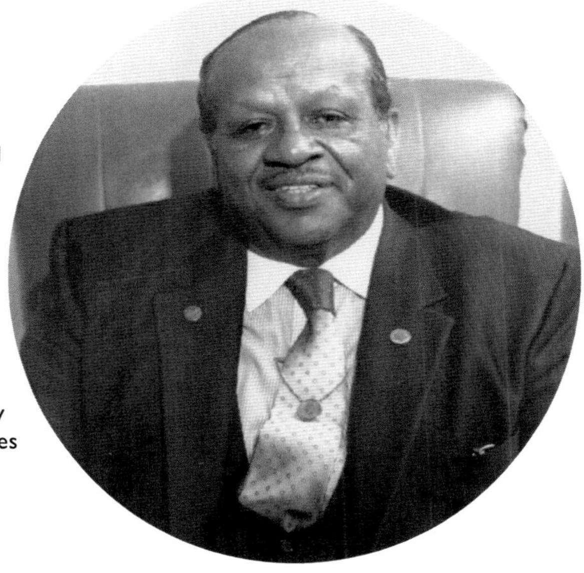

Surviving Jim Crow
Dr. Hobert Kornegay started his private dental practice started in 1948. In 1977, he became the first African American to be elected to city council. He became the first black supervisor in Lauderdale County in 1985. He was interviewed in an oral history conducted by the University of Southern Mississippi about living in Mississippi during Jim Crow and the civil rights movement. Kornegay fought for civil rights in Meridian. (Courtesy of Lauderdale County Department of Archives and History.)

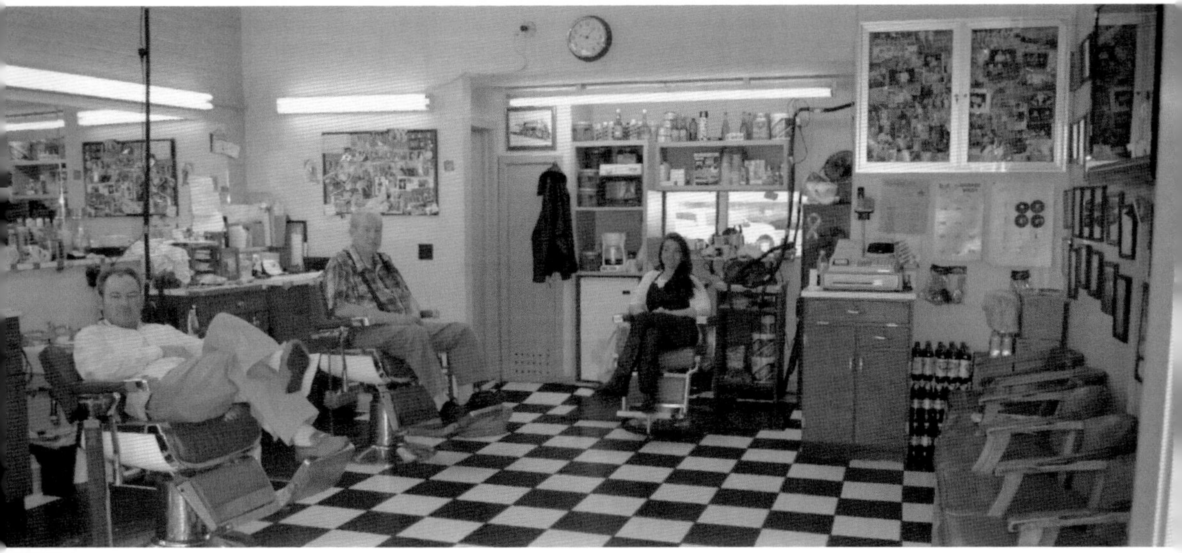

Clip Joint

"When I came to Meridian, all I had was change in my pocket," Bill Gordon said. Gordon and his wife lived in an upstairs apartment he had rented for $30 a month. He met his wife while attending barbering school in Memphis. "I had barbered in the Navy, so after three months at the school, the instructor thought I had enough experience and he gave me my diploma," Gordon said. Shown is the interior of Gordon's Barber Shop. (Courtesy of June Davis Davidson.)

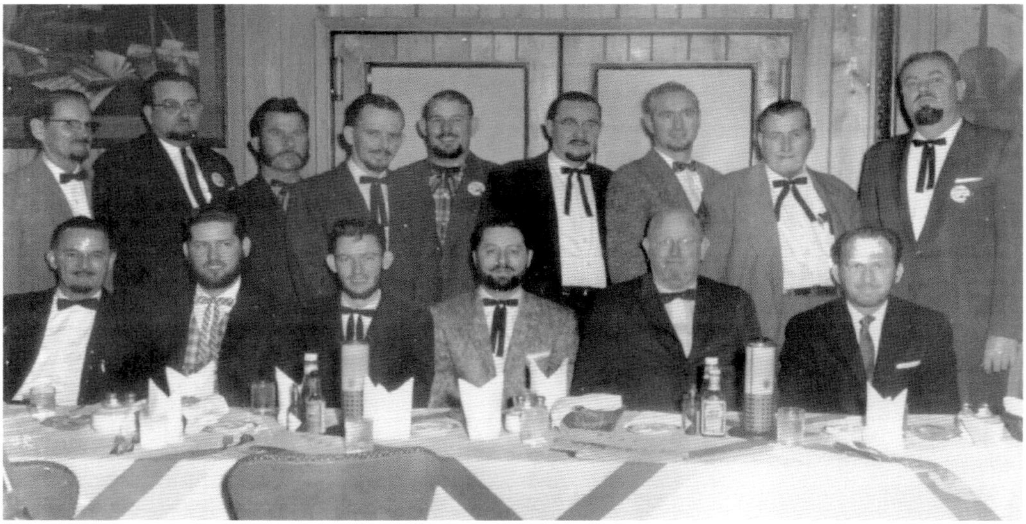

With a Clipper in Hand

Gordon's career in Meridian began at City Barber. For five and a half years, he barbered at Sam Tinesley's shop before he opened Gordon's Barber Shop in its current location in 1957. Gordon, who raced horses, is also the owner of several local businesses in Lauderdale County. This photograph of Meridian's barbers during Meridian's centennial includes, from left to right, Mr. Peek, unidentified, Bill Ward, Jack Jackson, Howard Chapman, Norris Tensely, unidentified, E.E. Gunn, and Sam Dickerson. (Courtesy of Bill Gordon.)

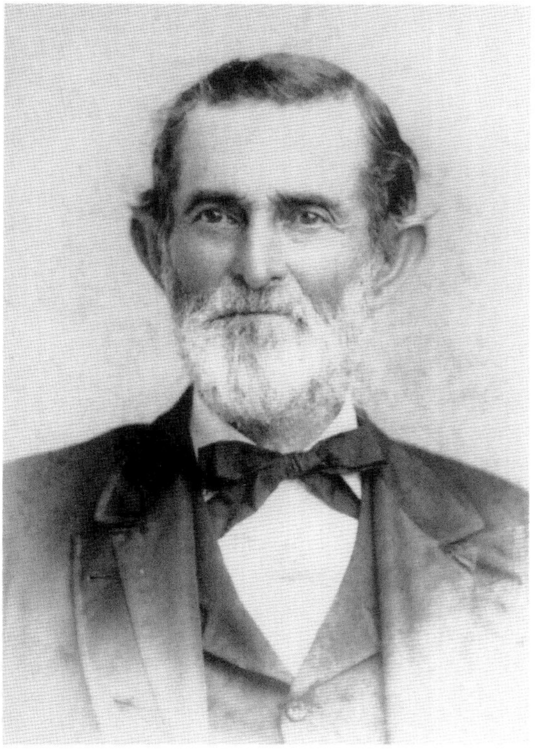

Daily Grind
On November 20, 1820, John Cooper Dunn, who was born 25 miles from Belfast, Ireland, boarded a ship called *The Jane* and set sail for Charleston, South Carolina. Records indicate that John, his siblings, and parents remained in South Carolina during most of his early boyhood before the family migrated to Alabama. He married a young widow, Elizabeth Ann (Hutchins) Kennedy, on April 6, 1852, in Green County, Alabama. (Courtesy of Ben Buckley.)

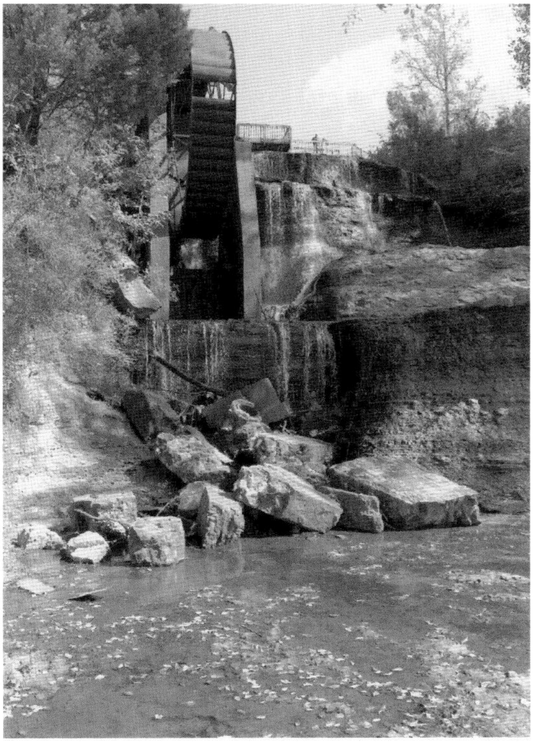

River of Dreams
John Dunn migrated to Lauderdale County and established a gristmill on the Chunky River. He was a lover of education and provided tutors for his children, Sue Pauline and Charles. The mill today is known as Dunn Falls, pictured here. The Confederate army, embroiled in the heat of the battle for Southern rights, often needed the resources of its citizenry to provide for Confederate needs. It is thought, but not proven, that the Confederates may have confiscated Dunn's mill or enlisted his help, for he did provide manufactured necessities for the war. John lost two of his brothers during the war: Charles Hayes Dunn and Alexander M. Dunn. (Courtesy of June Davis Davidson.)

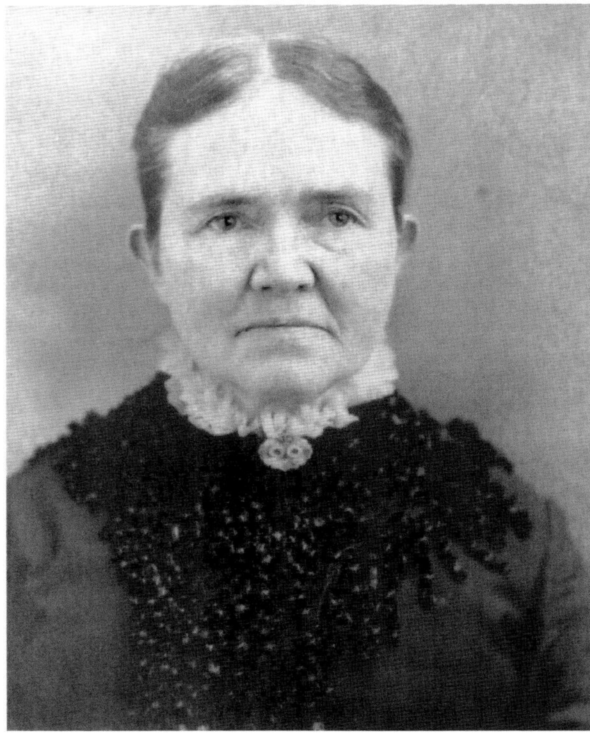

A Legacy
A few years before his death, John and Elizabeth moved to Forrest to be near his daughter Sue Pauline and her husband, Martin Leonidus Buckley. John Cooper Dunn died on the February 12, 1904, from pneumonia. His body was transported to Enterprise, where Dr. J.F. Jones of Meridian conducted the services. John Cooper Dunn is interred at Odd Fellows Cemetery in Enterprise. Elizabeth Dunn is pictured here. (Courtesy of Ben Buckley.)

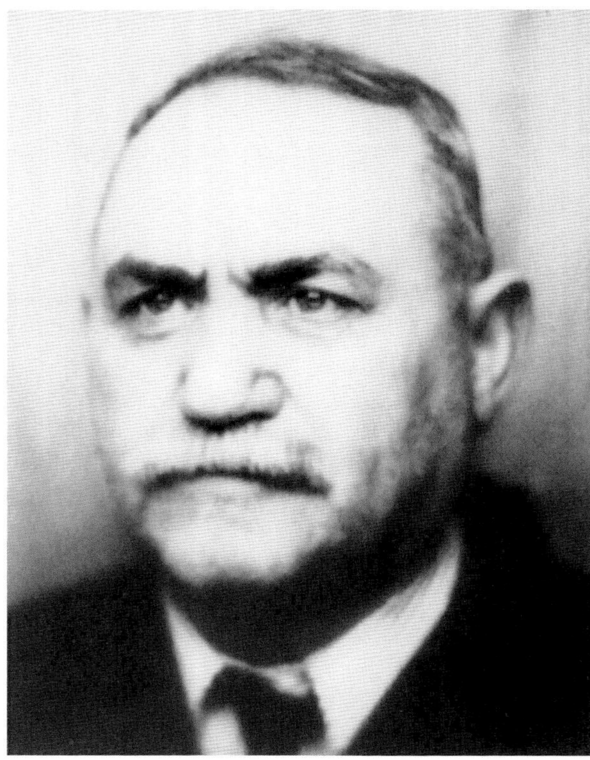

From Junk to Treasure
Marty Davidson's family first settled in America in the early 1900s when his grandfather, Russian-born Louis Davidson, immigrated and started the company that would become Southern Pipe and Supply, which is in its 72nd year of operation and its fourth generation of family management. Louis Davidson started a junk company in Meridian called St. Louis Junk Company. The company started selling bathtubs, and in 1938 Louis Davidson opened Southern Pipe and Supply with his sons Sammie and Meyer. (Courtesy of Marty Davidson and Southern Pipe and Supply.)

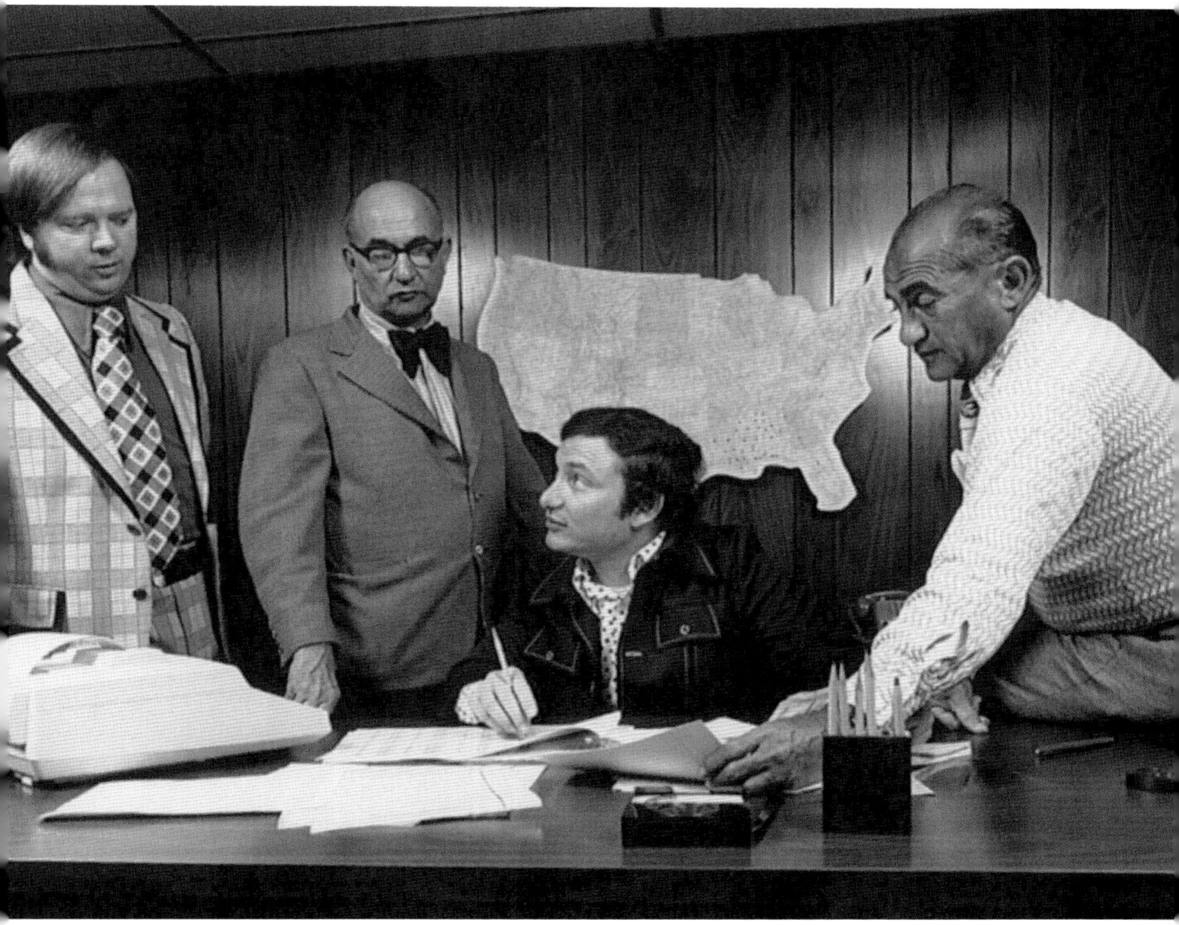

Legends Live On
Marty Davidson, the son of Meyer Davidson, started working at Southern Pipe when he was five years old and continued working summers until he left for college. He began working for the company full-time in 1962. In 1968, he purchased the company from his father. In that same year, Ku Klux Klan members bombed the home of Meyer Davidson because of his public stance against the bombing of synagogues and churches in Mississippi. In 48 years, Southern Pipe and Supply has grown from four branches in three states to 93 branches in seven states. In 2010, it was ranked as the seventh-largest distributor of plumbing supplies in the United States and the second-largest regional distributor by *Supply House Times*. Marty has been awarded the local Hartley D. Peavey Award for Entrepreneurial Excellence, the Neville Humanitarian Award, and Meridian Star Citizen of the Year Award, and is honored in the Mississippi Business Hall of Fame. He received the Ellis Island Medal of Honor, a national award sponsored by the National Ethnic Coalition of Organizations, in New York on May 7. Davidson represented the immigrant experience through his Jewish and Russian heritage and was the second Mississippian to receive the award. (Courtesy of Marty Davidson and Southern Pipe and Supply.)

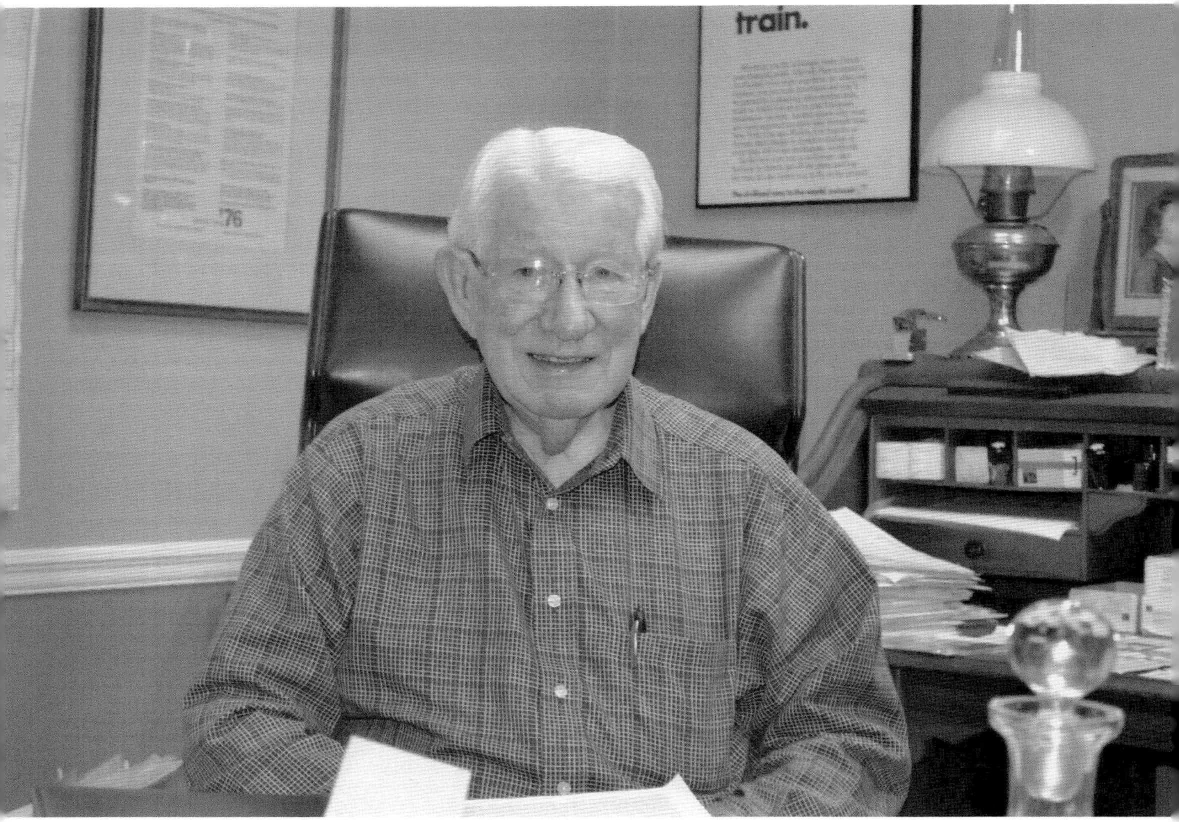

From Wall Street to Cars

In June 1950, Gil Carmichael became a field salesman for the *Wall Street Journal.* In this position, Gil taught men (not women) how to read the *Wall Street Journal* throughout his territory of New Orleans, South Louisiana, and South Mississippi. "I would go to the top floor of a building and talk to every businessman all the way down. I'd walk in and say, 'I'm Gil Carmichael with Dow Jones. We print the *Wall Street Journal.*' I would teach them how to read the *Wall Street Journal* and how it was laid out. I did that for eight years and helped build the circulation."

When his Cadillac dealer friend, with the help of Gil, became a FIAT distributor for five states, he asked Gil to come on board. "I left Wall Street Journal and moved to Shreveport to bring in FIAT automobiles. I brought them into the port of New Orleans and I would set up dealerships." But Gil wanted to be in business for himself.

Gil became a partner in a Meridian dealership and later bought all interest in that business. "That's how I started the Volkswagen dealership in Meridian. I built the Volkswagen building. I had Mercedes and Audi. And I had dealerships in Tuscaloosa." (Courtesy of Gil Carmichael.)

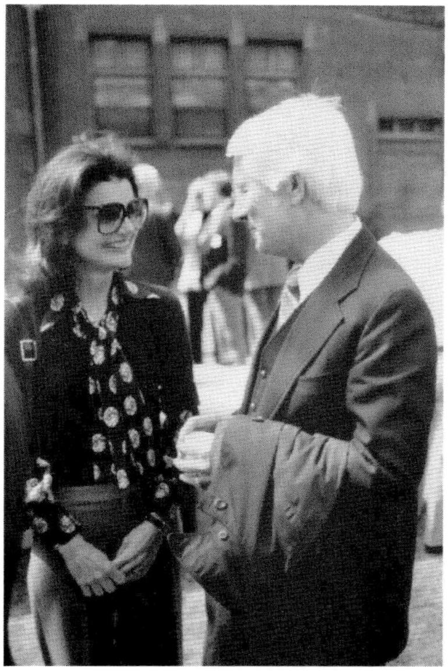

For Lease

When appointed federal railroad administrator by the first Bush administration, Gil Carmichael sold his two car dealerships in Meridian but kept his buildings. This became the nucleus of his real estate company, Missouth Properties. "When I finished my four years in Washington, I came home and took over our real estate company and have been expanding it ever since." (Courtesy of Gil Carmichael.)

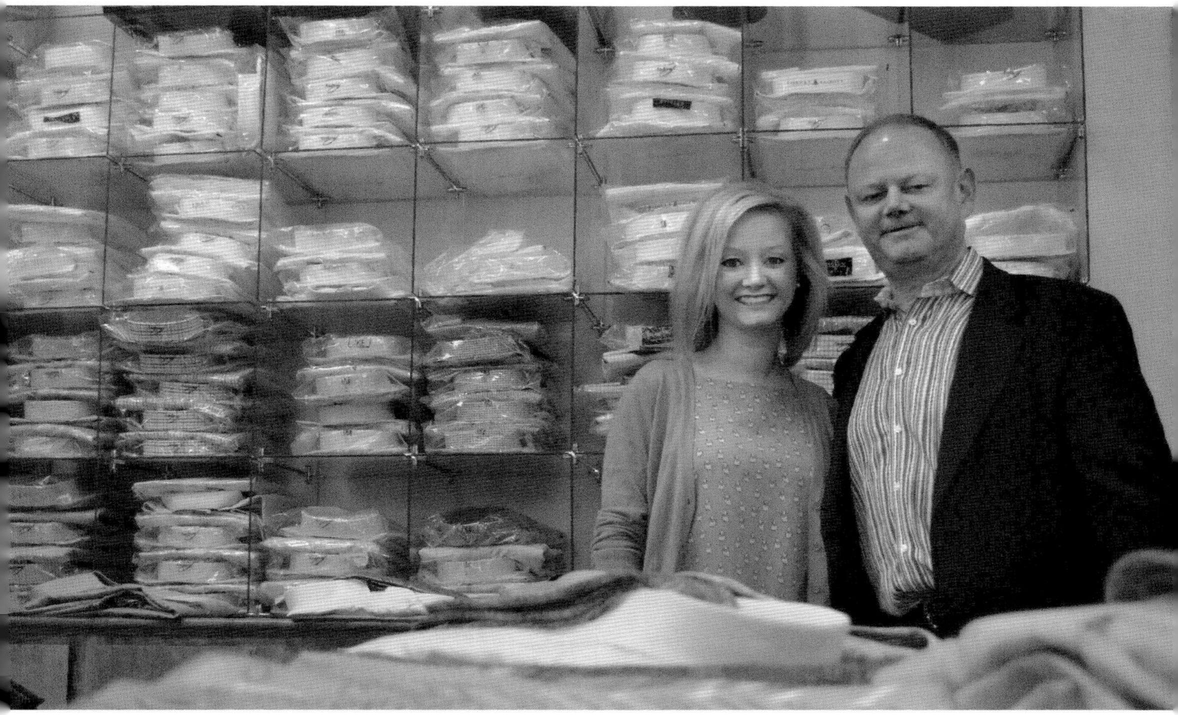

Dressing the Town

The Mayer family has sold clothes since the 1930s. They bought the old Alex Loeb Building in 1984 and were there until 2003. "We moved in our new building [on Highway 39] in January 2005," said Harry. Being a local business, 99.9 percent of his customers are "our dear, dear friends. . . . Over the years you develop many close relationships. We are not a transaction store; we are a relationship store." (Author's collection.)

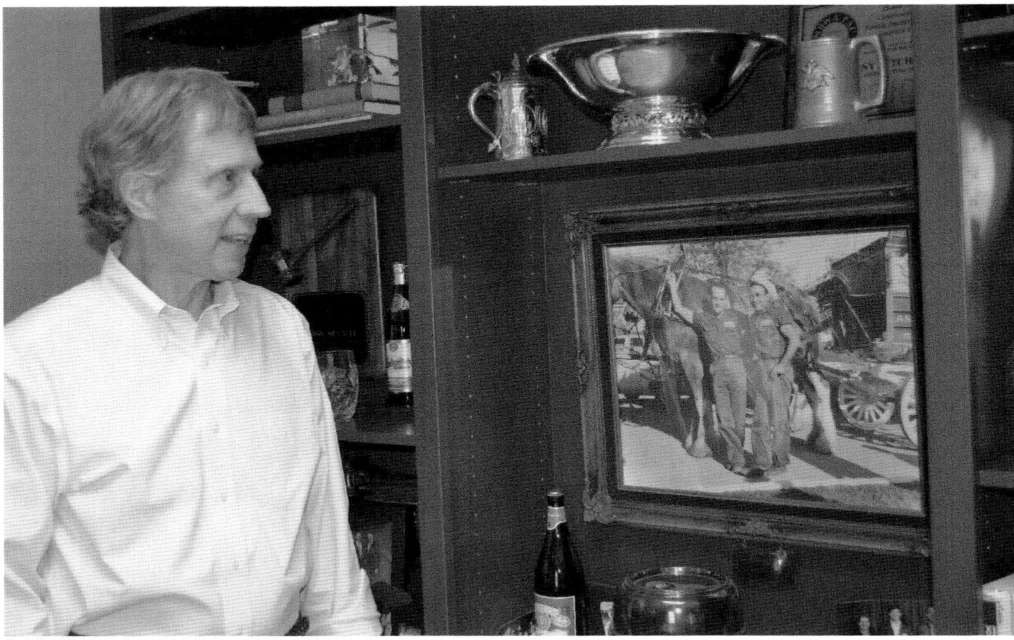

Have a Cold One on Me

When Manny Mitchell's grandfather E.J. Mitchell emigrated from Lebanon to America, they could only afford to bring their oldest child, leaving seven in Lebanon. Settling in Meridian in the 1920s, the Mitchells had six more children, including Mann Mitchell (Manny's father) and Bilbo Mitchell (father of Meridian attorney Bilbo Mitchell). Their general store, which opened in 1931, was in the vicinity of the current Mitchell Distributing Company, an Anheuser-Busch distributor. Mann became a distributor of Falstaff Beer in Lauderdale County and, later, a distributor of Budweiser. Since his father's passing, Manny has run the business. Longtime supporters of the Meridian community, Manny and his wife, Melanie, set up the Mitchell Boys and Girls Club Endowment. (Above, courtesy of Manny Michell; below, author's collection.)

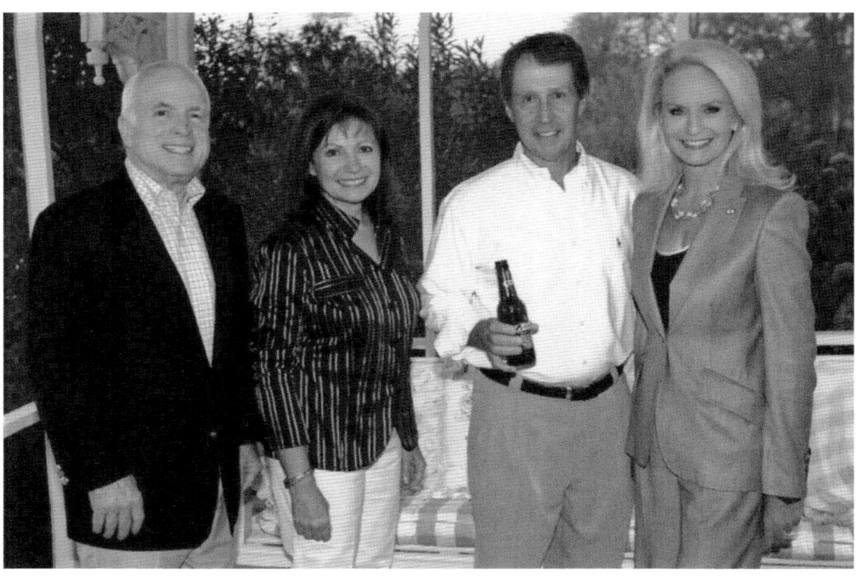

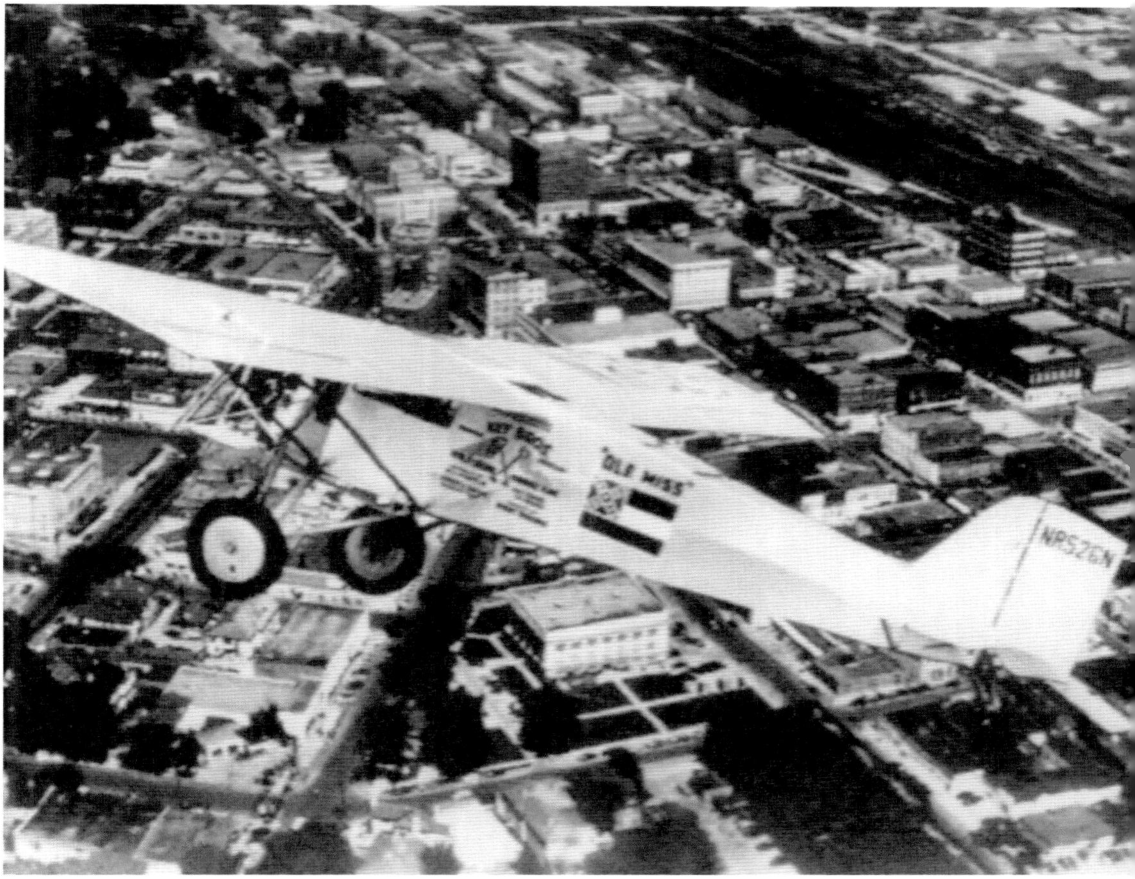

Inventor

Inventor and mechanic A.D. Hunter invented a spill-free fueling system, a valve on the end of the fuel nozzle. During fueling, if the nozzle was removed from the tank, the fuel would automatically stop flowing because of Hunter's special valve. This technology allowed Keys Brothers to refuel in midair as they flew 52,320 miles of nonstop flight, covering 653 hours and 34 minutes. The Key Brothers still hold the flight endurance record, thanks to Hunter's genius invention. The US Army Air Corps later adopted this nozzle, and it is still in use today.

"A.D. Hunter was quietly confident in his abilities without being arrogant at all, and was not in the least bit concerned with the world's opinion of him," said Calvin Lott, whose father was Hunter's good friend. "If you met him face to face, you would have thought he was homeless. He was swarthy complexioned, usually dressed in greasy work clothes, and always had a short cigar in his mouth." A.D. told Calvin that he had been able to solve problems dealing with machining metal, in large part because of a book. "He brought out a large book, and the title of it was something like *A Survey of Machine Work in America*. The copyright date was around the 1850s." He told Calvin that "as time progresses, everything changes and people often forget how things were done in the past." (Courtesy of Lauderdale County Department of Archives and History.)

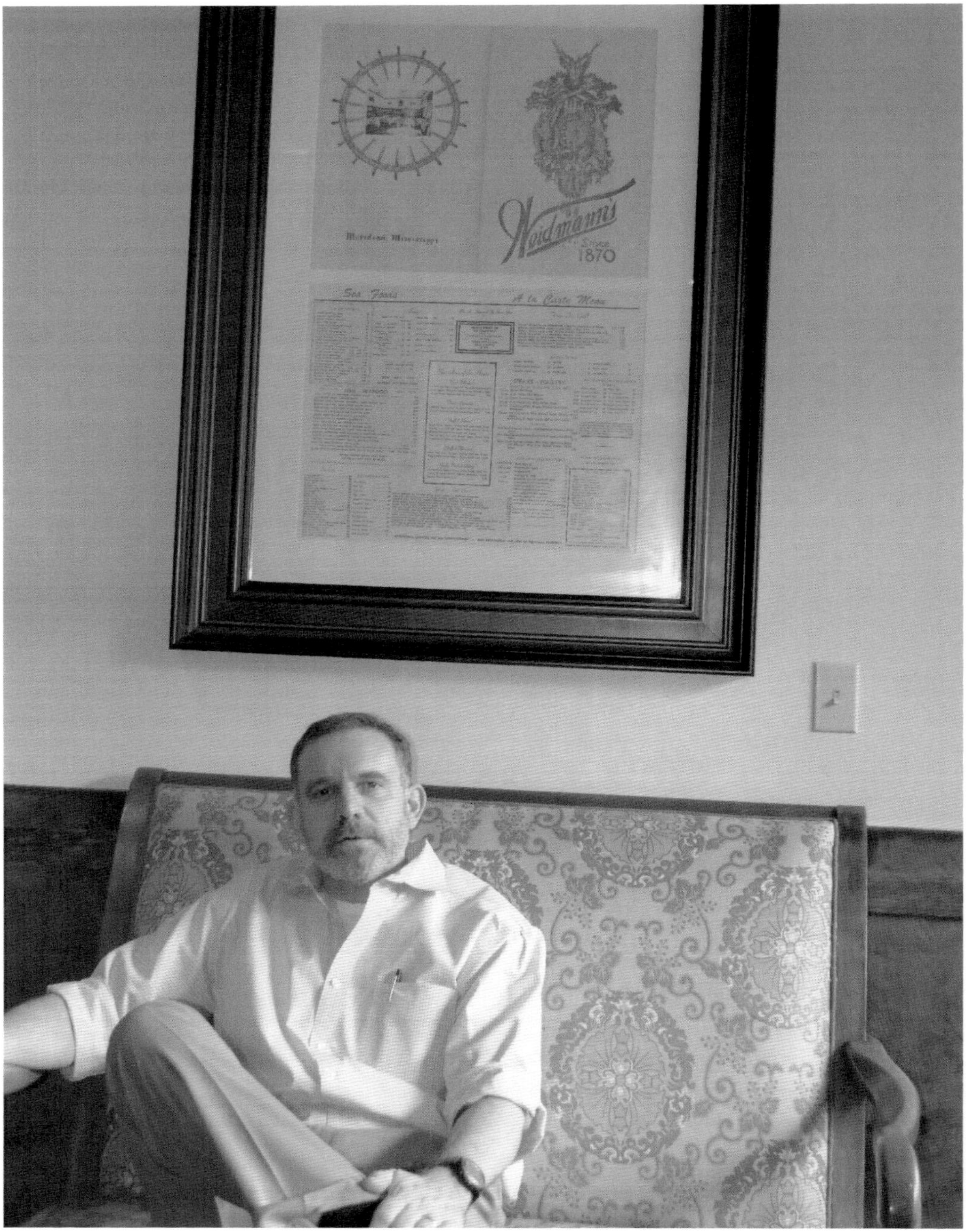

Rebuilding a Future and a Past

Charles Frazier was managing a restaurant in New Orleans when Katrina struck, forcing him and his family to evacuate to Hattiesburg. He ended up in Meridian as operations manager of the Crescent City Grill before serving as general manager for five years. Because Charles loved history and the downtown revitalization, he accepted the offer to manage Meridian's oldest and most famous restaurant establishment, Weidmann's. "The brand is the history," said Frazier, "and it has been since 1870." (Author's collection.)

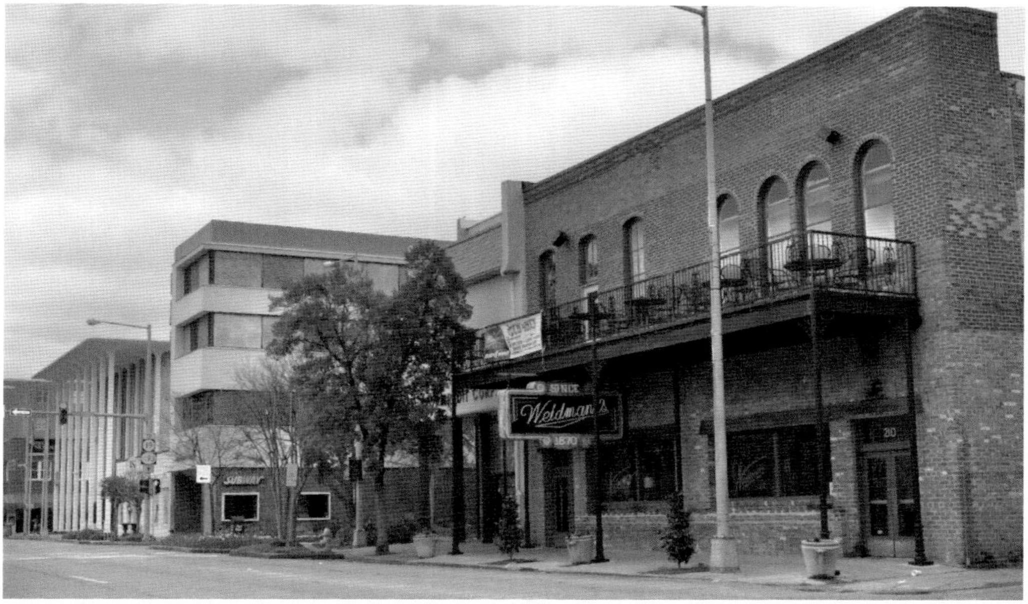

New Management

When Charles Frazier took over, his goal was to bring back the early Weidmann's. "People have been very generous in bringing pictures back, and we've put them back up on the walls." The Weidmann's sign also hangs in front as it did years ago. (Author's collection.)

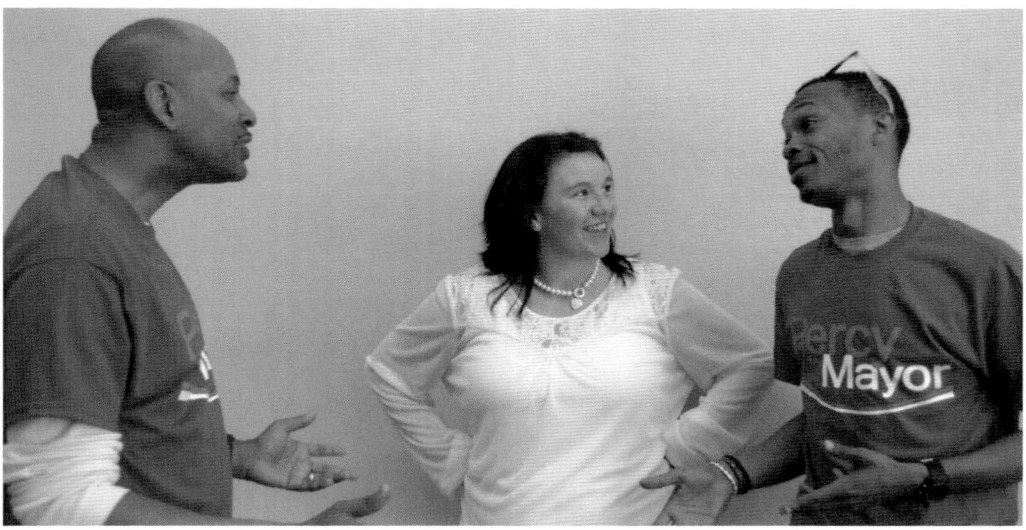

Mentor

Percy Bland, owner of a State Farm Insurance Agency in Meridian, is a former adjunct professor at Mississippi State University (Meridian Branch) in the Healthcare Administration Department. He serves as a mentor to youth and plays a lead role in dropout prevention programs in the community. He helped to start the first Tee Golf Program for minorities within the inner city. On June 4, 2013, Percy Bland made history by being elected the first African American mayor of Meridian. Pictured are Percy Bland, Derrick Sims, and Kristen Eakes. (Author's collection.)

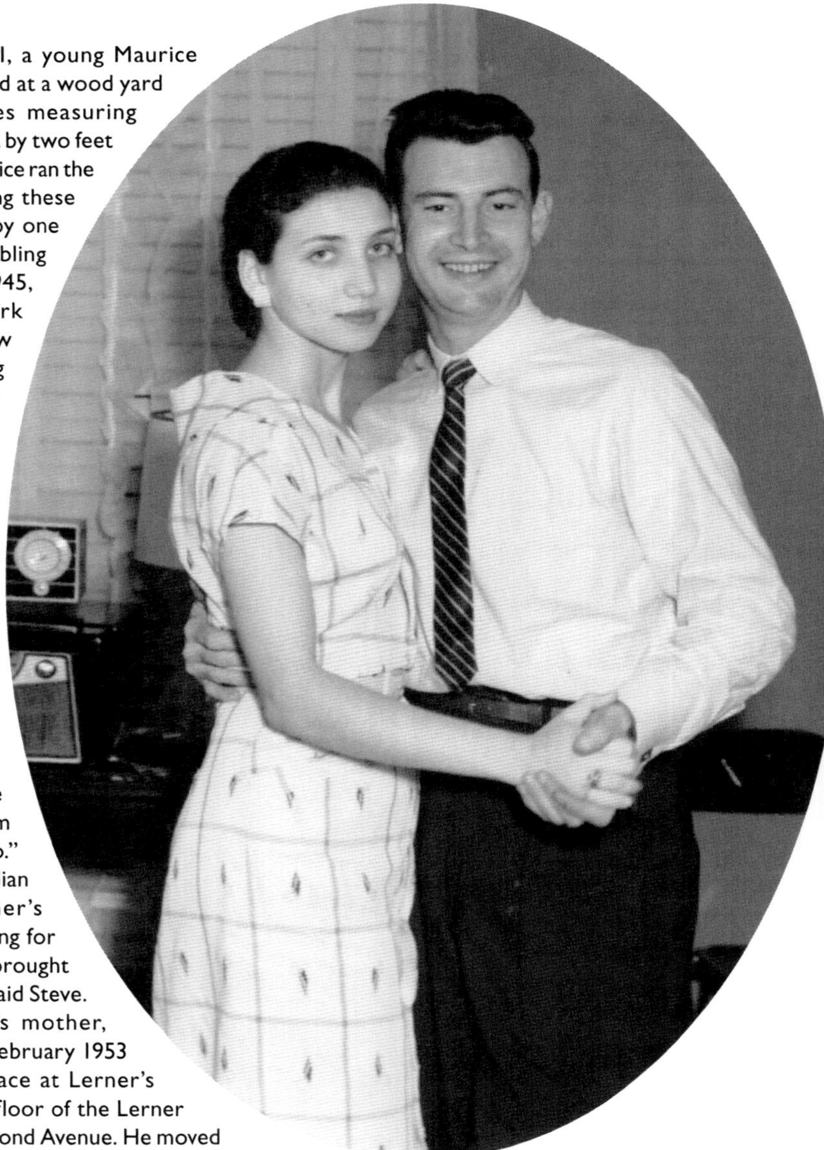

The Family Jewels

During World War II, a young Maurice Jerome Labiche worked at a wood yard where grenade boxes measuring approximately two feet by two feet were constructed. Maurice ran the wheelbarrow delivering these wood squares, made by one guy, to the guy assembling the boxes. Around 1945, Maurice went to work at Woodrow's of New Orleans, sweeping floors and doing menial tasks. There, 18 men worked on jewelry, each one having a specific job. "Each could do their specific job really well but didn't have enough knowledge to go into business for themselves," said Steve LaBiche, Maurice's son. "They took Maurice under their wing, and Maurice learned from all of them how to do what they do." Maurice came to Meridian around 1953. "Lerner's Jewelers was advertising for help, and that's what brought my dad to Meridian," said Steve. According to Steve's mother, Elizabeth LaBiche, in February 1953 Maurice occupied space at Lerner's Jewelers on the third floor of the Lerner Building on Twenty-second Avenue. He moved to the location on Fifth Street and Twenty-first Avenue across from the courthouse, where he worked on the second floor before Lerner's moved to the Threefoot Building. (Courtesy of Elizabeth and Steve LaBiche.)

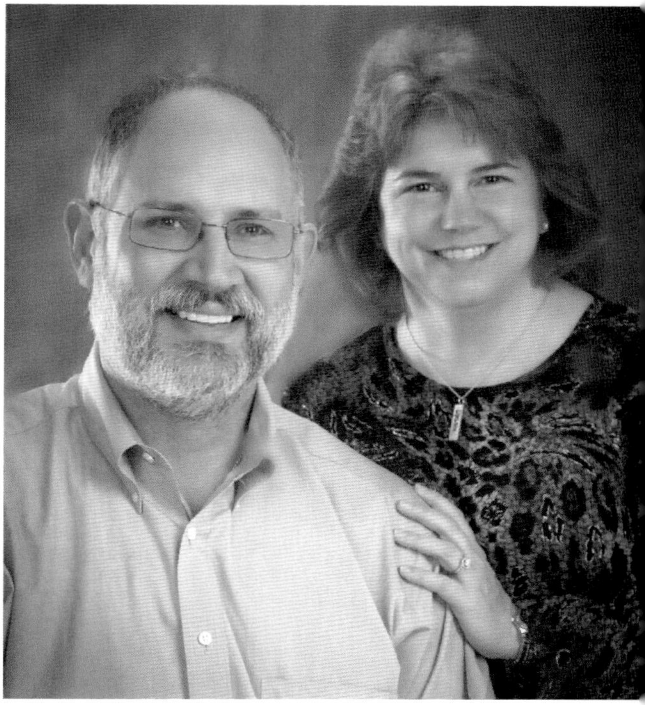

Fulfilling the Legacy
In July 1986, the LaBiche family bought their current location on Eighth Street. Though Maurice passed away on March 31, 2007, LaBiche Jewelers remains a major homegrown Meridian business. (Courtesy of Randy Rives of Rives Photography.)

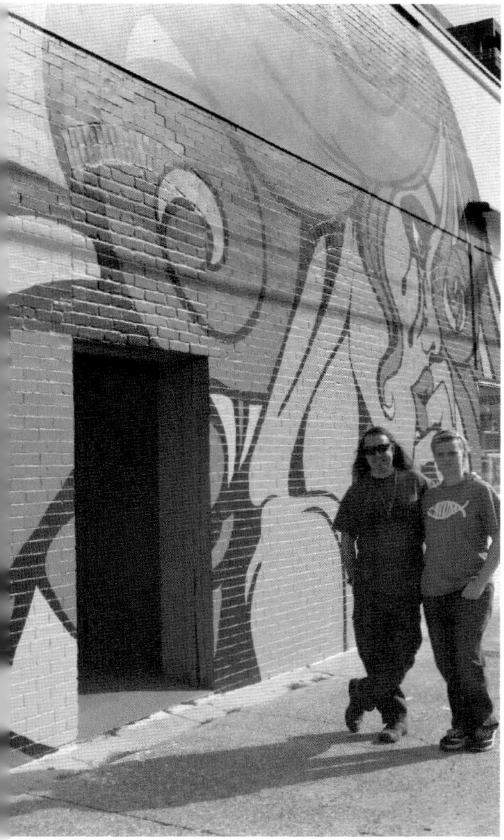

MUM's the Word
About 17 years ago, Wayne and Stacey Williams started Meridian Underground Music (MUM) in the old Peavey Building on Twenty-second Avenue. What is unique about MUM's new location on Twenty-third Avenue, which has been open for four years, is its incredible exterior mural by local artist Jason Cooper, of Black Heart Studios in Meridian. "We're real proud of that mural," said Wayne. (Author's collection.)

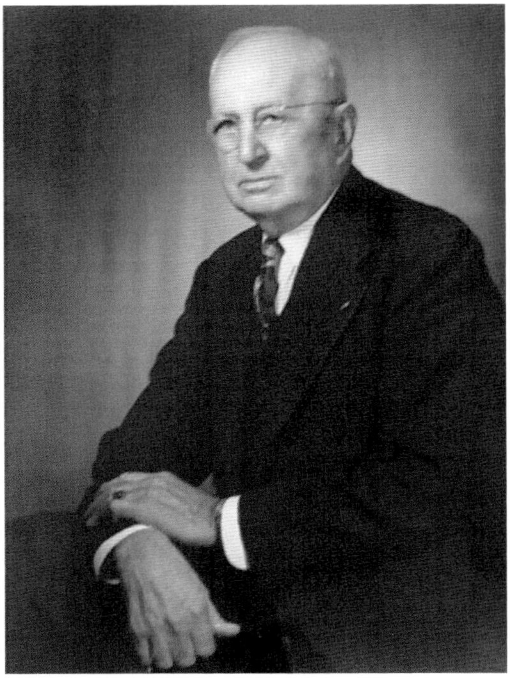

Healing the Sick

In 1910, Meridian was a bustling town of thriving businesses at the crest of its golden age whose focus on education led to more than one college in the city and a health care facility, Turner Hospital. But by 1917, the country entered World War I and our hometown boys would be sent to the battlefields of France while our patriotic farmers would grow food for the war effort instead of cotton. In 1928, a young physician, Dr. William Jeff Anderson, purchased the 30-bed Turner Hospital and renamed it Anderson's Infirmary. (Courtesy of Anderson Regional Hospital.)

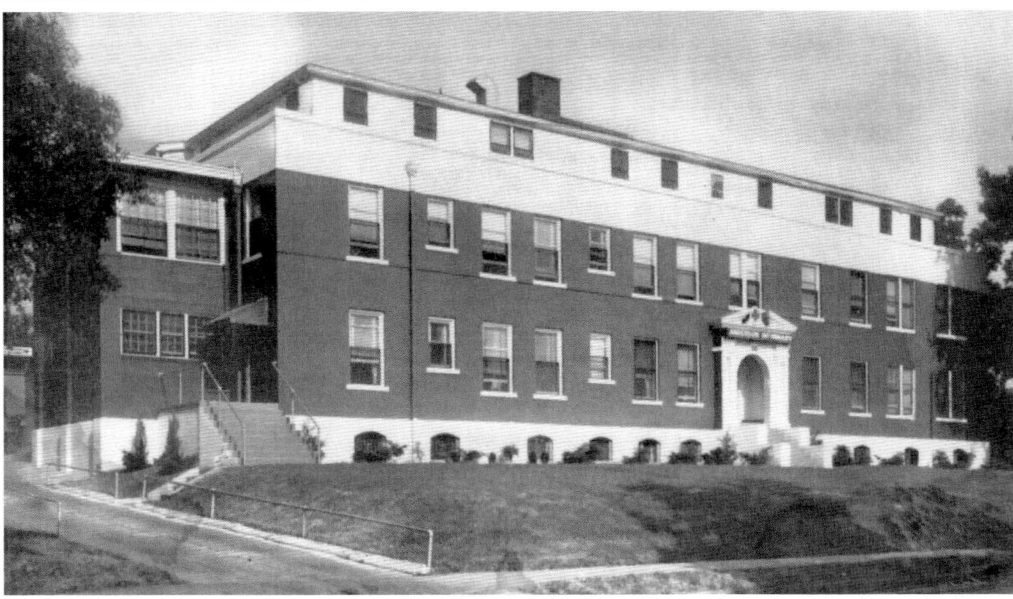

A Man with a Dream

With a staff of three physicians, nurses, a laboratory, and two operating rooms, the hospital would withstand the ravages of the Great Depression. Through the determination of Dr. Anderson, the hospital remained open. He mortgaged his home to care for the medical needs of the community. As economic recovery began, Anderson's Infirmary expanded its medical facilities. An X-ray department and air-conditioning was added, and by 1951 the staff of physicians had grown to more than 24. The original Anderson's Infirmary is pictured here. (Courtesy of Anderson Regional Hospital.)

70

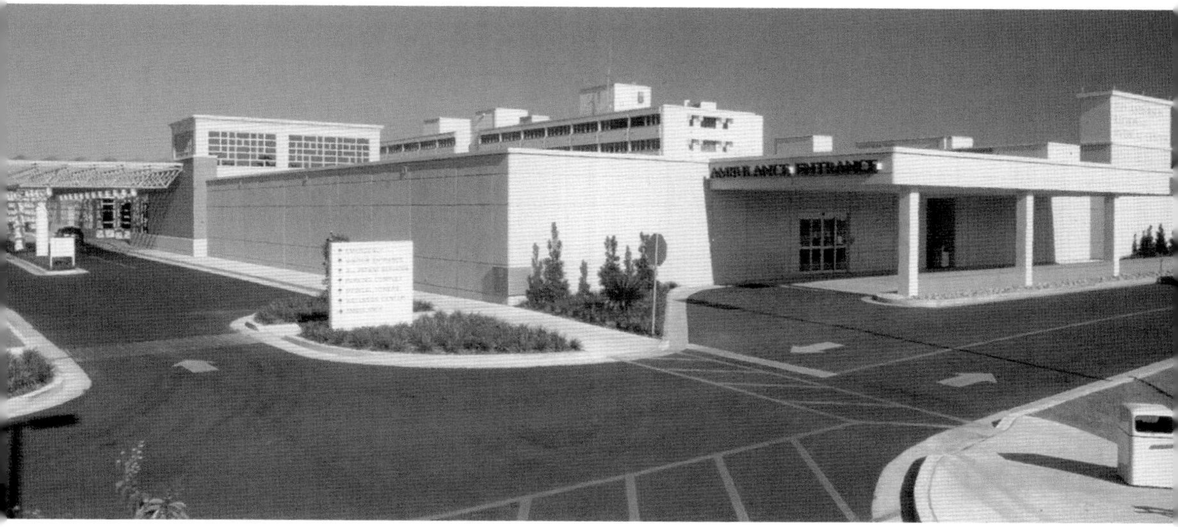

Healing Hands
Dr. William J. Anderson Jr. continued in his father's footsteps. The hospital, renamed Jeff Anderson Memorial Hospital, expanded to a 120-bed facility. By 1965, Anderson Memorial became East Mississippi and West Alabama's largest medical facility. From a small two-story, red-brick building once known as Turner Hospital in 1910, today's Jeff Anderson Regional Medical Center, pictured here, is a state-of-the-art medical facility—a milestone for the dedicated personnel who played an important role in the services the hospital provides. (Courtesy of Anderson Regional Hospital.)

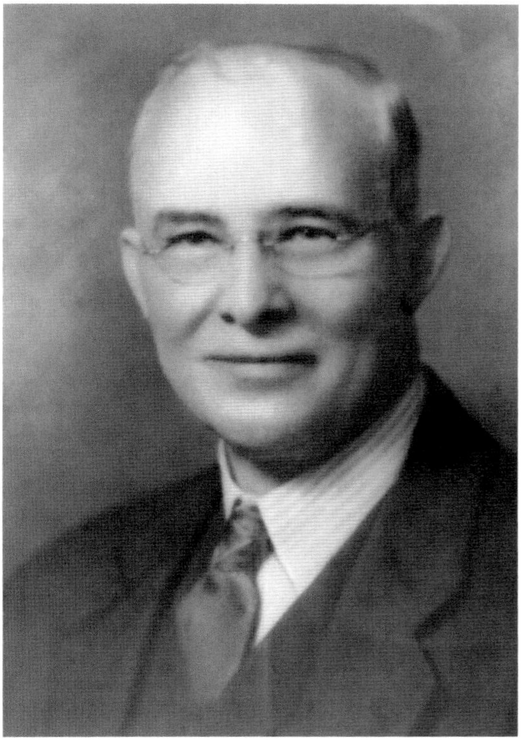

Say "Ah"
Dr. Jesse Hackley Rush, pictured, founded the newly constructed 18-bed Rush Infirmary in 1915 to meet the growing medical needs of east central Mississippi. His small staff consisted of his wife, Mary Hunnicutt Rush, a registered nurse, and six student nurses. (Courtesy of Rush Foundation Hospital.)

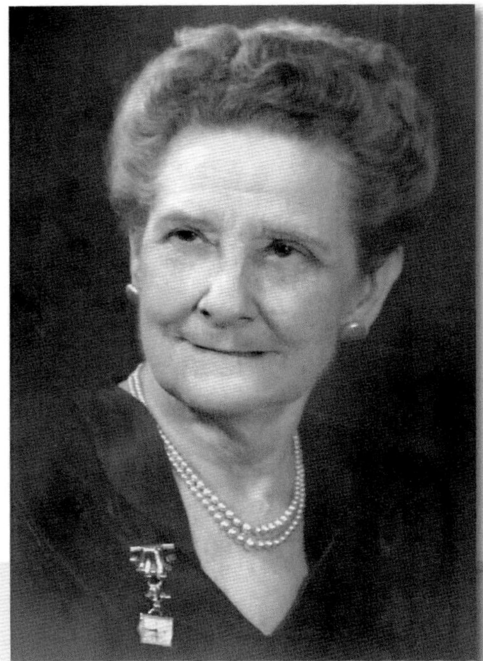

Mary Hunnicutt Rush

In the early years, Mary, the wife of Dr. Jesse Hackley Rush, worked with her husband at Rush Infirmary. With 98 years of growth (1915–2013), Rush Infirmary's 18-bed facility has grown from a small facility to today's Rush Foundation Hospital, a modern, nonprofit medical center covering four city blocks. (Courtesy of Rush Foundation Hospital.)

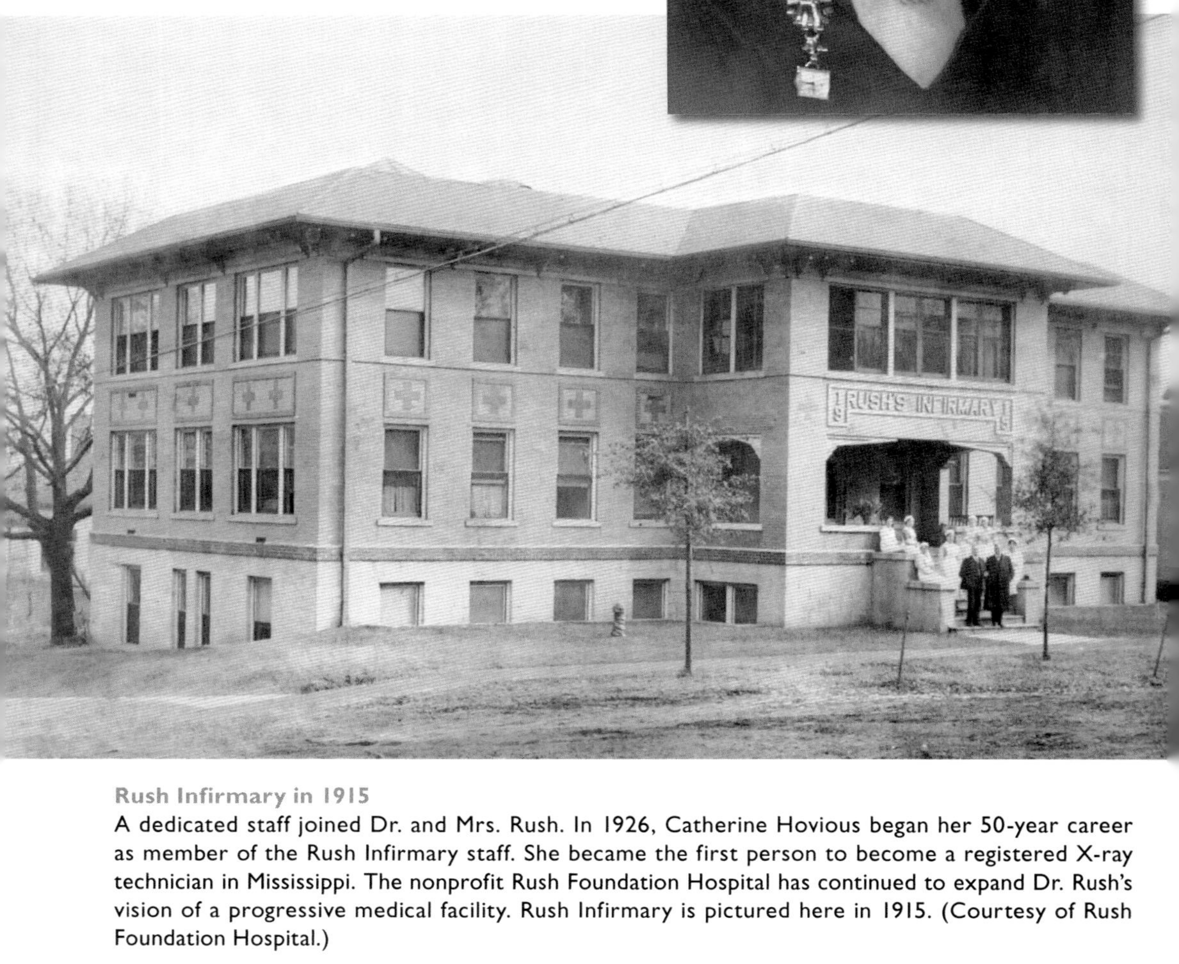

Rush Infirmary in 1915

A dedicated staff joined Dr. and Mrs. Rush. In 1926, Catherine Hovious began her 50-year career as member of the Rush Infirmary staff. She became the first person to become a registered X-ray technician in Mississippi. The nonprofit Rush Foundation Hospital has continued to expand Dr. Rush's vision of a progressive medical facility. Rush Infirmary is pictured here in 1915. (Courtesy of Rush Foundation Hospital.)

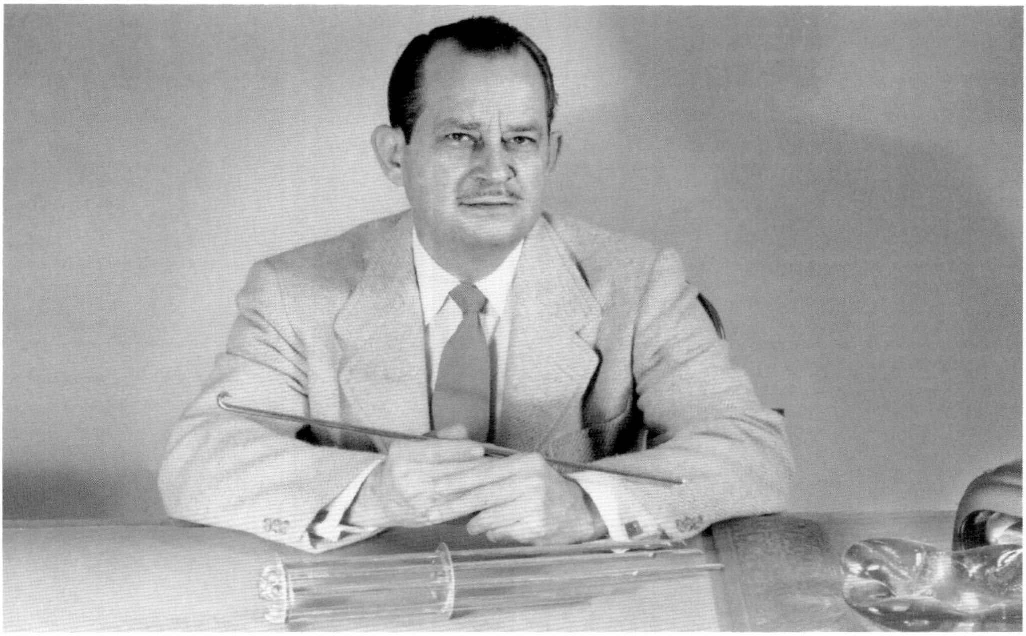

Pinned
In 1927, Leslie Vaughn Rush joined the staff at his father's hospital, Rush Infirmary. The health care facility would make medical history in 1936, when Dr. Vaughn Rush invented an orthopedic pin used for pinning bone fractures. He performed the first bone-pinning surgery in the United States in 1936. The revolutionary Rush pin is still used today. The hospital is known statewide for its successful ventures. In 1944, Catherine Hovious, Dr. H.M. Ivey, and Dr. Leslie Rush joined forces with Meridian Community College to create the first junior college nursing program in the state. Dr. Leslie V. Rush and his wife, Katherine, were the parents of two children, Beryl and Vaughn. Dr. Leslie Vaughn Rush is pictured here with his invention, the Rush pin. (Courtesy of Rush Foundation Hospital.)

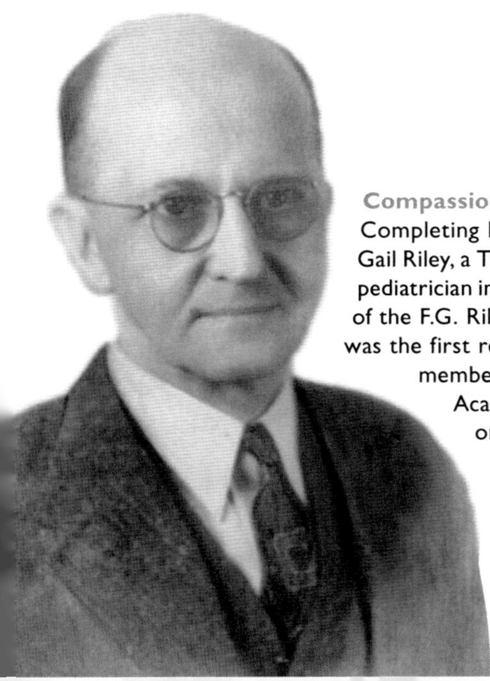

Compassion
Completing his residency at University of Pennsylvania, Dr. Franklin Gail Riley, a Tupelo native born in 1889, became Meridian's first full-time pediatrician in 1922. In 1930, the World War I veteran opened the doors of the F.G. Riley Hospital, a 12-bed maternity and children's facility. He was the first residency-trained pediatrician in Mississippi and a founding member of the American Board of Pediatrics and the American Academy of Pediatrics. He established the hospital as a nonprofit organization. (Courtesy of The Riley Foundation.)

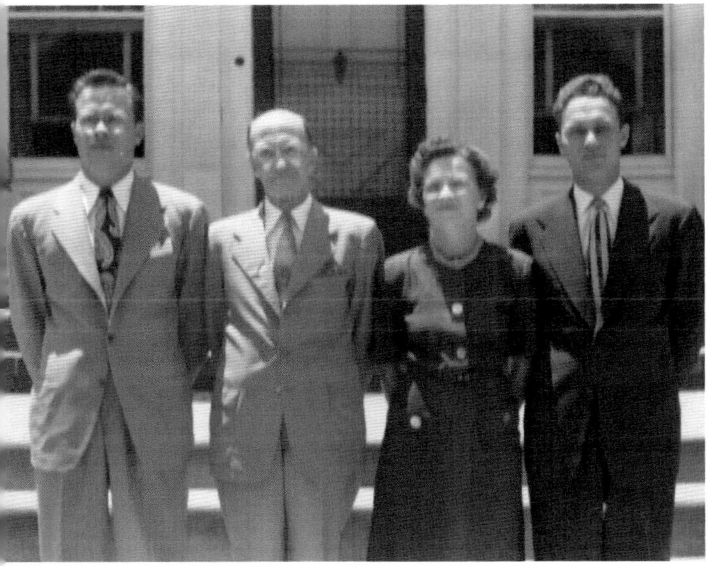

Children's Helper

Franklin Gail Riley married Harriet Gardner and had two sons. Dr. William Gail Riley, born June 14, 1922, was a graduate of Vanderbilt University and the Vanderbilt School of Medicine in 1945 and served as a flight surgeon in the Air Force during World War II. In 1950, he returned to Meridian and joined his father's practice. In 1998, he and his brother Richard sold Riley Hospital to Heath Management Associates of Naples, Florida, before they formed the Riley Foundation. Pictured from left to right are William Gail Riley, Dr. Franklin Gail Riley, Harriet Riley, and Richard Franklin Riley. (Courtesy of The Riley Foundation.)

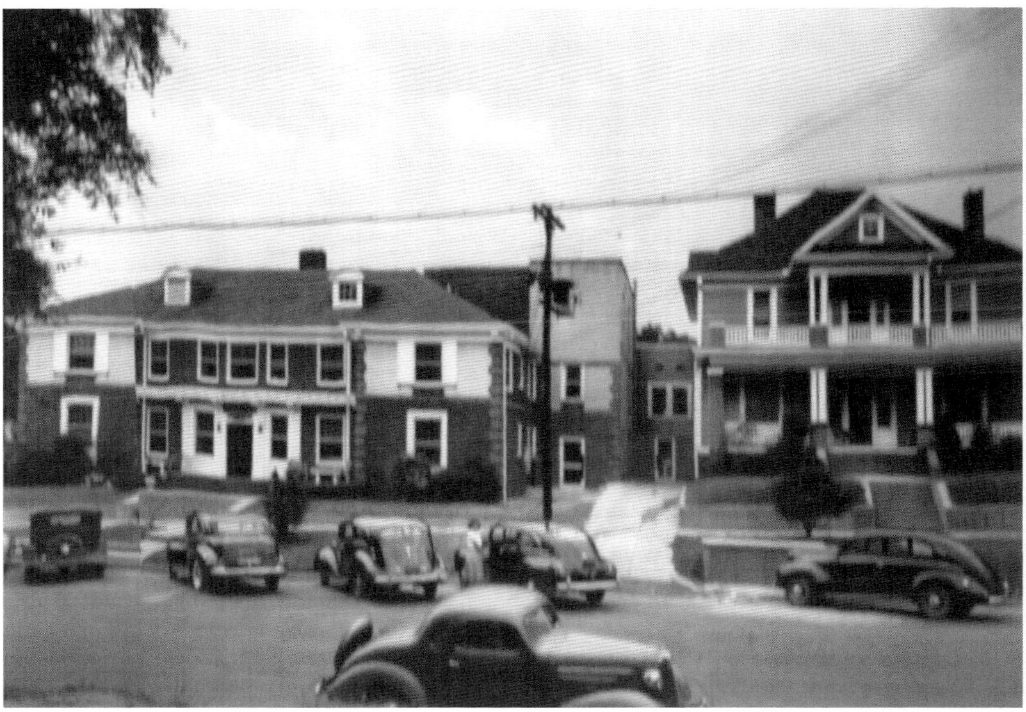

A Surgeon's Walk

Dr. Richard Franklin Riley, born in 1925, attended Vanderbilt University and Vanderbilt University of Medicine and served his internship at the University of Virginia Hospital. He served in Germany while a first lieutenant in the US Army Medical Corps. He married Mary Ann Bonner on December 1, 1956. Funds from Riley Hospital nonprofit foundation and the Rileys' generosity of charitable grants have left a lasting influence on Meridian and its neighbors. The original Riley Hospital is pictured here. (Courtesy of The Riley Foundation.)

CHAPTER THREE

Communities

Our community legends have a common bond: commitment, compassion, and a desire to serve. For generations, legends have lived by the same patriotic words spoken by Pres. John Fitzgerald Kennedy: "Ask not what your country can do for you—ask what you can do for your country."

People in our rural communities came from great-grandparents who picked cotton, plowed with mules, and drove hand-cranked Model Ts with solid-rubber tires across clay-rutted roads. They lived through the Great Depression and World War II. They watched as Neil Armstrong walked on the moon. They chilled milk in the well long before the iceman delivered blocks of ice.

They live in ancestral homes and have memories of grandma's wood stove and mom's microwave. They warmed by potbellied stoves long before central heat and sat in church pews that held hymnals and a paper fan used to stir a cool breeze. From the traveling store to the modern-day grocery, they taught the same values in their homes, schools, churches, and synagogues and witnessed American progress unfold.

They are donors who have helped others to live. They walk among us, or live on in our memories.

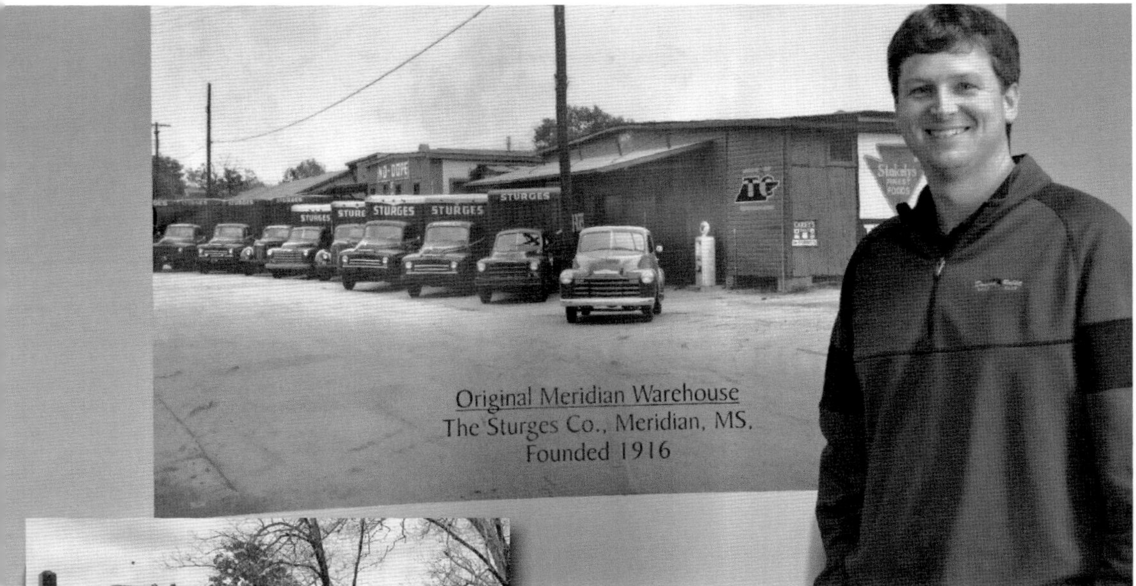

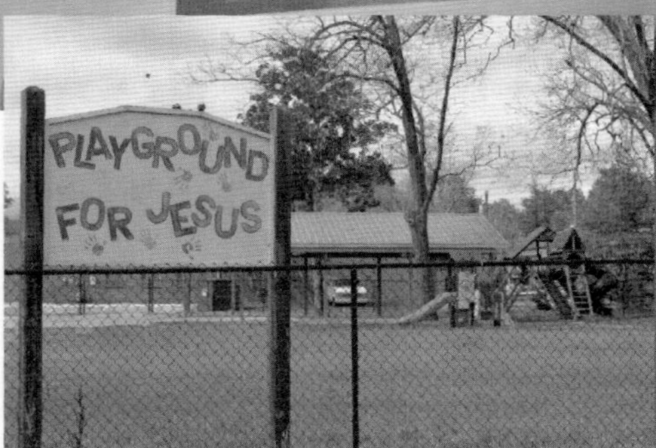

Let the Children Play

One day, Wesley House director Ginger Grissom showed Trey Long where some young boys had spray-painted guns on the sidewalk in front of the building.

"I didn't think this could happen in Meridian. But I went in the back of Wesley House and found an empty 12-gauge shotgun case that had been shot, and that Halloween, someone got shot behind Wesley House at the housing authority."

Trey's Sunday School class went down to clean up around the Wesley House and decided to build a small playground in the back, which would cost around $5,000. Someone offered to donate the money, but they wanted a plaque installed to advertise their company. Trey felt convicted because he had told the neighborhood children that God was providing the money. "I just didn't want to put a plaque that said the playground had been donated by a person or company," said Trey, so he turned the grantor down.

The next day, a grant came into the Wesley House for $5,000 earmarked for "recreational purposes only," and that encouraged Trey and his Sunday school class to build a big playground on the field beside Wesley House, where syringe needles were often found as well as old mattresses that were used for prostitution. The cost for a playground of that size would be around $45,000. Trey knew God was much larger than a dollar amount, so he sent an e-mail blast to all his contacts that read, "What could you do with $10. You could go to McDonald's, get a few snow cones, or you could help build a playground with $10 and provide a safe place to play for the people in our town."

"I hit 'send' and went to lunch. Within one month, I had over $60,000 coming into my mailbox. I got money from every single state." Trey asked the children what was the number one thing they wanted on the playground. They all said, "A fence."

The scripture I John 3:17 reads, "If anyone has material possessions and sees a brother or sister in need but has no pity on them, how can the love of God be in that person?"

"I don't remember ever reading it, but I was convicted by that verse." The I John 3:17 mission is still going strong. "God orchestrated all this. It's been over three years. I John 3:17 has never not met a need in those three years, paid in full. It's a God thing." (Author's collection.)

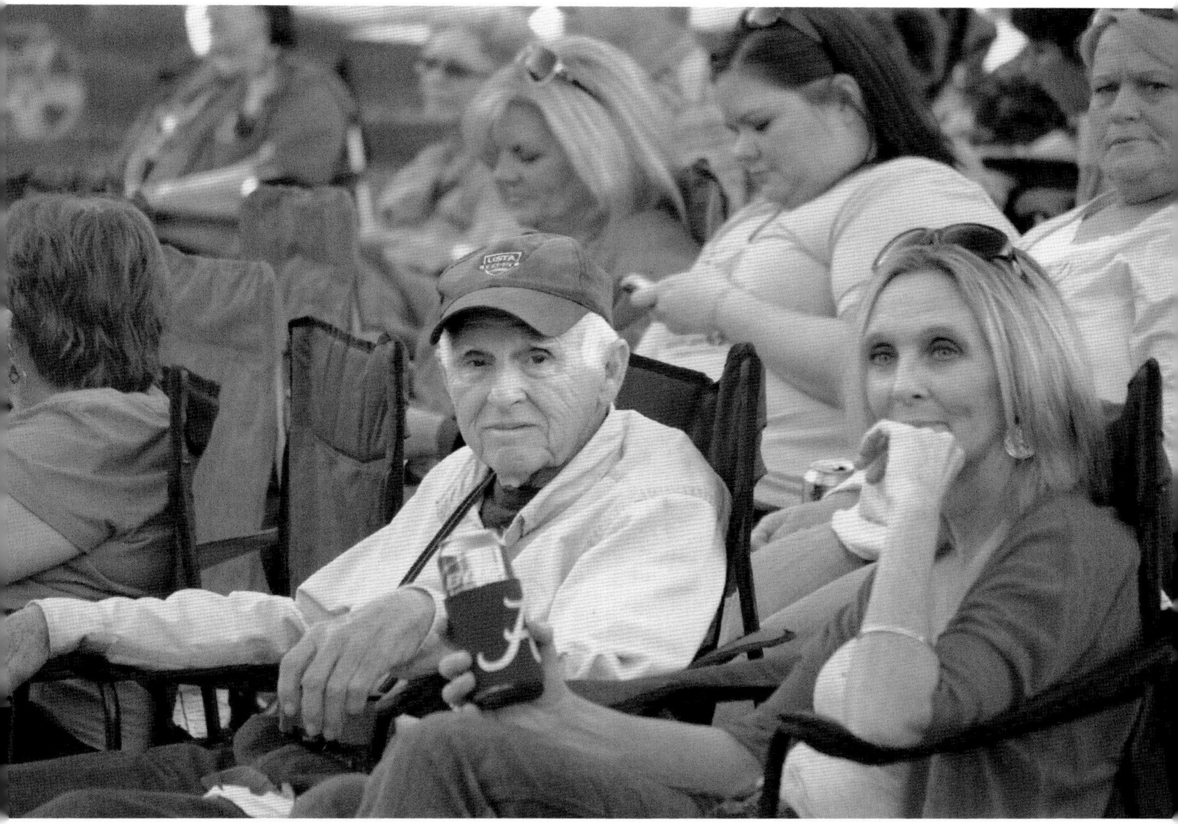

Quiet Supporter

Attend just about any local event in Meridian, and you'll find Tony Sansone. An avid supporter and leader in the community, he gets things done. He served as the first director of the Mississippi Junior Miss Pageant and for many years brought quality entertainment to his hometown through various events, such as the former Lively Arts Festival. He has been active in community theater and is father and grandfather to multitalented kids, including Patrick Sansone (see page 40) of Wilco and The Autumn Defense.

When Tony decided to bring Wilco to the Temple Theatre in Meridian, he did it not by the Internet, but the old-fashioned way—by US Mail. People sent Tony a check and a self-addressed envelope, and he, in turn, mailed their tickets. Within three days, the 1,500 seats in the Temple Theatre had sold out.

Talent is genetic in the Sansone family. At the age of four, Tony's mother, Marguerite Sansone, won a talent contest on the stage of the Temple Theatre. She became a professional singer, performing on cruises, singing with big bands, and playing the Blue Room of the Roosevelt Hotel. She also had her own live radio show in New Orleans.

Sansone, who says the genetic talent skipped his generation, is known by all, but not because he puts himself out there for recognition. A quiet supporter, he gets things done with hard work and by caring about his community and its people. Tony was presented with the National Exchange Club's Book of Golden Deeds Award, their highest honor celebrating unsung heroes for tireless work in their communities. In this photograph, Tony is enjoying a Meridian Main Concert Series in Dumont Plaza. (Author's collection.)

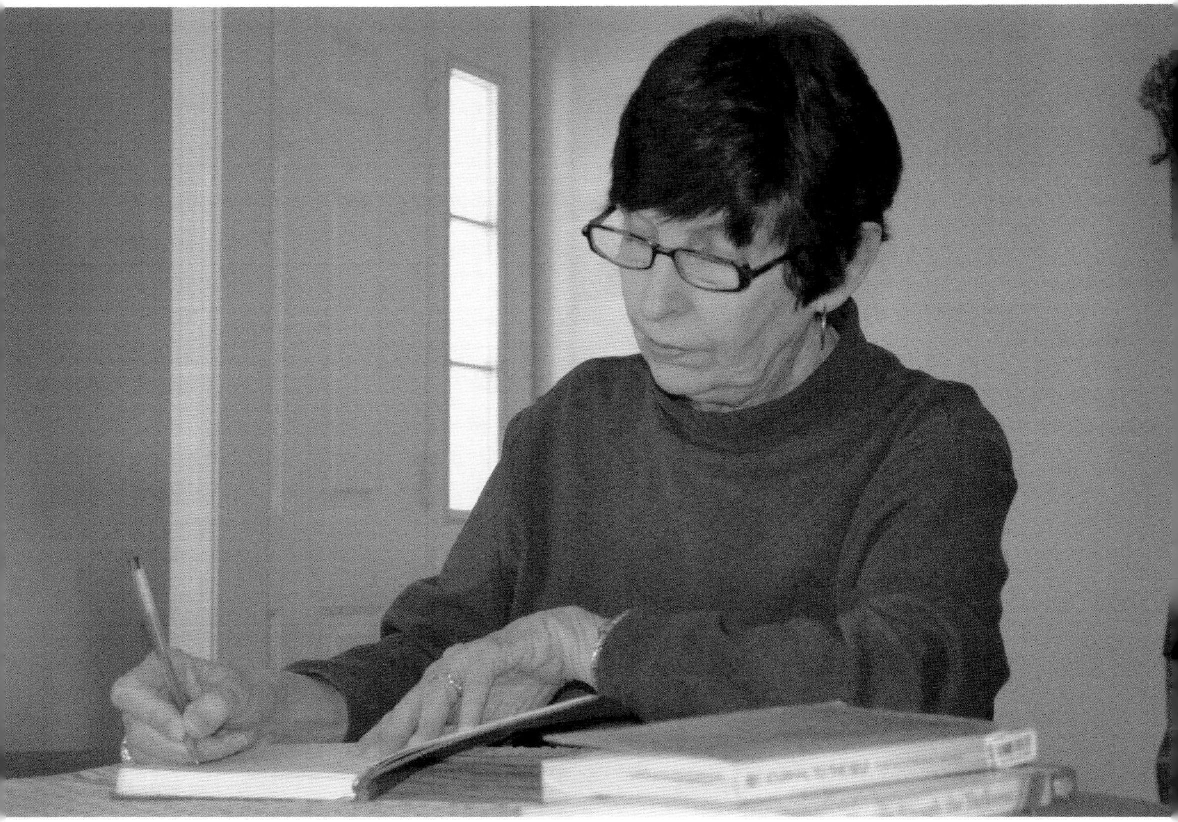

Write On
Author Virginia Dawkins loves to journal—not so much because it's fun, but because it empties her of negative feelings and pain while also allowing her pages to praise and glorify God. She began a Wednesday-night recovery group at her church called "Beginners." She uses the Life Recovery Bible and the 12-step program and volunteers at the Lauderdale County Juvenile Center. "It is a personal thing. It has nothing to do with correct English or grammar. It has everything to do with your experiences and how you feel." (Author's collection.)

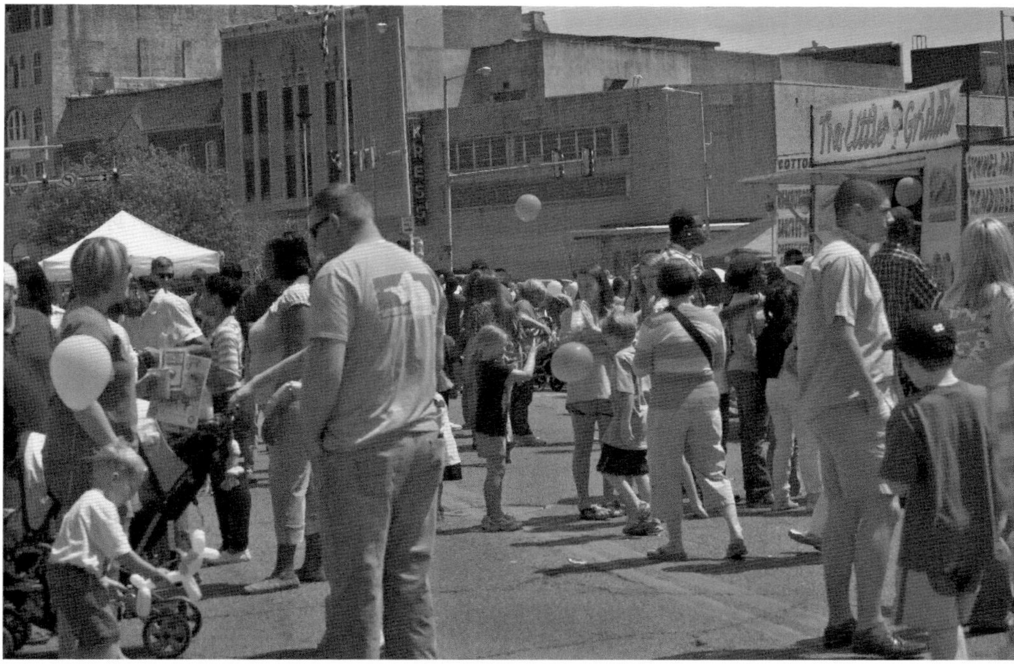

The Annual Threefoot Festival

Held every year on the first weekend in April, "The Threefoot Festival is important to our community because it not only allows the public the opportunity to purchase fine arts," according to Meridian Council for the Arts president Zena Limerick, "but it also gives our children a chance to explore the arts and expand their knowledge of the arts." With live entertainment by talented local singers, musicians, and performers, the day is rounded out with all aspects of the arts. "This is a very important event evidencing our never-ending pursuit to support and grow the arts in our community. People should take advantage of it." (Author's collection.)

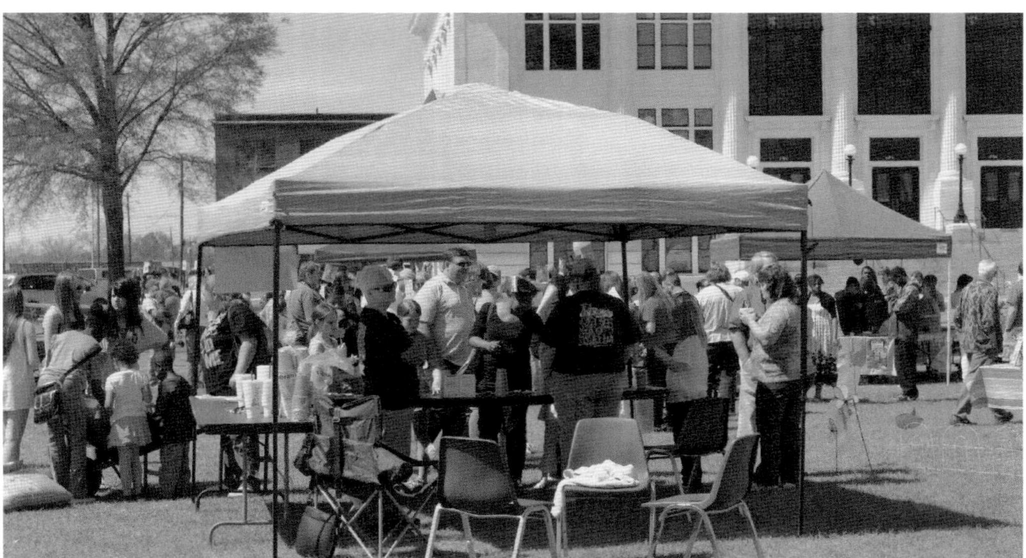

A Community Need, Indeed

The second Saturday of each month, the foot-stomping sound of music drifts above Wilson's Grand Oak Bluegrass and Gospel Hall located on the Whynot–Causeyville Road. Owner Larry Wilson, pictured here, felt there was a need in the community for a social hall where the coffee is always on and musicians tune up, then play Gospel, bluegrass, and country music. (Courtesy of June Davis Davidson.)

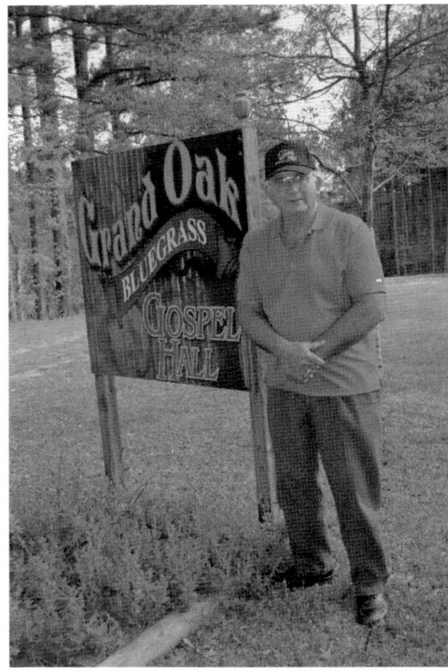

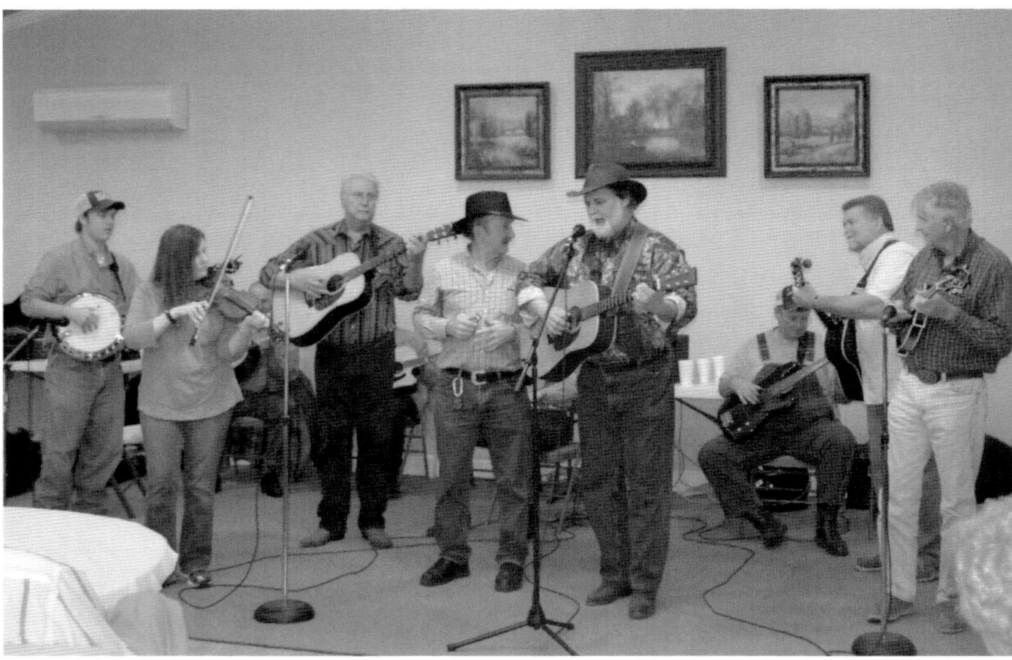

Picking Time

Grand Oak Bluegrass and Gospel opened its doors in December 2007. "Occasionally, we ask for a donation if we have a special group of musicians," Wilson said. For those who have a hankering for downhome picking and singing, come on out, sit back and relax, and tap your foot—you're sure to be humming along with a familiar tune. Pictured center stage is Andy Linton, at the microphone and playing guitar. (Courtesy of June Davis Davidson.)

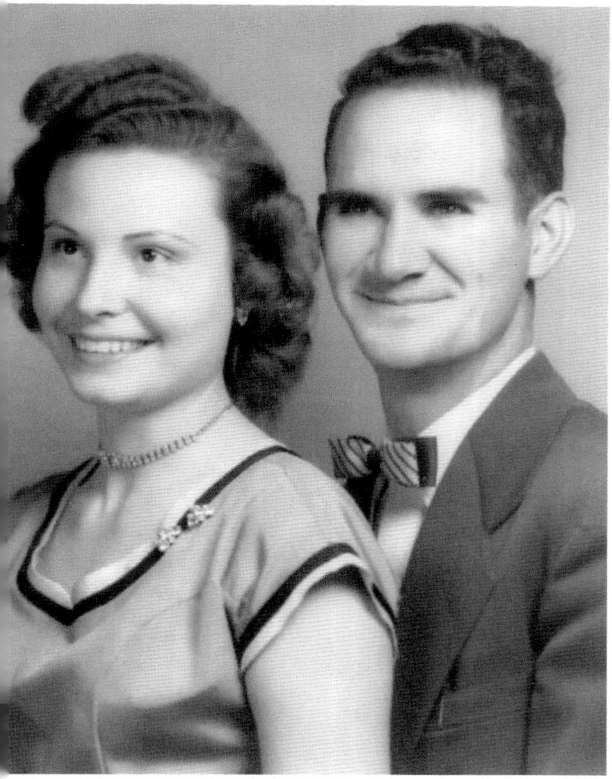

A Man and His Bible

In the 1950s, Melvin L. Boles earned his living as a salesman for Lott Furniture on Front Street, aided by his wife, Rosie, who worked at Alden Mills. Melvin's love for gospel led to his first church, and his fiery sermons aired on local radio in the early 1960s. He practiced the charity he preached by filling gas tanks and feeding the hungry. Melvin and Rosie are pictured here in earlier years. (Courtesy of Melvin Boles.)

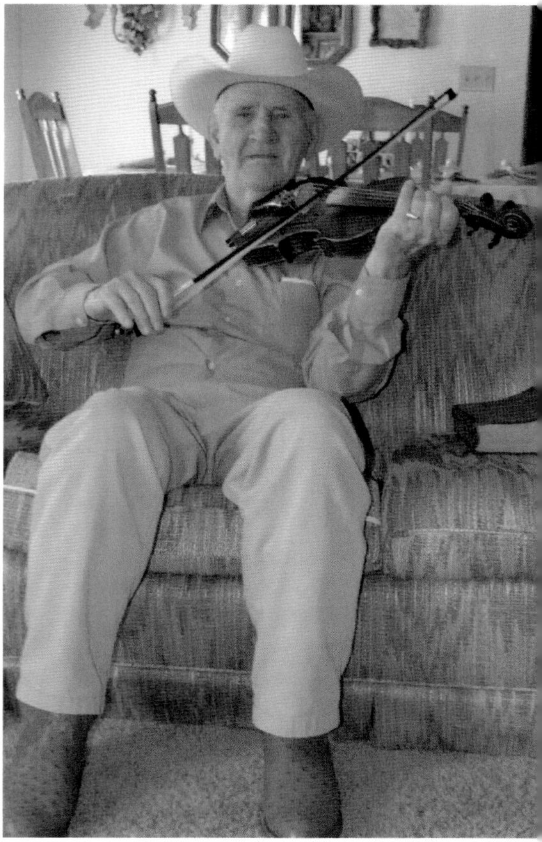

Where Angels Fly

The Reverend Melvin Boles, born on July 11, 1923, is now retired from the pulpit. His son Mike has stepped into the pastoral position, continuing in his father's footsteps and going far beyond by building a state-of-the-art auditorium for Sunday worship services and theatrical productions. The auditorium's cable system, used to fly angels, cost $1 million. Today, the members of the Boles family are involved in Christian moviemaking. Here, Melvin Boles plays fiddle at his home in 2012. (Courtesy of June Davis Davidson.)

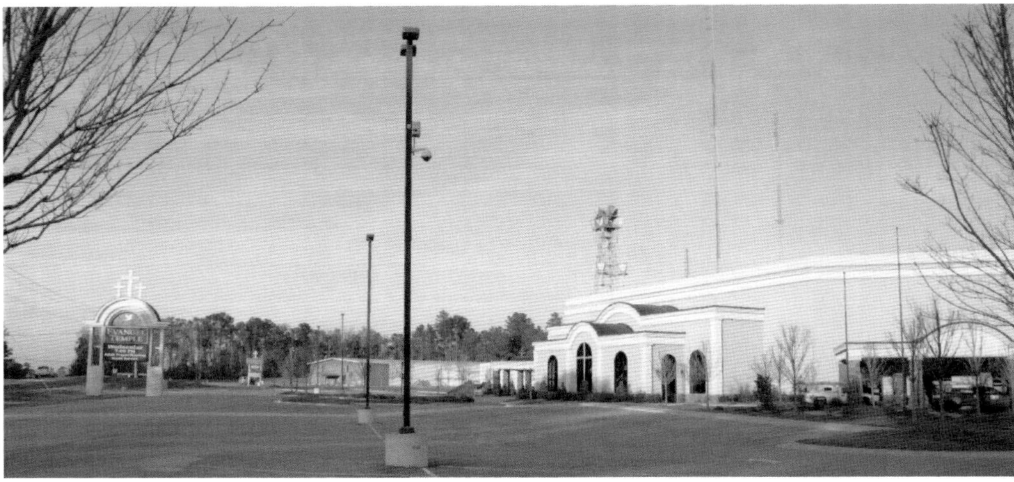

A House of Praise

Melvin Boles established the Evangel Temple, a nondenominational church located on Highway 45 South. As his congregation grew, so did the vision for Christian theatrical productions. The popularity of the themed productions, including *The Life of Christ* and *Deceived,* among others, led to an overflow of seating capacity. Pictured is the Evangel Temple on Highway 45 South in Meridian. (Courtesy of June Davis Davidson.)

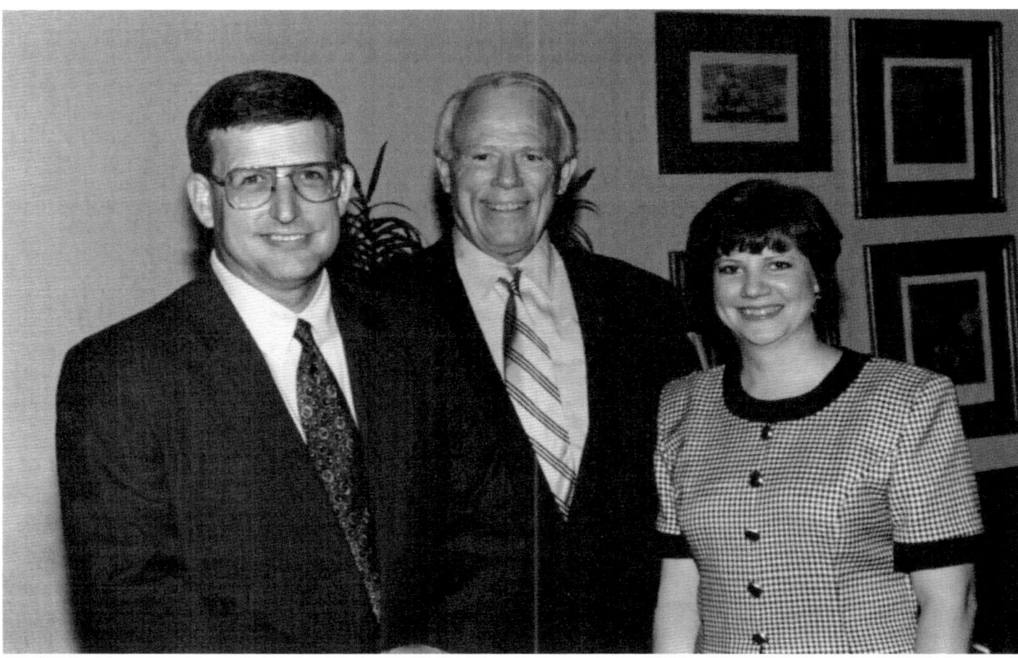

The "A" of A-Team

Bill Crawford acted as coordinator of the Navy/Meridian Team, otherwise known as the "A" Team, which worked diligently get the 32-year-old Meridian Naval Air Station off the list of the 31 major military bases slated for closure. When the vote came in to keep the base open, Bill, his wife Lynn, and the A Team returned home to a joyous crowd and an ecstatic hometown. (Courtesy of Bill Crawford.)

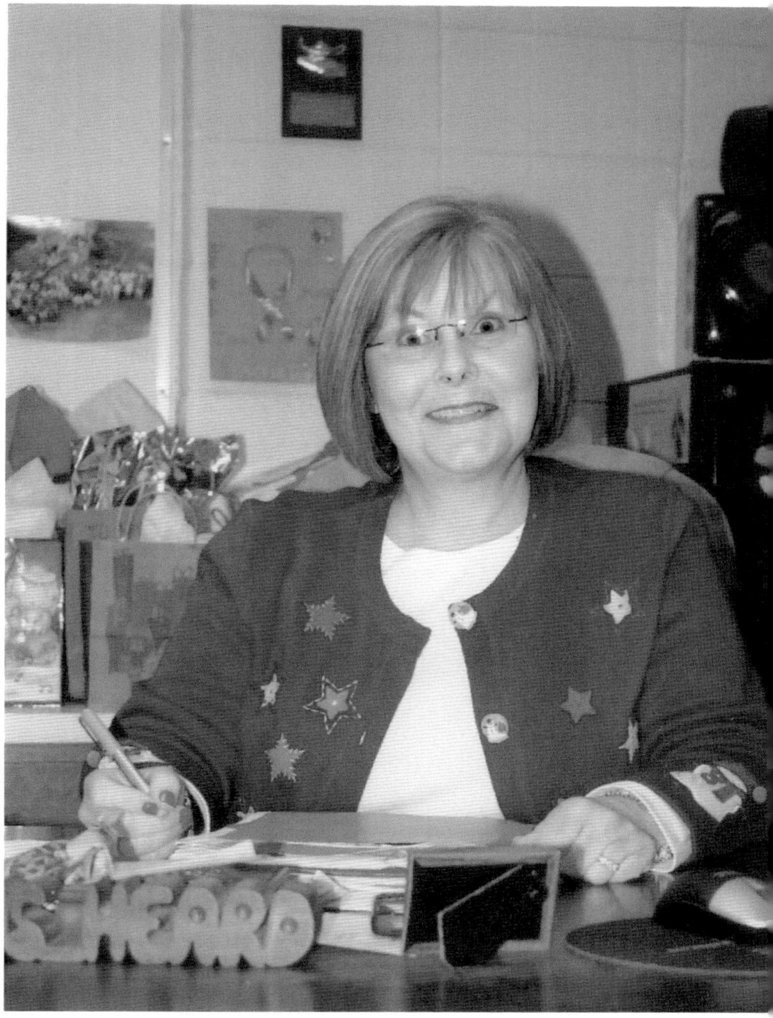

Dedication to Education
Every school has a teacher who is held in high regard, and if you ask the people at Clarkdale Attendance Center, that person is Camie Heard. Dr. Roy McNeil, who is the principal of Clarkdale Middle School, said, "Camie Heard may be the single most inspiring person I've ever met." She is more than a teacher, wife, mother, and grandmother; she is a long-term, battle-scarred warrior who has, along with her physicians, waged an 18-year assault on cancer during her teaching career. (Courtesy of Debbie Fant.)

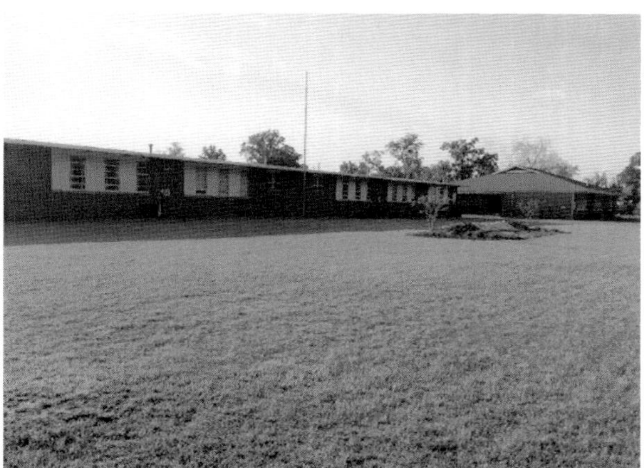

Perseverance
Camie fought this battle while she continued to teach fifth-grade mathematics at Clarkdale Attendance Center. "When I would teach a difficult math skill, I could see a little light go off in the children's faces when they 'got' it," she said. The sweetest words Camie probably ever heard were those of her students: "We prayed for you." Camie still wages her battle, but she does not do it alone. She is surrounded by love and prayers of her many friends, former students, and family. (Courtesy of Debbie Fant.)

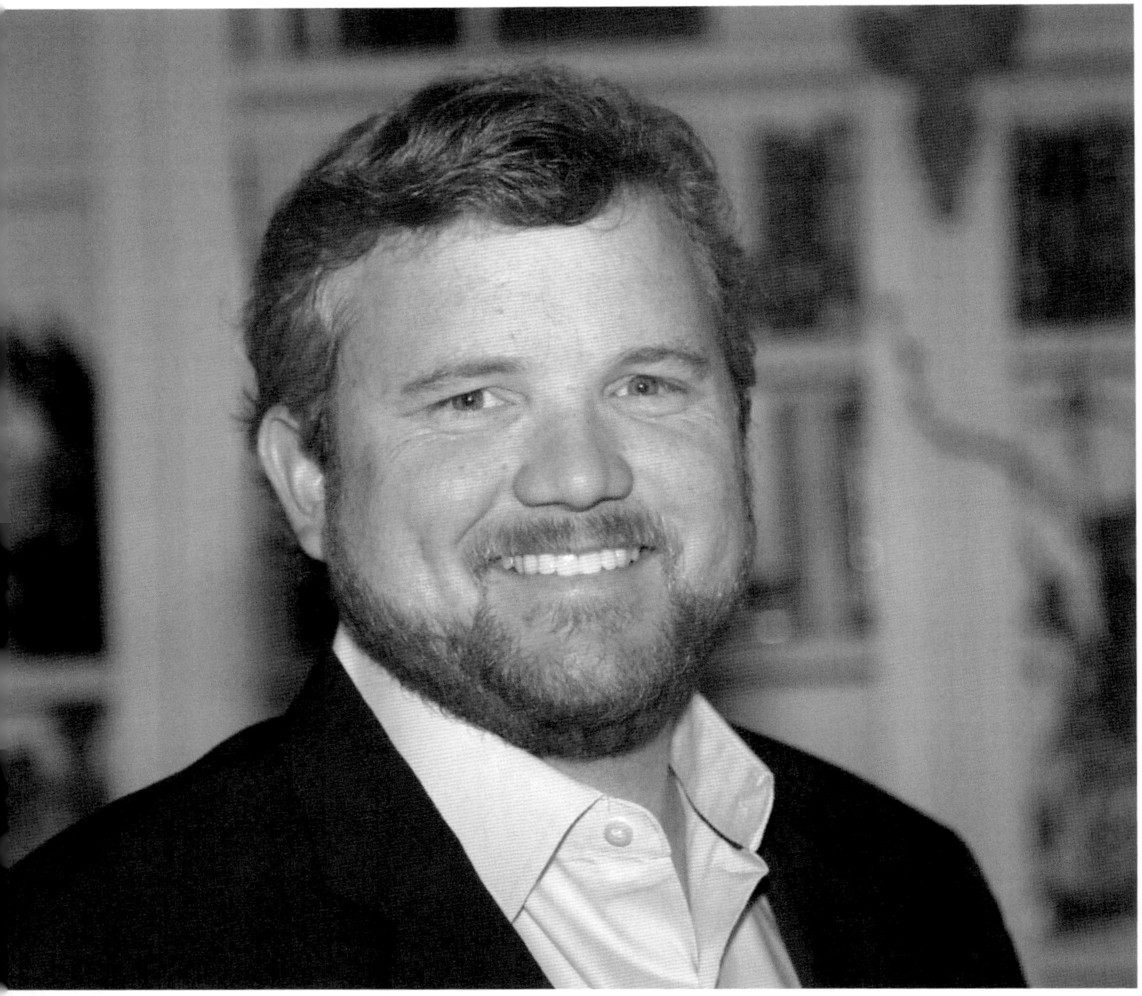

Involved Parent
In 2012, the Meridian City Council approved the appointment of Michael Van Veckhoven, who had been named the 2011–2012 Parent of the Year, to the Meridian School Board. Michael's dream is for every school in Meridian to be a star school. "I think we often place too much responsibility on public education itself to right the wrongs of society," he said. "The job of the teacher is to teach. Yet, we force our teachers to do much more." (Courtesy of Michael Van Veckhoven.)

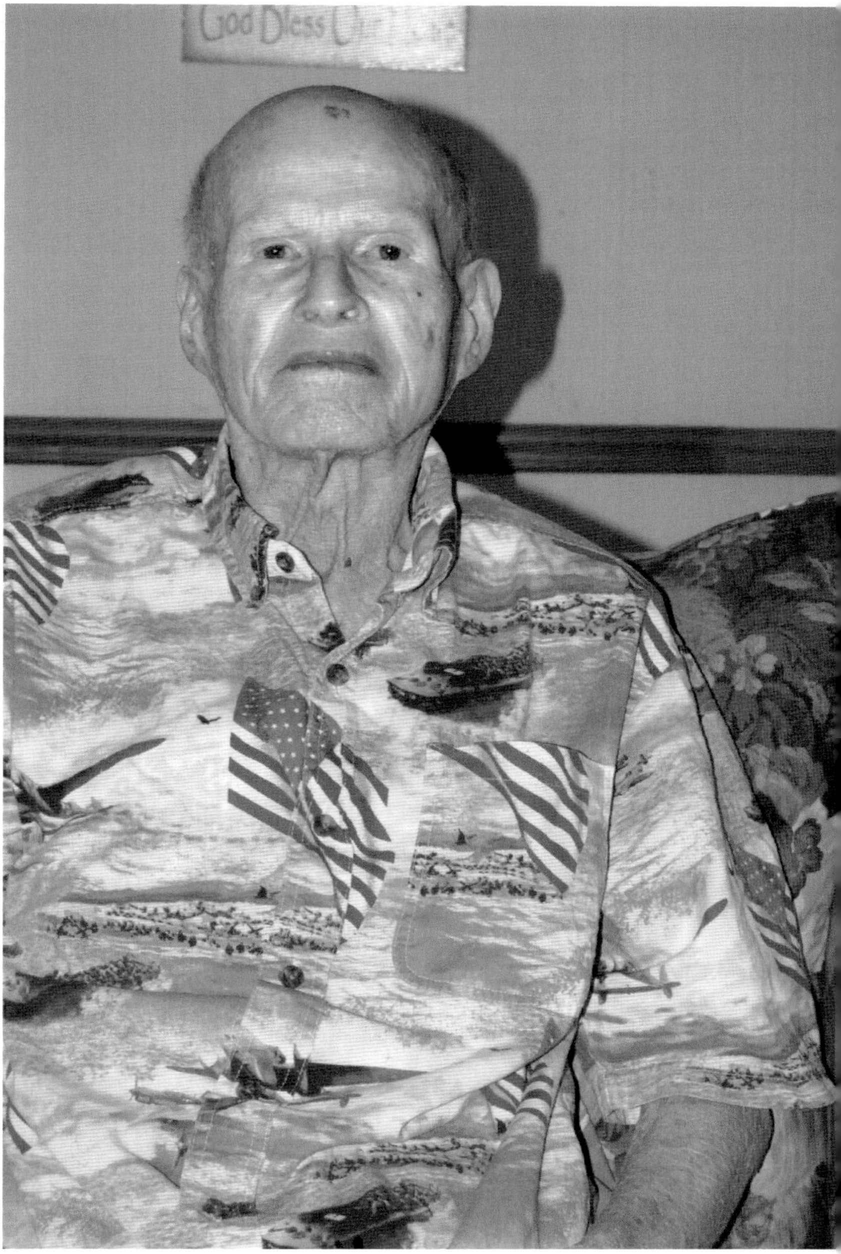

Camp Time

Russell Camp, who is over 100 years old, reminisced about his youth: "My granddaddy died when I was eight years old. He fought in the Civil War and was shot through the jaw in Tennessee. The musket ball went in one side of his jaw and came out the other. It knocked his teeth out. When he was in Vicksburg, the captain gave them each an ear of corn. One of the men asked for two ears because he was so hungry. Granddaddy knocked on a lady's door and asked for food, but she didn't have anything much to eat herself. One of the men with him saw a goose in the field; they chased it down and cooked it over an open fire near the creek."

For over 100 years, Russell Camp resided on the same property near Vimville that his father, John Camp, owned.

"When I was young, my daddy had a blacksmith shop and he farmed too. I used to help my mother make lye soap; you couldn't touch it with your hands; it would eat them up," he said. During the early 1900s, families often traveled by horse and buggy. "My brother Norman had a fine carriage with a top edged in black-fringed tassels. When we were boys, my brother R.V. and I made a cart to ride down the hill. He used a black gum log to fashion the wheels from," Camp said.

"We played pole vault and marbles during recess at Vimville School. We used steel bearings or clay balls that had been baked in the fire for marbles. Clay marbles would do in a pinch." He laughed and said, "We played basketball outdoors on a dirt court, too."

The first car we owned was a Model T that was given to my mother by her brother."

He served as an MP (Military Police) during World War II and married Aline Culpepper, a longtime organist at Hebron Baptist Church. (Courtesy of June Davis Davidson.)

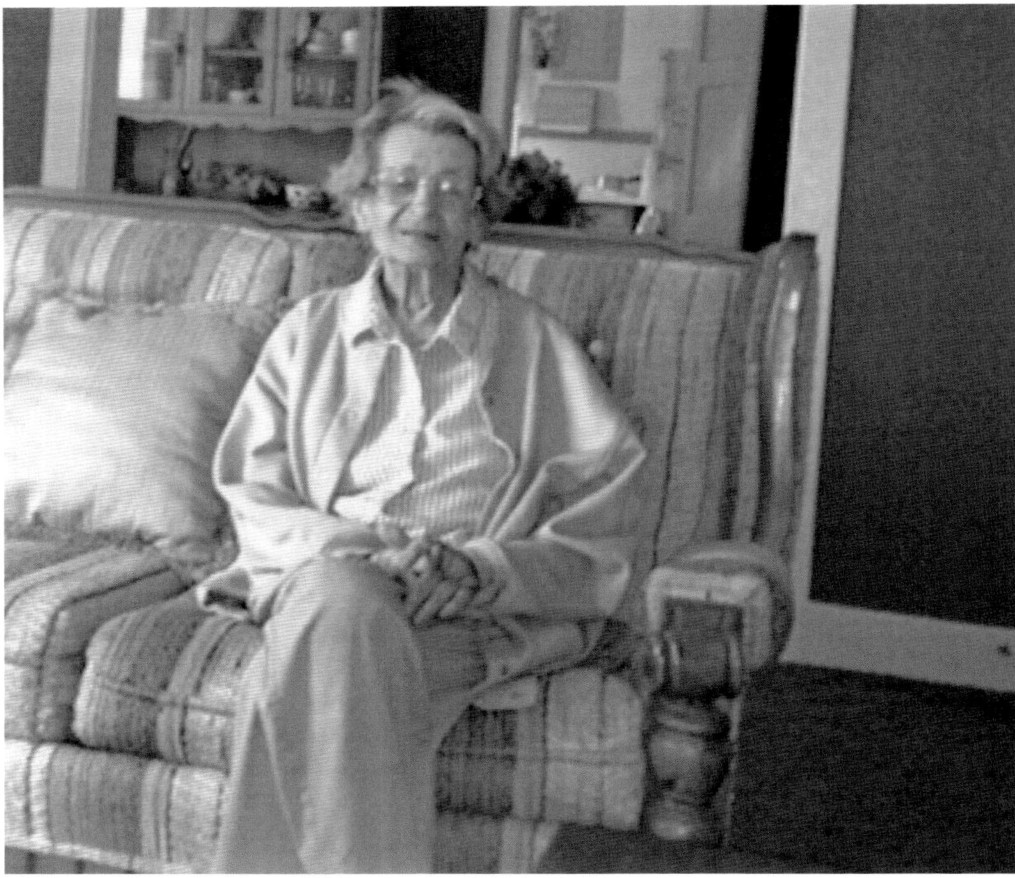

A Century Ago

Louise Thompson drew her first breath in Lexington. She weighed just 2.5 pounds when she was born 100 years ago.

"I remember riding to church in daddy's touring car that had curtains instead of glass windows. In the winter, we heated bricks and placed them in the floorboard to warm our feet."

Louis was about nine years old when her family moved to Whynot near her grandparents William M. and Sarah Miller. She attended Whynot School, a two-story wood structure with an outhouse. Most of the children rode the school wagon, unless snow and ice froze the wheels; then school was canceled. "Girls wore dresses with a ruffled band around the neck. Material cost 10¢ a yard then, for quality material," Louise said.

"During the Depression, Whynot closed the 11th and 12th grade. After that, Wyness McRae and I went to Meridian High. We paid Mrs. Brown, who worked at Metropolitan Insurance in the Threetfoot building, a dollar a week to ride into town with her. Meridian High's tuition was $3 a month. When I graduated, I attended Holmes Junior College." Louise taught music at Vimville School for almost three years.

"During World War II, my husband, Woody, and I were at the store in Vimville. An announcement came over the radio reporting the plight of Jews in Nazi concentration camps. No one said a word. We were shocked. My brother A.H. Miller was overseas. He drove an ambulance and picked up the wounded on the battlefield."

Louise celebrated her 100th birthday in 2012 at a reception held in her honor at Hebron Baptist Church. Louise Miller Thompson is the daughter of Albert H. and Evie (McNees) Miller. She and Woody Thompson have two children, Gerald Wayne and Betty Carol Flanagan. (Courtesy of June Davis Davidson.)

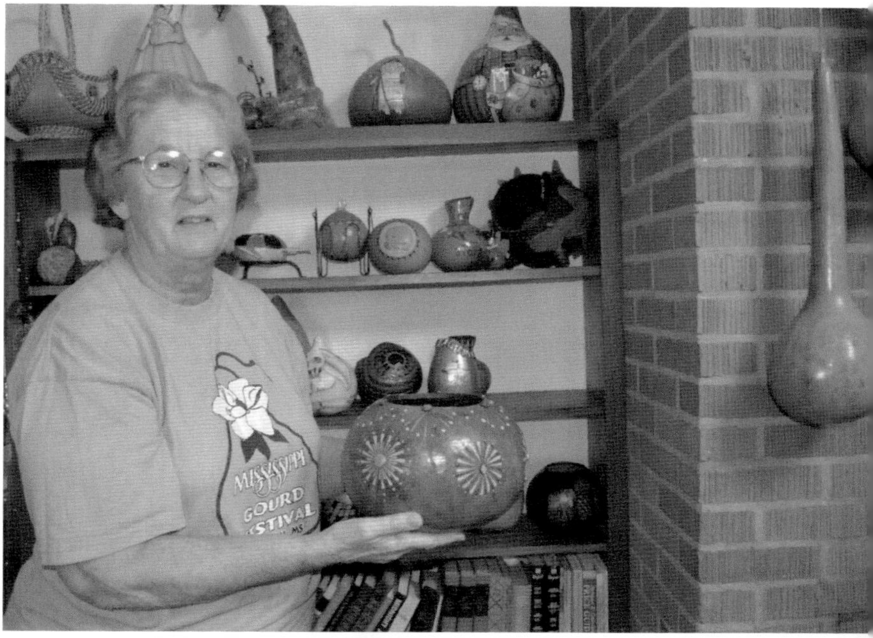

Painted Faces
Ray Davis and her husband, Jerry, raised gourds that were shipped nationally and internationally. She soon discovered that gourds were not just for purple martin houses but also for a unique art form. Ray's interest in gourd art led to the first gourd festival in Mississippi. The festival was held in 2004 at the Davis family's "Gourd Gracious Farm" in Collinsville. (Courtesy of June Davis Davidson.)

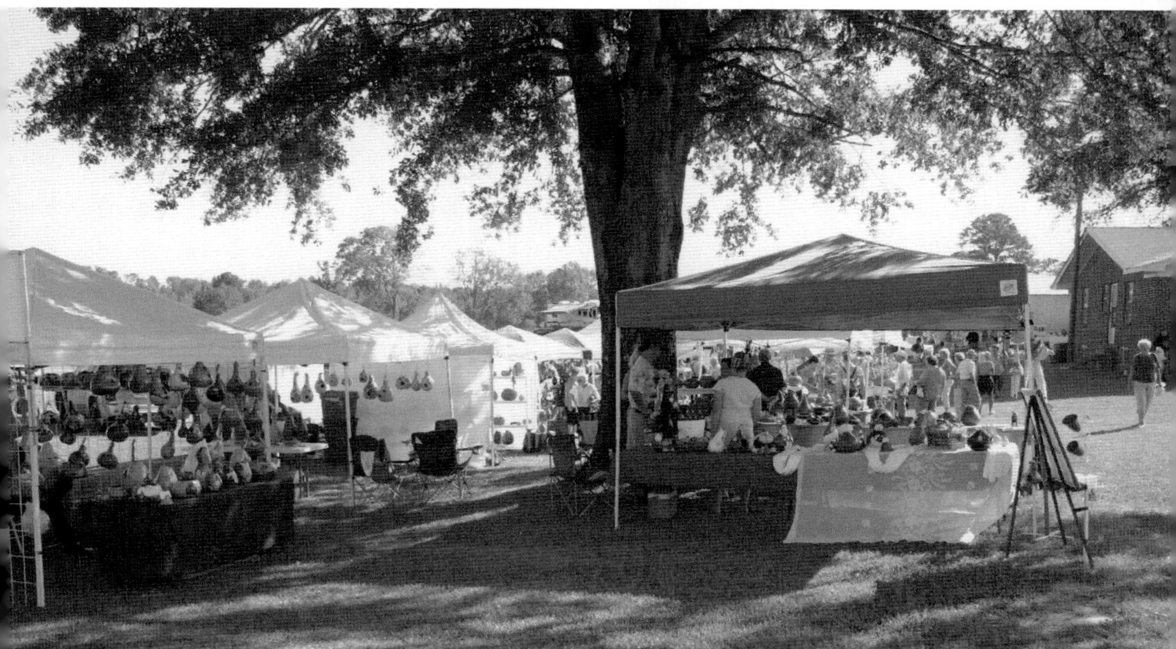

Gourd Festival
Over 200 gourd lovers and crafters attended the festival, encouraging the Davises to host an annual festival. Gourd art classes were added to the slate of activities. The Mississippi Gourd Society, formed in 2007, continued the festival in Raleigh after Jerry's illness in 2010 prevented the couple from hosting the festival. The Raleigh festival attracts over 600 gourd artisans and purple martin lovers. (Courtesy of Ray Davis.)

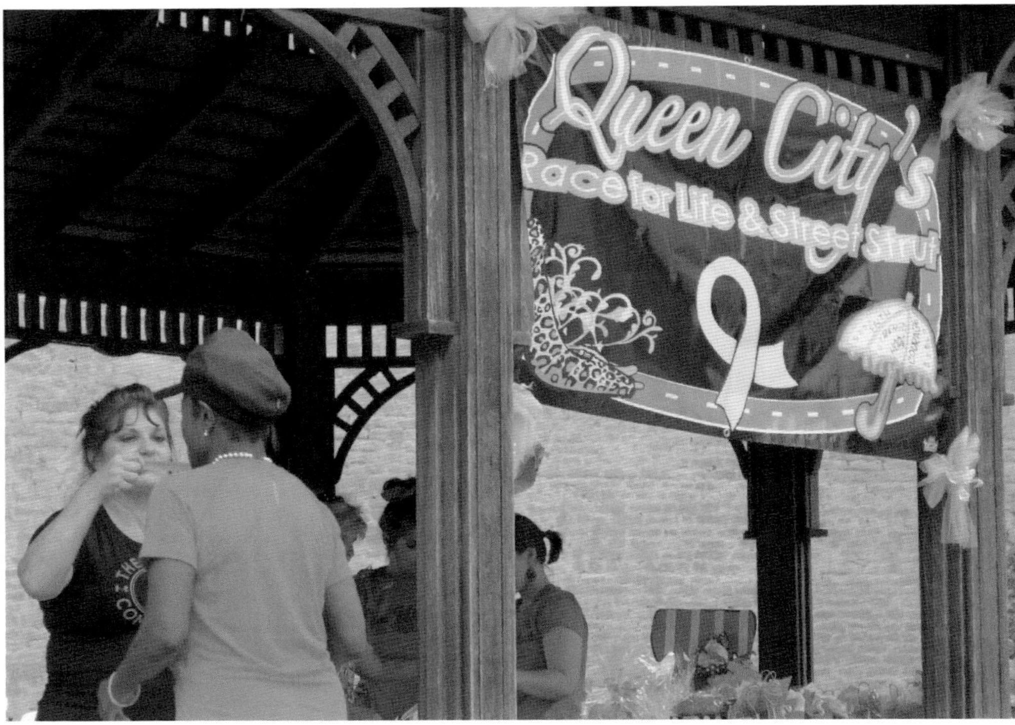

Cancer Run
Cindy Shrock started the annual Queen City Race event in honor of her sister Judie Bounds, who has battled breast cancer since 2005. "I'm very passionate about the fight of breast cancer. I have made so many new friends. There are times I get emotional just talking about my passion and the inspiration from all the new friends and their stories on their journey with this horrible disease." (Author's collection.)

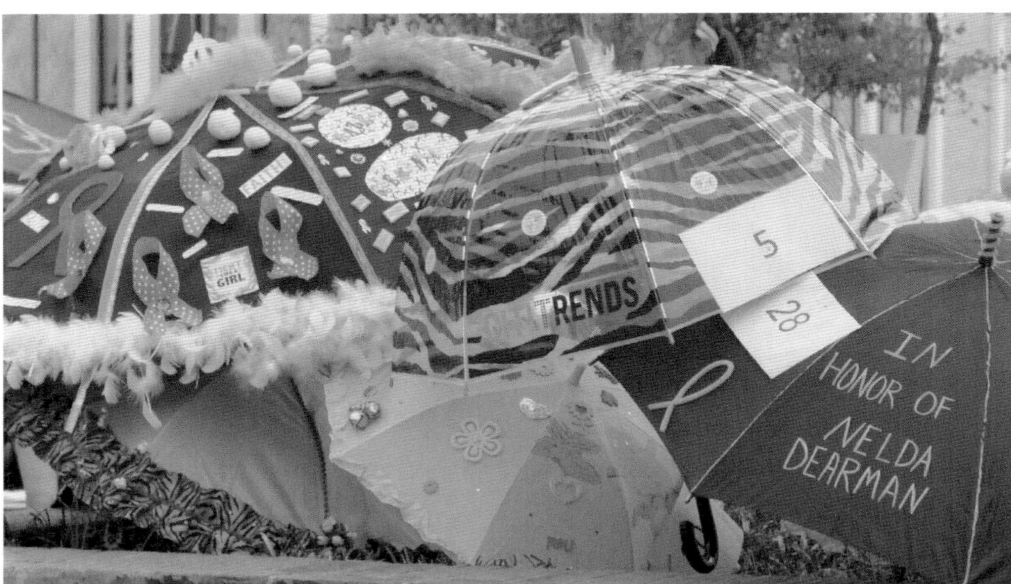

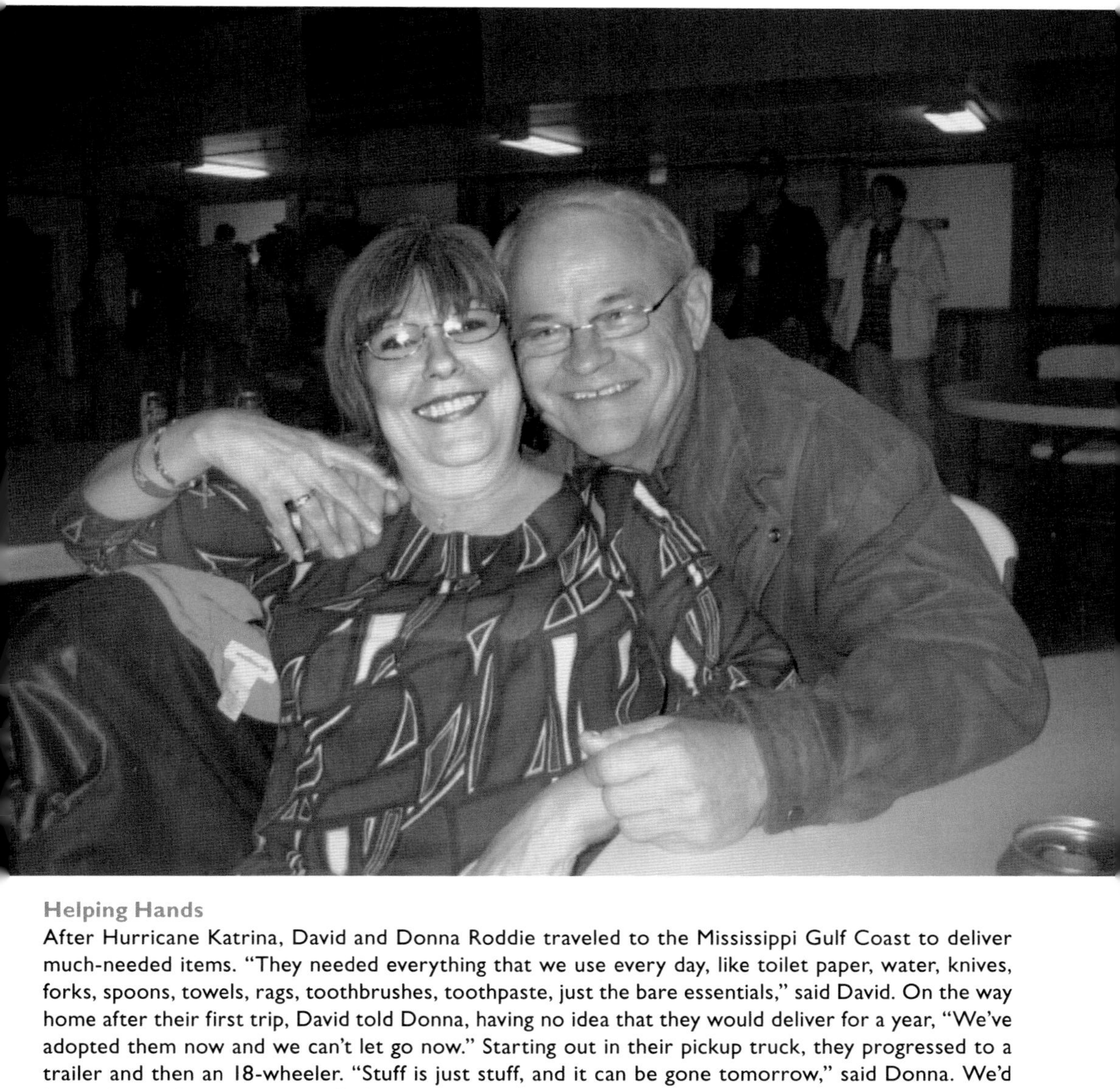

Helping Hands

After Hurricane Katrina, David and Donna Roddie traveled to the Mississippi Gulf Coast to deliver much-needed items. "They needed everything that we use every day, like toilet paper, water, knives, forks, spoons, towels, rags, toothbrushes, toothpaste, just the bare essentials," said David. On the way home after their first trip, David told Donna, having no idea that they would deliver for a year, "We've adopted them now and we can't let go now." Starting out in their pickup truck, they progressed to a trailer and then an 18-wheeler. "Stuff is just stuff, and it can be gone tomorrow," said Donna. We'd better have relationships with God and with the people we love, because that's what counts in the long run." (Author's collection.)

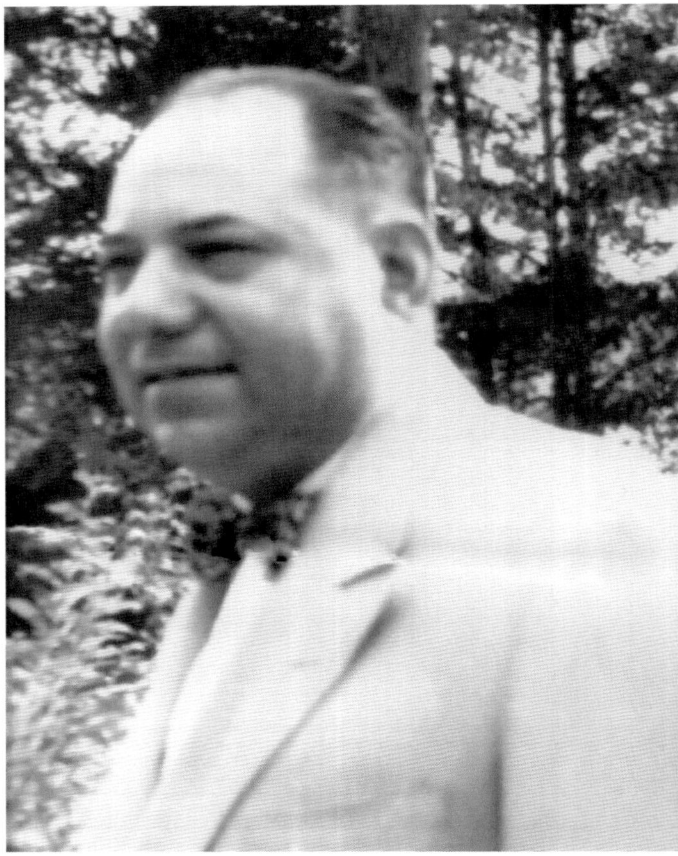

Around the World
As a father, Sy Rosenbaum exposed his children to worlds far beyond their hometown, researching beforehand the places they would visit so his family could experience the world far beyond the tourist attractions. "He gave us a true love of other cultures, history, and architecture." He played tennis up until two weeks before he passed away, and he loved being outdoors and fishing out on the lake. "He always inspired my sister and me and to do the best we could," said Rosenbaum's daughter Barbaree Heaster, "and to be good people. That was really important to him." (Courtesy of Barbaree Heaster.)

Like Father, Like Daughter! (OPPOSITE PAGE)
Barbaree's love for architecture came from her father, Sy Rosenbaum. "We would be walking, looking up at the buildings and talking about the architecture and the design of the buildings." When Barbaree restored the Rosenbaum Building, the restoration of the Grand Opera House had not taken place yet. Therefore, the refurbishing of the Rosenbaum Building was the first effort in revitalization in downtown Meridian. "To me, you must save different kinds of architecture, because once they're gone, your grandchildren will never see them." (Courtesy of Barbaree Rosenbaum Heaster.)

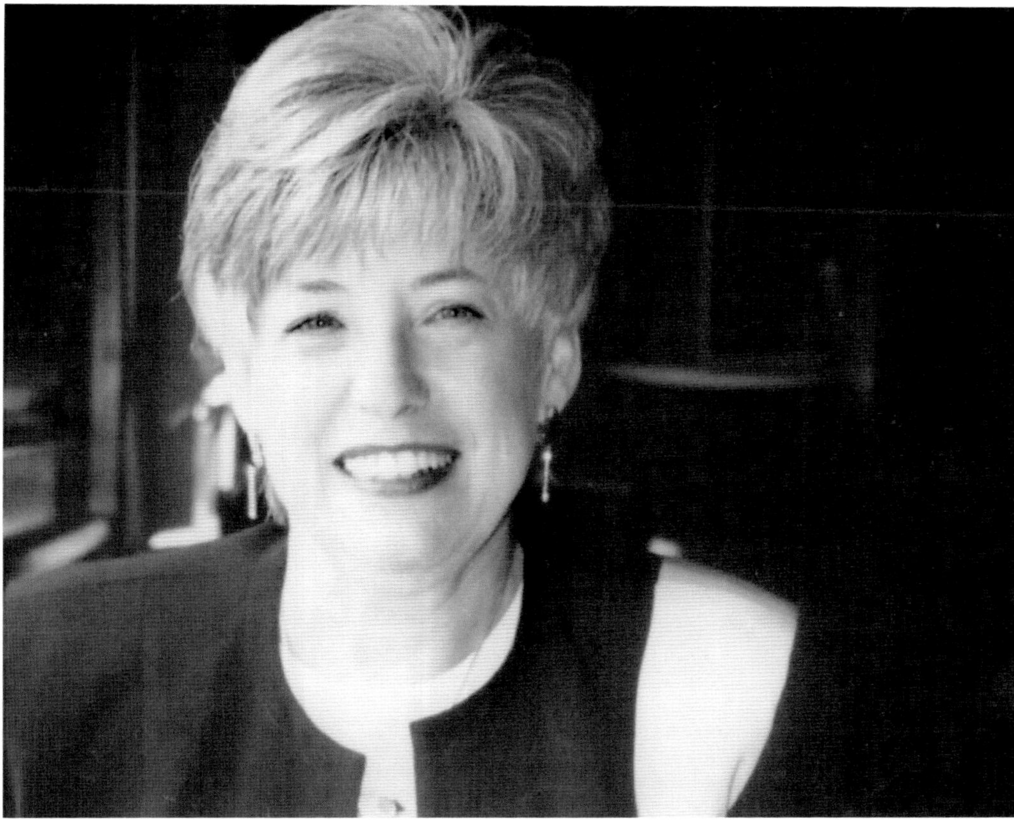

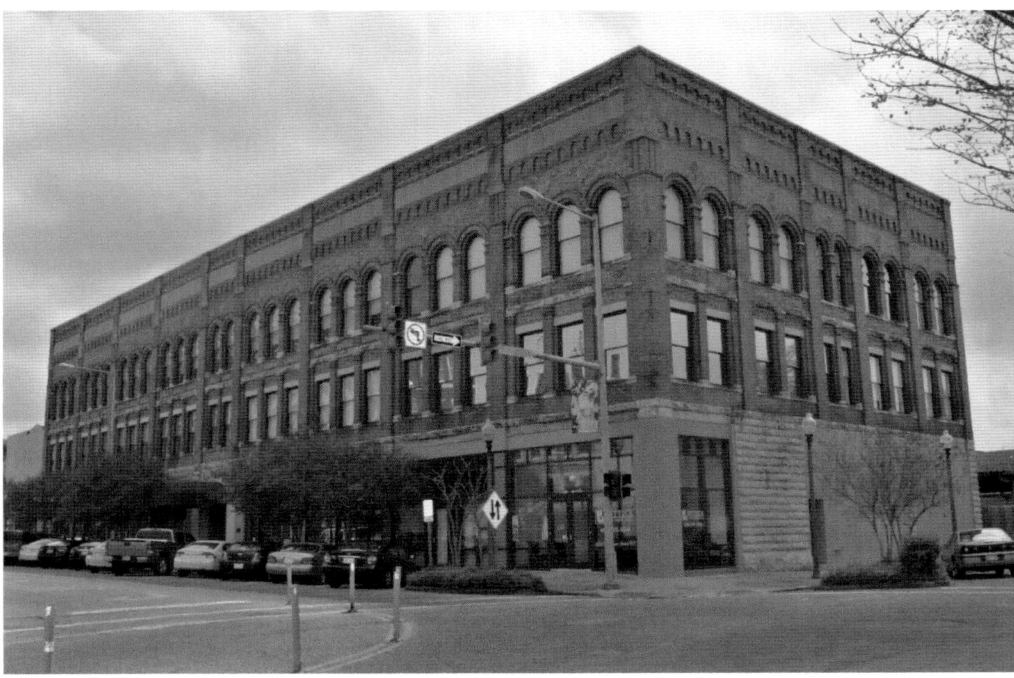

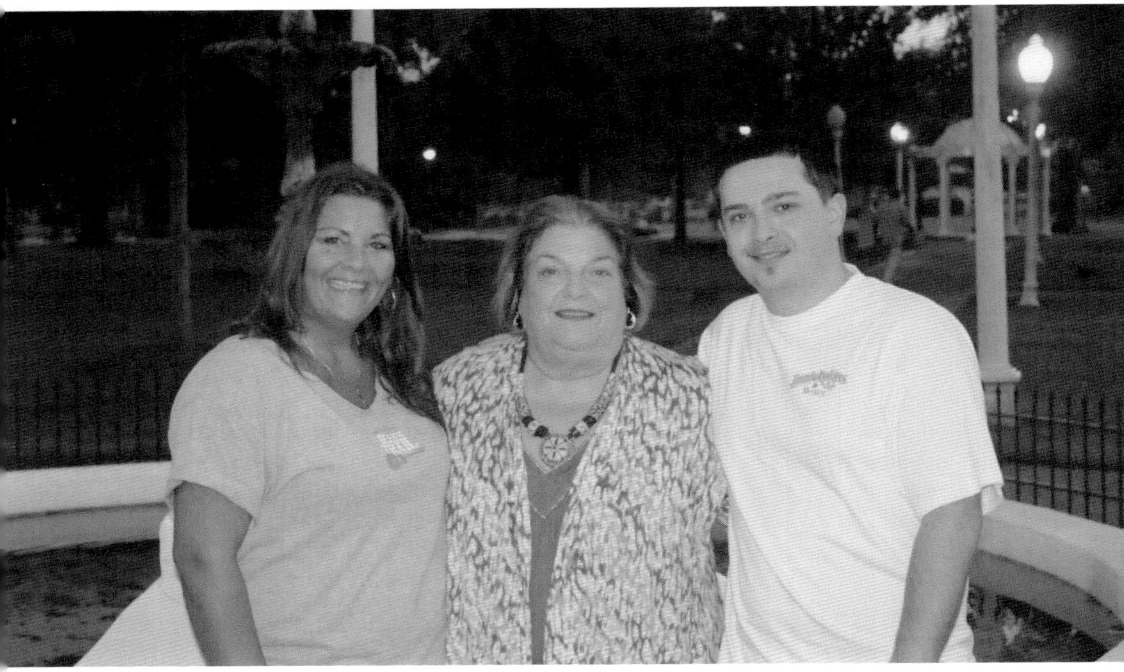

Keeping History Alive

Betty Lou Jones serves as president of Meridian's jewel from the past: Merrehope, a refurbished Victorian mansion from Meridian's golden age. One section of Merrehope, however, was built in 1858 by settler Richard McLemore. "The antebellum part will now be authentically furnished for the 150th anniversary of Sherman's March through Meridian," said Betty Lou, who also serves on the Jimmie Rodgers Board and Meridian Arts Council, and is an active volunteer for the American Cancer Society in Lauderdale County. "In 2011, we had 22 bus tours. In 2012, we had 44 that represent 41 states and nine countries." Betty Lou is pictured here between the great-grandchildren of Jimmie Rodgers, Dixie Haslett and James Cody Court. (Author's collection.)

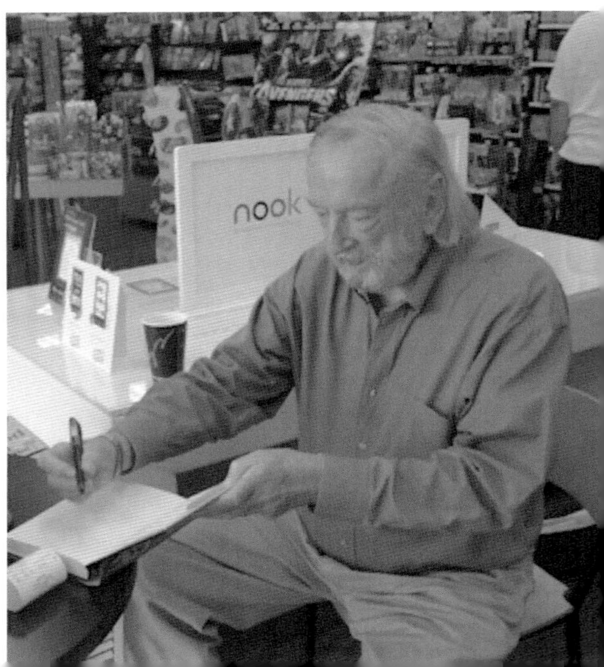

The Snoop

Hewitt Clarke is a man of talent, a sleuth who has unwrapped Meridian's most notorious crimes of passion and wove them into a compelling tale of intrigue. He is well known locally for his books on Lauderdale, Neshoba, and Kemper Counties. A former reporter for the *Wildcat* and a graduate of Meridian High, Clarke attended the University of Mississippi and earned his bachelor of arts in business. His investigative skills were honed while he served in the Army as special agent in the Army Counter Intelligence Corps. He currently resides in Texas and is a frequent visitor to his former hometown of Meridian.

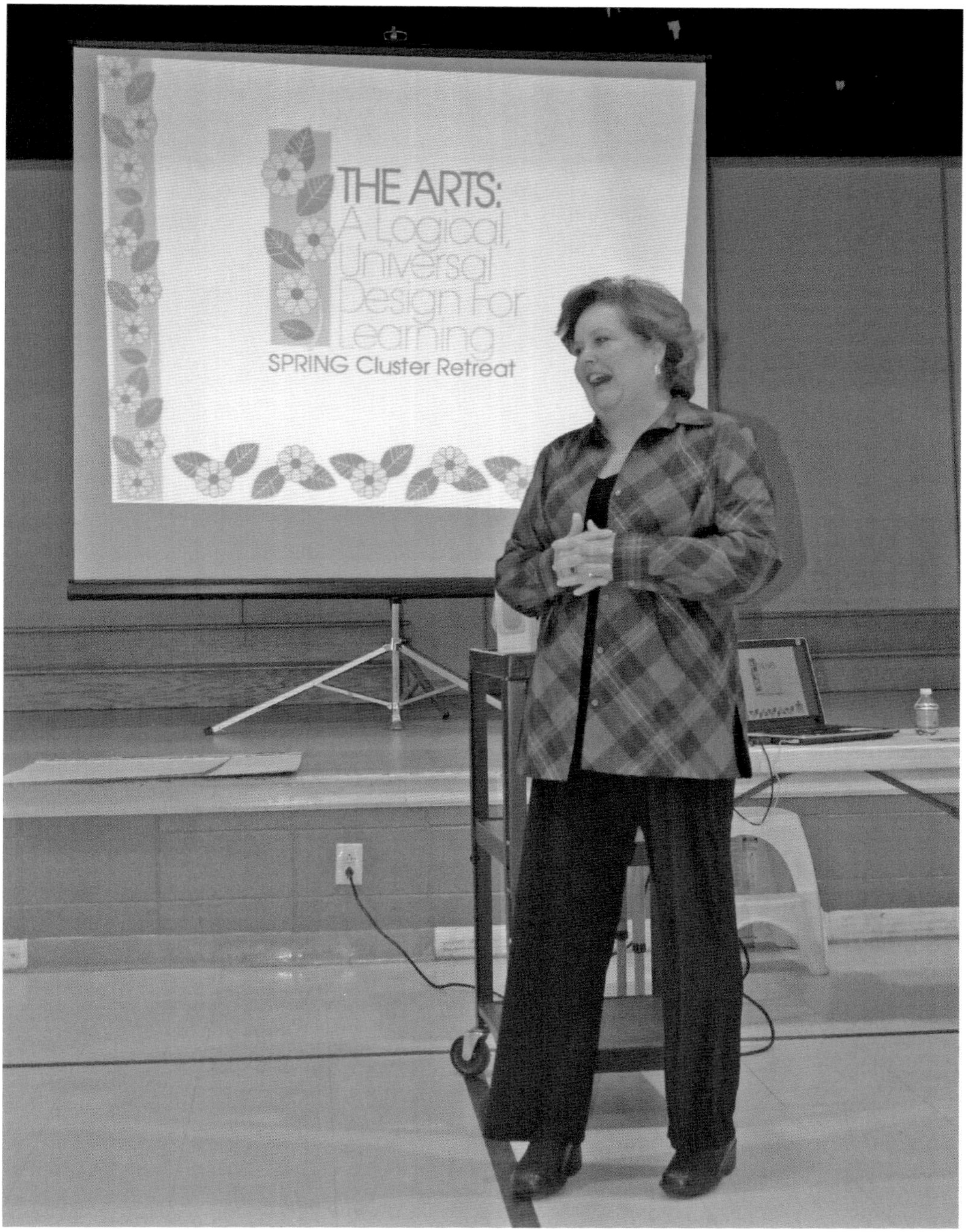

Arts for Learning

Dr. Charlotte B. Tabereaux, education director of Meridian's MSU Riley Center for Education and the Performing Arts, believes in Arts in Education. As director of federal programs and arts supervisor for Mississippi's Rankin County School District, Charlotte developed an art program that earned the school district the 2004 Governor's Award for Excellence in the Arts. Charlotte continues to teach Arts in Education to teachers and students throughout Mississippi. (Author's collection.)

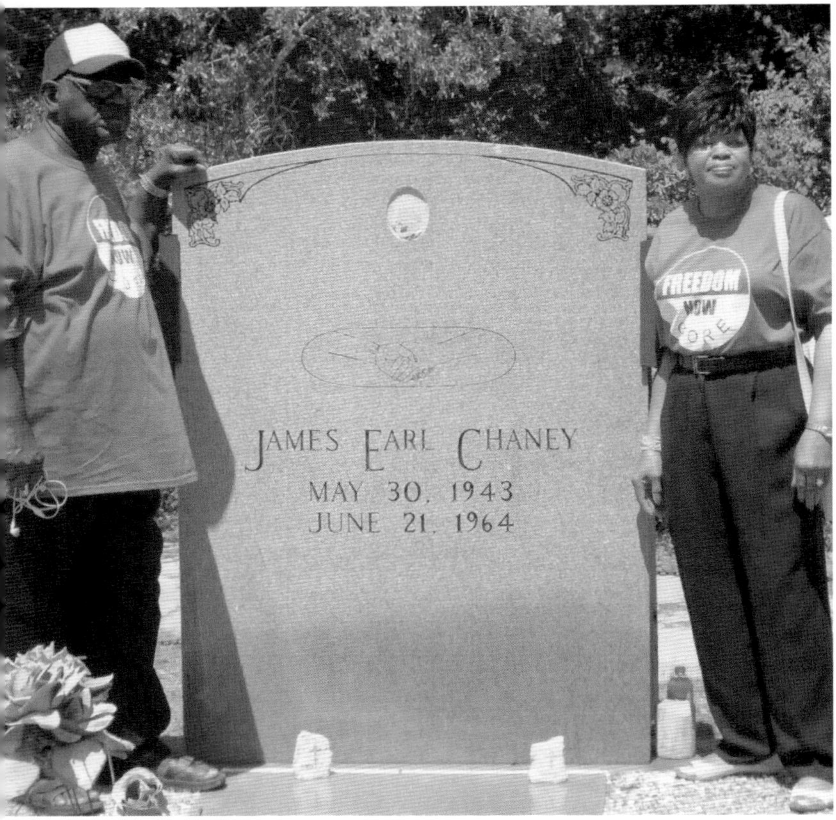

George and Louise Smith at James Chaney's Gravesite
George Smith was project director of the Congress of Racial Equality (CORE) Meridian operation from 1964 to 1967. His wife, Louise Moore Smith, also a native of Meridian, was a Mississippi civil rights movement veteran. Both remember when martyr Mickey Schwerner said at a meeting, "Look at me. Even though I'm white, I'm not free. Not one man is free until all men are free." George and Louise still fight for the rights of the slain of civil rights workers Schwerner, Goodman, and Chaney, asking the State of Mississippi to bring charges against the people who were never charged for their murders. Now a resident of Fort Wayne, Indiana, George and Louise travel to Meridian each year on the annual pilgrimage to remember Freedom Summer and the three who were killed. Nevertheless, George and Louise focus not on the deaths of the civil rights workers but on their lives, saying, "because they lived, we can face tomorrow. Meridian was a very segregated place in the sixties, and we wanted to see a change." George and Louise Smith marched with Dr. Martin Luther King Jr. and worked with James Chaney, Andrew Goodman, and Michael Schwerner. They believe it is important to see the historical places and remember so that history will not be repeated. James Earl Chaney was born on May 30, 1943, in racially segregated and economically depressed Meridian. An active participant in church activities at St. Joseph Catholic Church, he attended school there from kindergarten to ninth grade before attending Harris Jr. College High School in Meridian, Mississippi, where he was an avid sportsman. As a young man, he became involved in the civil rights movement. He dared to wear a paper badge that spelled out *NAACP* and, consequently, was suspended from school. James became involved in the Freedom Bus Rides in 1962 and joined CORE (Congress of Racial Equality) in 1963, helping organize voter education classes in Meridian, Mississippi. As liaison to Michael Schwerner, he took care of COFO's (Congress of Federated Organizations) Voter Education program in southeast and east-central Mississippi. On June 21, 1964, James Chaney, Andrew Goodman, and Michael Schwerner, after investigating the ruins of Mount Zion church, were ambushed and murdered by members of the Ku Klux Klan. The murders were orchestrated by Edgar Ray Killen, a Neshoba County preacher. Over 19 suspects were brought to trial, but as of this date Edgar Ray Killen is the only one who has been tried and convicted—but for manslaughter, not murder. This conviction was not made until 40 years after the murders. (Author's collection.)

The Greek

Kris Gianakos, also known as "The Greek," started his training at Columbus Air Force Base, where he became an instructor pilot. He and his family lived overseas for three years, but came back to Columbus. "I volunteered for Columbus because no one ever wanted to go. I was rewarded with my first command position. I was a flight commander."

Kris went to England Air Base in Louisiana, and from there he and his flight squadron served two deployments: Desert Storm and Desert Shield. After that, at Ramstein Air Base in Germany, he coordinated the "bed down" of the US forces. "Where do we put the airplanes and people?" Kris explained with a question.

Again, Kris ended up at Columbus Air Force as commander of the flyer squadron. "It's so rare in the Air Force that you come back to the same place more than once, but to come back a third time with all that previous knowledge about weather patterns, how things work, the people, it was a really good time," said Kris. His squadron volunteered at the local animal sanctuary. "We took abused tigers, cougars, and exotic animals that people bought and didn't take care of."

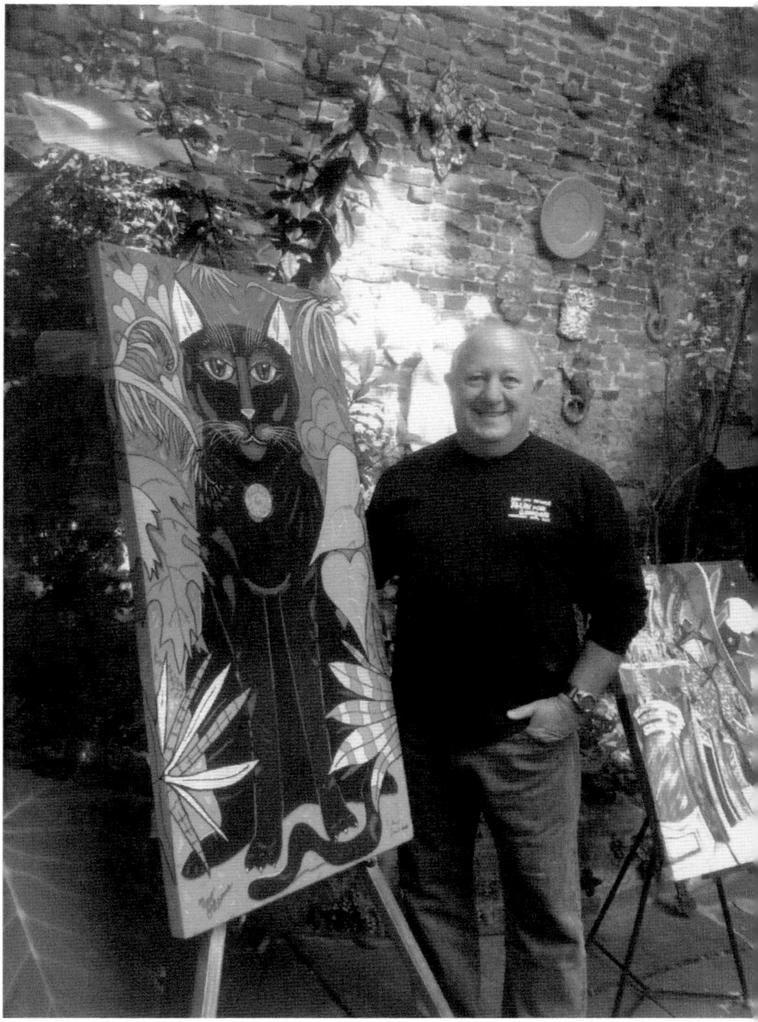

Now a retired colonel, Gianakos returned to Meridian because of family. Since then, he has been heavily involved in the arts, serving as president of the Meridian Council for the Arts, the Meridian Museum of Art, and the Meridian Performing Arts Center. He is also a commissioner for the Mississippi Arts Commission.

Kris loves Meridian because "it still has a small town atmosphere. I have the ability to breathe in and breathe out, and there is a sense of freedom." (Courtesy of Kris Gianakos.)

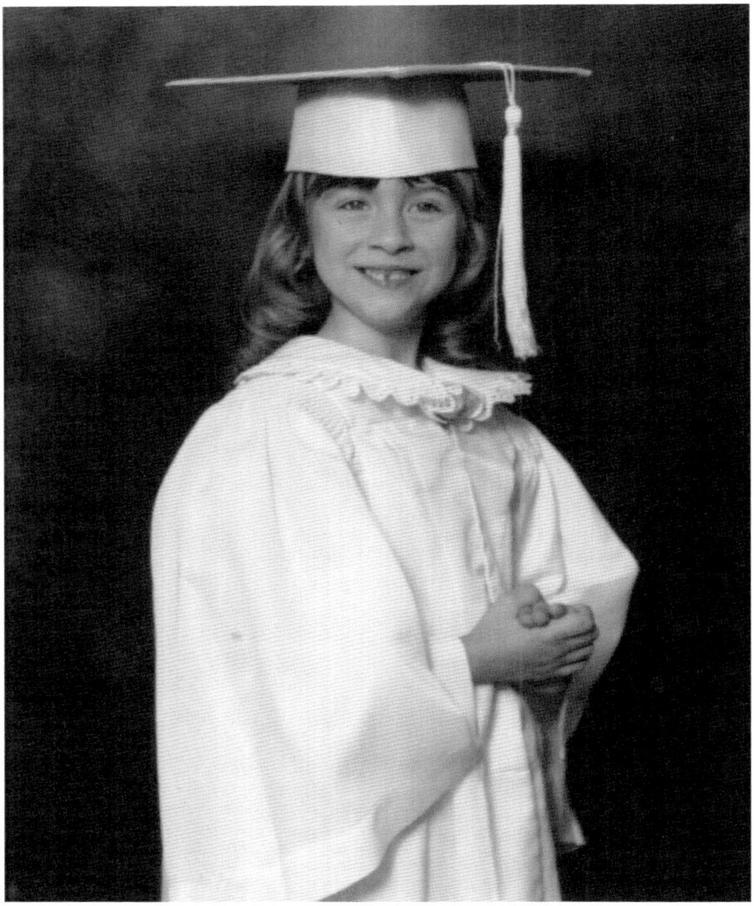

The Gift of Life

"Everyone has their own idea of what a hero is or what it means to be a legend," said Stephanie Denham, Lorien Lea's mother. "My legend and my hero has been a nine-year-old child." More than 22 years ago, Lorien Lea saw her mother's renewed drivers license and asked what organ donation was. Lorien listened carefully as Stephanie explained. "About a half hour later, Lorien returned to the room and seriously expressed her wish to donate her organs if anything happened to her." Barely three months later, Stephanie returned to this conversation. One month after Lorien turned nine years old, her life was cut short by the preventable crime of drunk driving. She lay for five days in a coma, kept alive by a ventilator. When the doctors declared Lorien brain-dead, Stephanie contacted the Mississippi Organ Recovery Agency. Her daughter's heart went to an 11-year-old boy in Pittsburgh; her left kidney to a young man in Mississippi; and her left cornea to a woman in Mississippi. A young man with hepatitis received his miracle liver at Emory University in Atlanta. Three weeks after his surgery, he was out of his coma and out of the ICU.

Lorien's wreck happened on Palm Sunday, March 24, 1991. She died on Good Friday, March 29, and was buried on April 1. Lorien lives through her gifts of life to people that she never met. Lorien was one of the first multiple organ donors and one of the first children donors in Meridian. "I dedicate myself to promote organ donation, to educate about the dangers of drunk driving and help with legislation to curb this crime. Many people all over the world and country have heard Lorien's story and her gifts through her life and her death. I did it so people would know and remember my daughter, Lorien Lea Denham." (Courtesy of Stephanie Denham.)

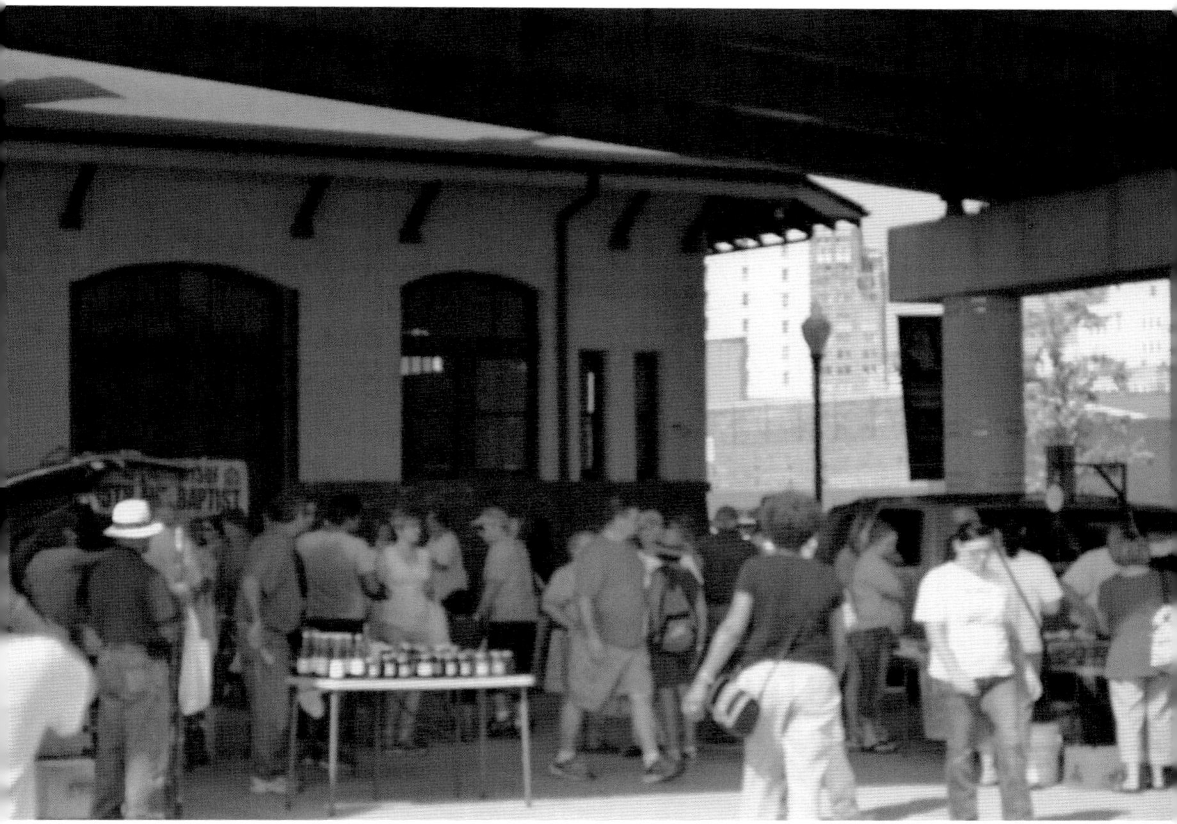

Earth's Bounty

For four consecutive years, Meridian Main Street (MMS) received awards from Mississippi Main Street Association for downtown revitalization. In 2013, the MMS Earth's Bounty Festival (shown here) received the Best Public/Private Partnership Award in the Economic Restructuring category, which includes projects and programs best exemplifying how the public and private sectors work together to enhance downtown and boost its economy, attract visitors, and provide significant downtown opportunities for residents.

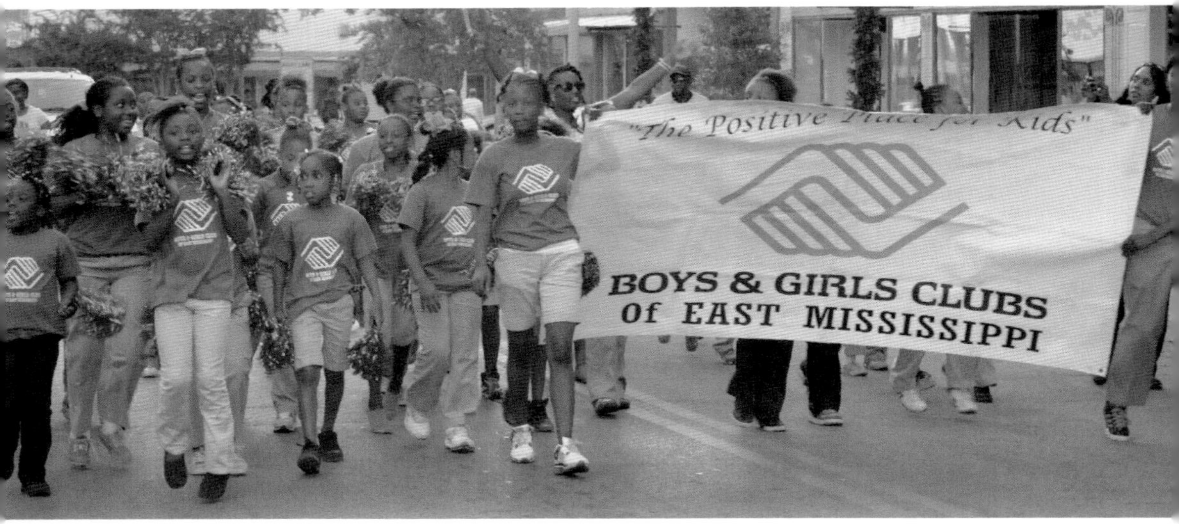

It Takes a Village

Ricky Hood's "village" is the Boys and Girls Club of East Mississippi, where he reaches, teaches, and affects the lives of many children. Since 1989, he has formed lasting relationships with the kids of Boys and Girls Club and their families. "No child deserves less than the best opportunity we can afford them to becoming successful in life," said Hood. "You have to build relationships with the children and their families." (Author's collection.)

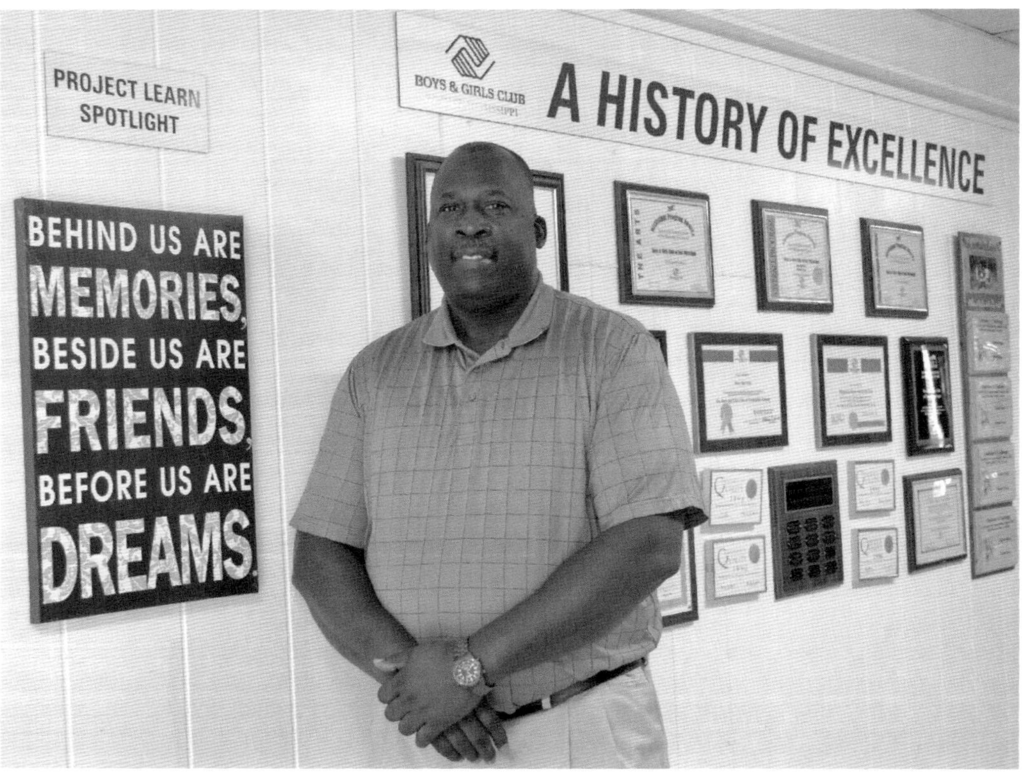

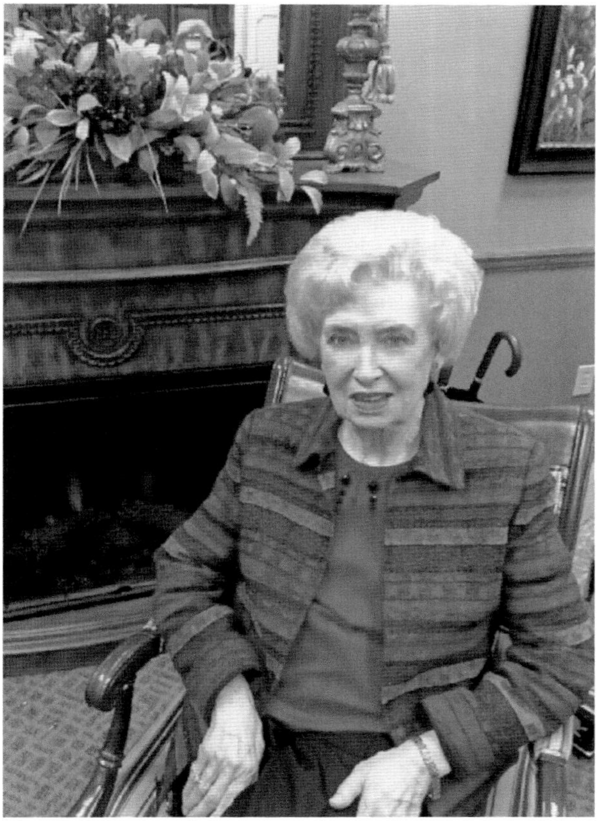

Selfless Worker
Since 1904, Wesley House has survived many difficult times. In the 1960s, when the facility was threatened with closure, Nell Grissom stepped in as a volunteer to oversee the Wesley House until a deaconess could be found. She became director, serving for over 40 years. Under her direction, Wesley House thrived and grew. In 1986, her daughter Ginger Grissom, who grew up in Wesley House because of her mother's work, took over the helm. The mission has grown into many different areas of education, victim and health services, and community services like scouting, clearinghouse, clothes closet, parenting, food pantry, and much more. Ginger has since received the 2007 and 2009 Readers Choice Woman of the Year Award and the 2010 Humanitarian Award. With a calling to serve, Ginger worked closely with Meridian resident Trey Long, who facilitated the fundraiser to build Wesley House's Playground for Jesus. (Courtesy of Ginger Grissom.)

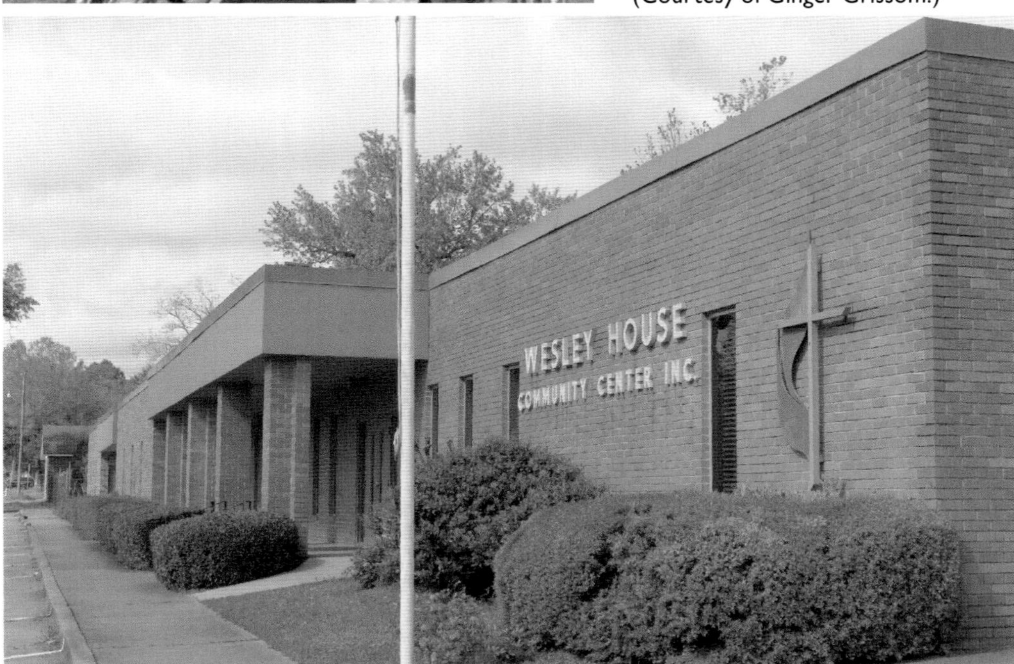

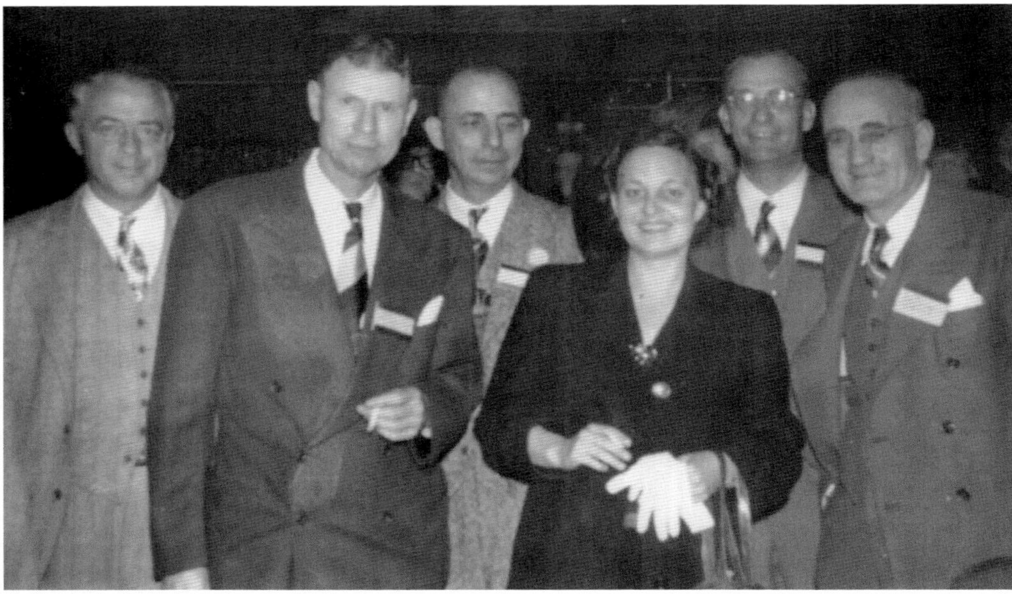

Breaking Bread

In the 1930s, Phil Hardin purchased a bankrupt bakery business in Meridian, Mississippi and grew it into a corporation with plants in Meridian, Jackson, and Tupelo. His natural entrepreneurial spirit was accompanied by a selfless, community-minded spirit and strong sense of citizenship. To support education, he offered tours of the plant to elementary schools and provided every student with a miniature Hardin's loaf of bread. In the 1940s, when floods struck northeast Mississippi, Hardin delivered bread at no cost to the devastated areas. He understood that markets are never static and that technologies and business practices are always changing. In 1953, Hardin sponsored a country music program featuring Danny and the Dudes playing "The Hardin's Bread Boogie" on WTOK, Mississippi's second television station. In the 1970s, Hardin constructed his state-of-the-art production and distribution center in Meridian. (Courtesy of the Phil Hardin Foundation.)

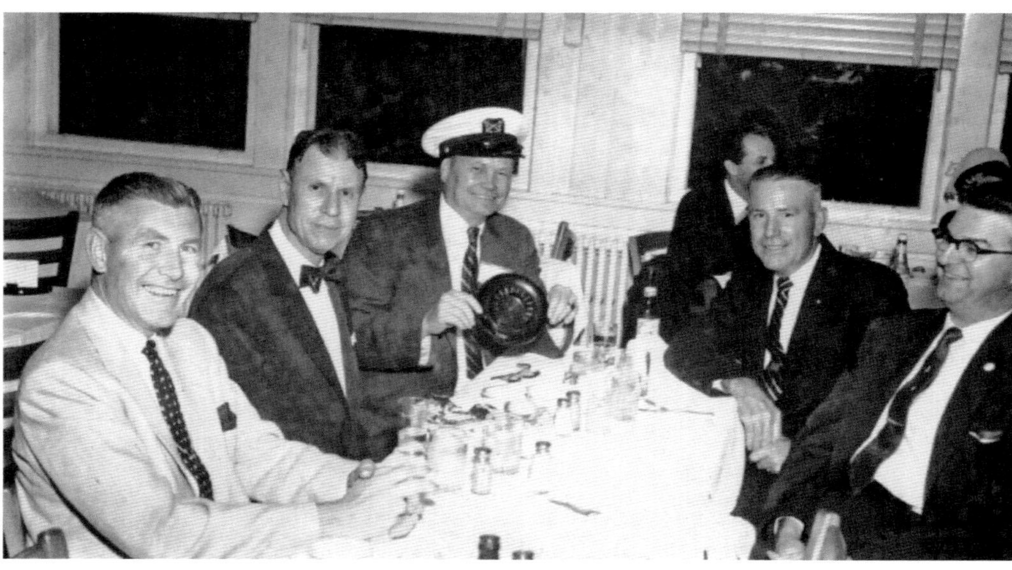

Phil Hardin Foundation

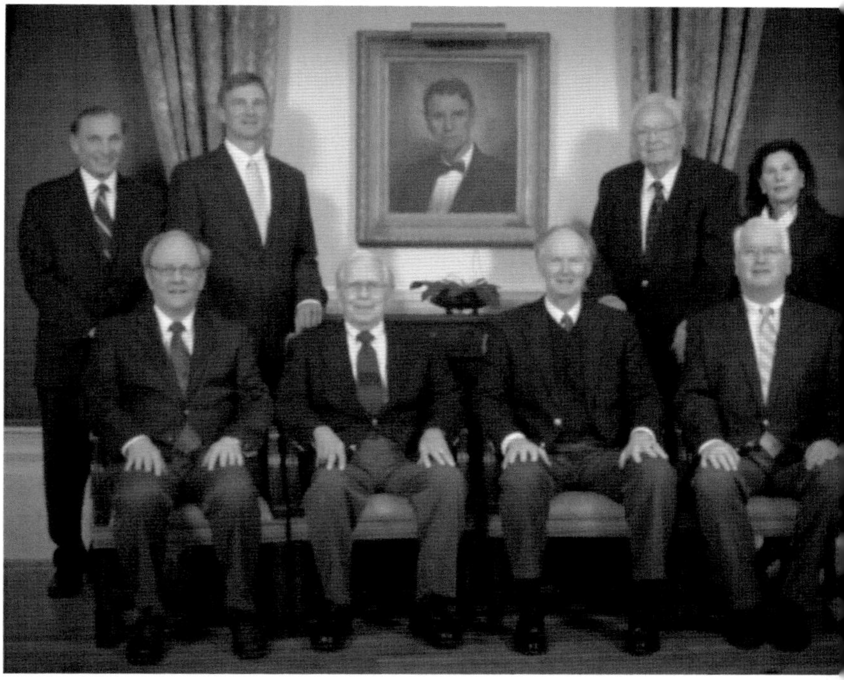

Phil Hardin established the Phil Hardin Foundation in 1964. Recorded in the foundation's first minutes are Hardin's words: "My material wealth has been principally acquired by the operation of my bakery business in the State of Mississippi and from the good people of the state. For a long time I have been considering how my estate could be best used after my death. I have finally conceived the idea of creating a charitable foundation through which the bulk of my estate can be used for furthering . . . the education and Mississippians. Upon his death in 1972, Phil Hardin left virtually all of his assets to the Phil Hardin Foundation. Since its inception, the organization has provided grants and loans exceeding $38.8 million, all focusing on the education of Mississippians. From left to right are (first row) Stephen O. Moore, R.B. (Bob) Deen Jr., Robert F. Ward, and Ronnie L. Walton; (second row) Marty Davidson, Jim McGinnis, Dr. Joe S. Covington, and Rebecca Combs-Dulaney. (Courtesy of the Phil Hardin Foundation.)

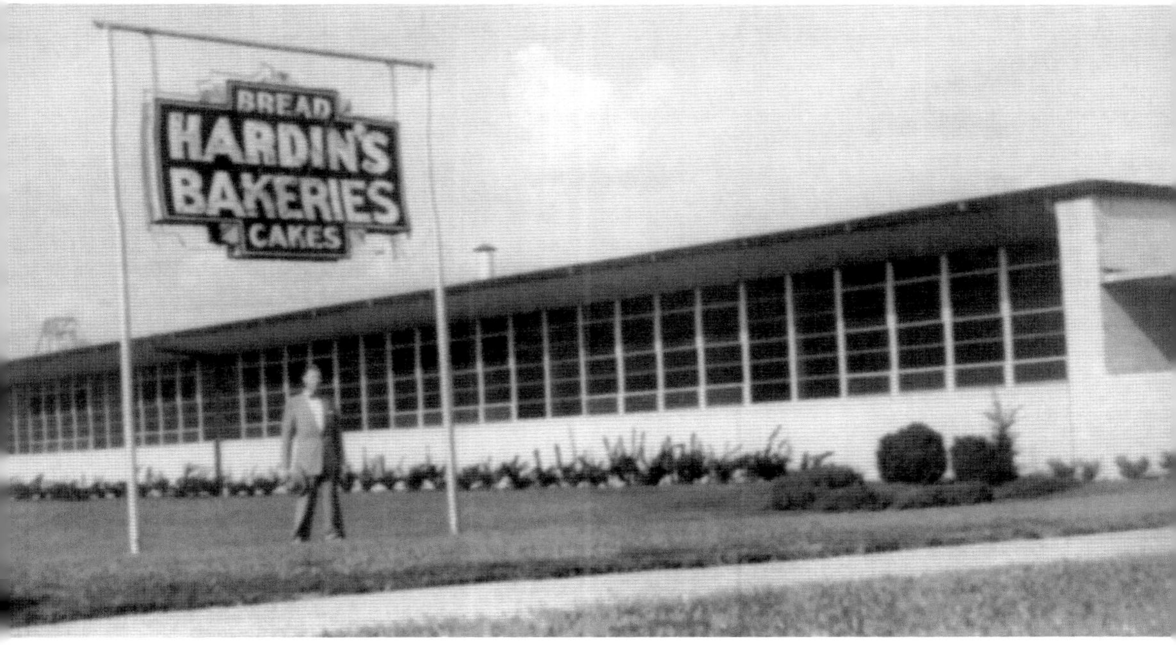

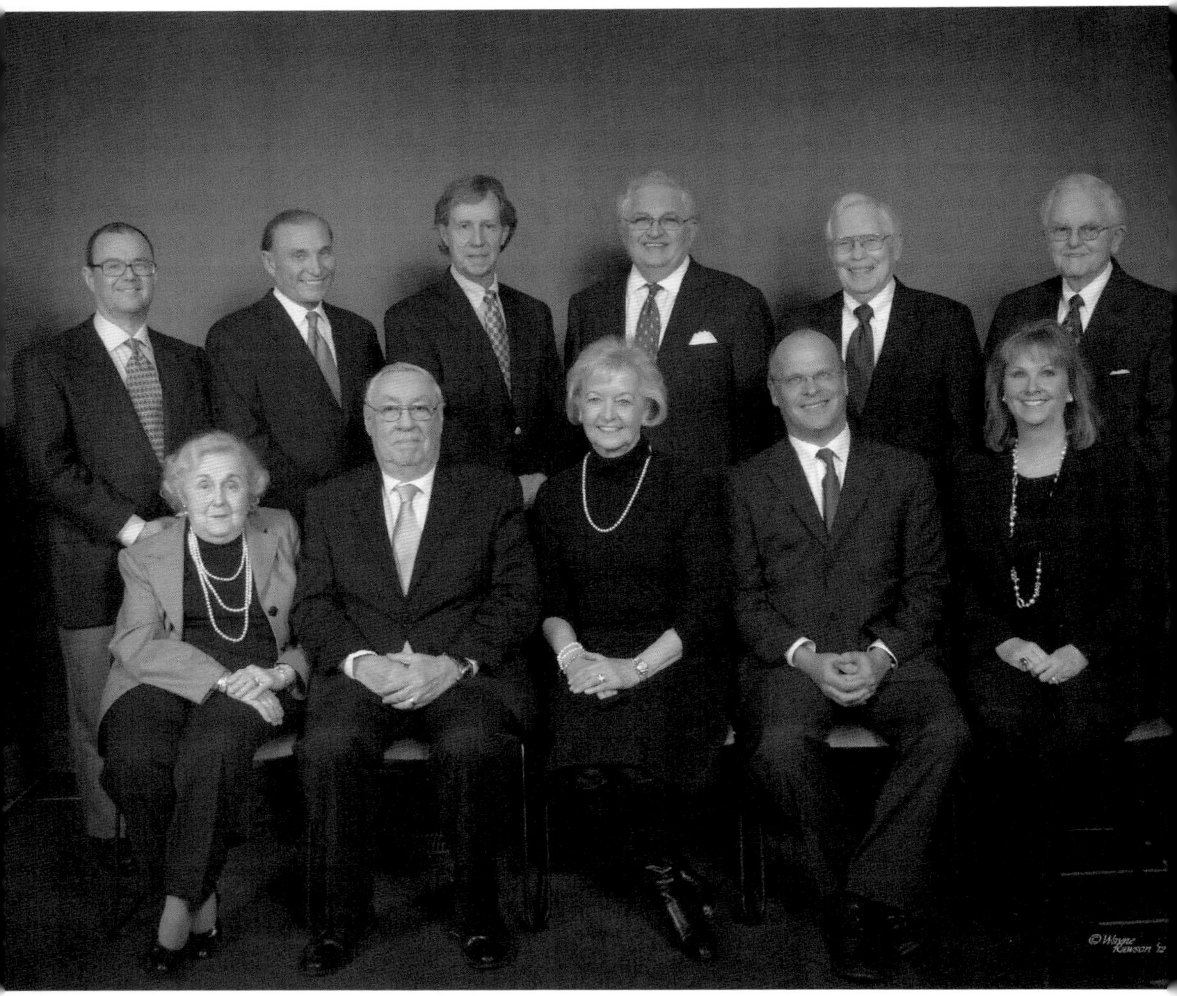

The Riley Foundation

Chartered in 1998, the Riley Foundation is the largest foundation in Mississippi. The vision, however, began in 1930 with Dr. Franklin Gail Riley, the first residency-trained pediatrician in Mississippi. In 2000, the foundation awarded a $10-million grant to restore the 1889 Grand Opera House and the Marks Rothenberg department store into a fully restored opera house, a studio theater, and a 30,000-square-foot, state-of-the-art conference facility. Opening in 2006, the facility is now the MSU Riley Center for Education and Performing Arts Center because of a partnership with Mississippi State University. The crown of downtown Meridian, the performing arts center offers high-quality entertainment year-round and attracts visitors throughout the Southeast. The 2012 directors pictured here are, from left to right, (first row) Mary Ann Riley, Tommy Dulaney, Christine Riley, Gail Riley, and Becky Farley; (second row) Richard F. Riley Jr., Marty Davidson, Manny Mitchell, Malcolm Portera, Bob Deen, and Edwin Downer. (Courtesy of The Riley Foundation.)

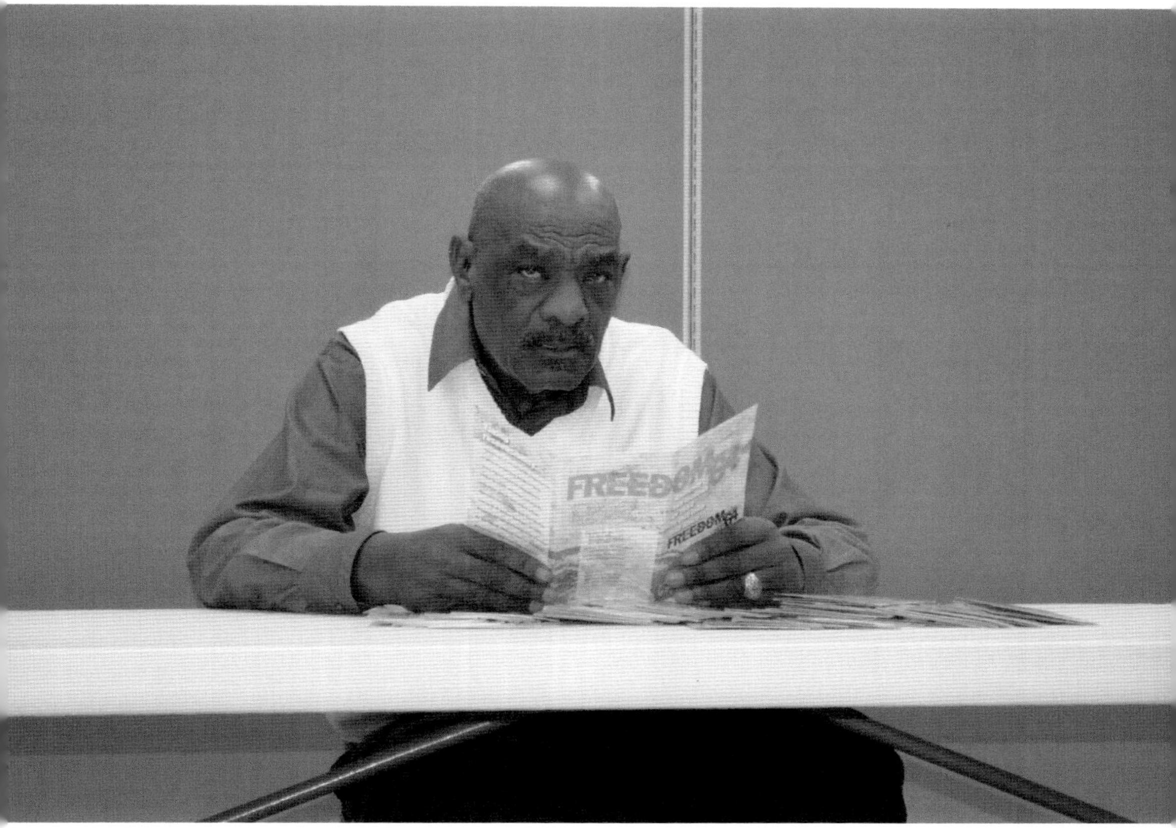

Civil Rights Activist

Roscoe Jones remembers seeing the integration of the Little Rock and the Freedom Riders sit-ins on television. At 13, Roscoe joined NAACP and became active in the Youth Council that was led by photographer Ralph Darden. Mickey and Rita Schwerner came to Meridian in January 1964 to form a Council of Federated Organizations (COFO) at the old Fielder & Brooks Drugstore on the corner of Fifth Street and Twenty-fifth Avenue. Later, James Chaney started working with Mickey and Rita. From January to May, they learned about the movement and the techniques of nonviolence. "We learned how to do sit-ins," said Roscoe, "because we had plans to go to Woolworth and Kress and J.J. Newberry's, which all of them had lunch counters. We were going to go to the lunch counters and demand to be served and we were going to go to Meridian Public Library." On May 30, 1964, they had their first sit-in at Woolworth in Meridian. Thirteen were arrested. At that time, the old city jail was under city hall. The main jail was by Kate Griffin and was segregated. "We were held, booked, and sent to jail. That Sunday, May 31, Fannie Lou Hamer came to speak about the Freedom Democratic Party challenging the regular Democratic Party. Since Roscoe and the others were still in jail and could not hear Fannie Lou speak, "Mickey got Fannie Lou to go to the jail where she cried and sang outside the jail," said Roscoe. In 1964, Roscoe met Fannie Lou Hamer at the Democratic Convention in Atlantic City. Roscoe has always been about equality for all people, not integration. To him integration was a by-product and something that could be controlled. "We've always mixed. If my grandmother worked for your grandmother, they were together. Many black women kept the white children when parents would go out of town." Meridian has always been an integrated, multicultural city. "We just refused to see it." (Author's collection.)

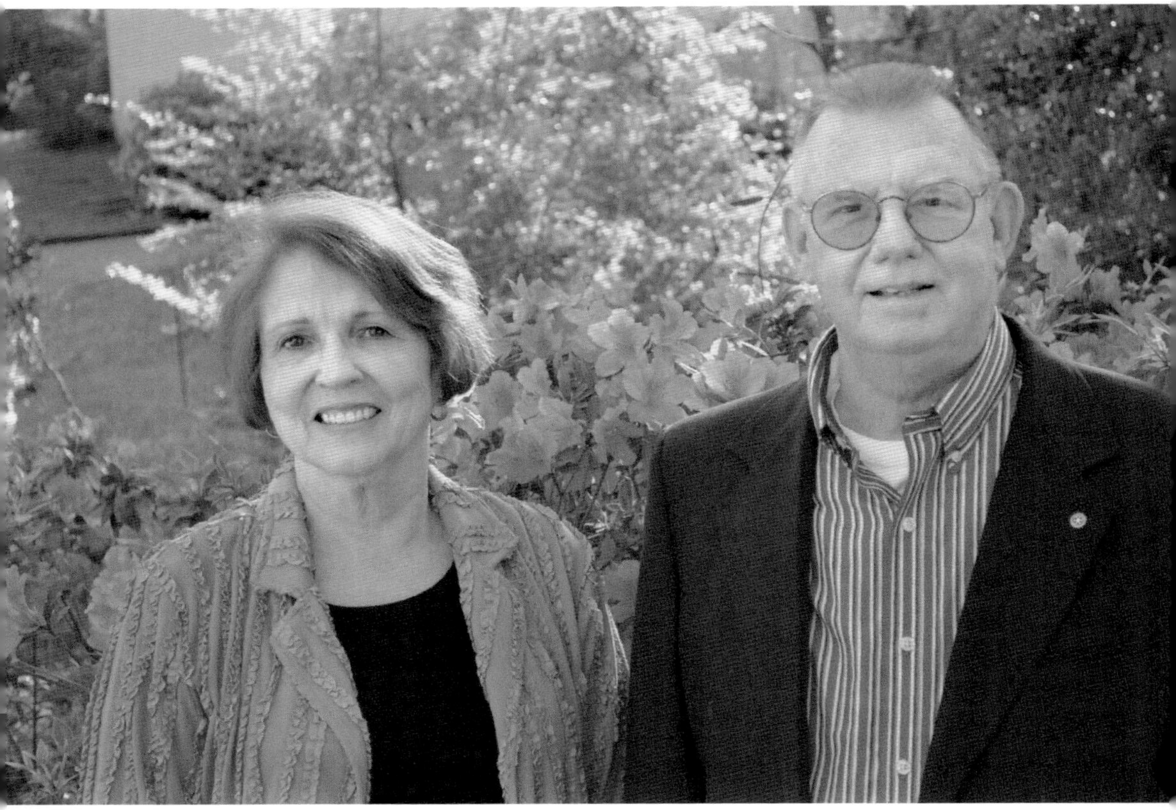

I Will Survive

In 1993, Tom Mayor suffered a stroke. Because Meridian did not have a rehab here, he had to go to the Methodist Hospital in Jackson. He stayed there for 30 days. "On my exit interview in Jackson, they said to come to Meridian and join a stroke support group." But when Tom returned home, he discovered that there wasn't one. "I asked the administrator of the hospital if the hospital would sponsor one." The hospital agreed, and the Meridian Stroke Support Group has been around since 1994. "We have members that are stroke survivors and their caregivers." The group also has speakers. It could be a pharmacist, or a physician or a physical therapist, said Tom, adding that they share with each other about their challenges and the successes. "It's very important for caregivers to talk to other caregivers to get ideas on treatment and what's going on, the frustrations, and so on." It's all about connecting. Support groups are important because "you're not alone. It's good to know what other people are going through and have gone through." Tom and his wife, Ann, also facilitate the hospital's Alzheimer's group and their caregivers. "Anderson's provides the meeting place and the food for the meetings," said Ann, "and Tom lines up the program." Because everyone is at different stages of recovery, they help each other see where they can be in time and how they can handle or confront different issues. "Years ago, when the group was so big, we divided into groups, with the caregivers being together. A seasoned caregiver can counsel a new caregiver on things to expect or anticipate." Tom and Ann got everyone in the group to write down something they discovered that worked well, and they compiled it into a book of hints. "These are things that doctors won't think to tell the stroke survivor or the caregiver." Tom provides this book to stroke survivors and their families. (Author's collection.)

CHAPTER FOUR

Sports

A river of dreams flows . . . and spreads its star-studded tributaries throughout our communities where local legends are born. They are Lauderdale County's golfers, fishermen, hunters, ballplayers, and racecar drivers who are among local and national legends: Oil Cab Boyd, Jonny Barr, Tommy Noblin, and Derrick McKey. They breathed excitement into sports and left a lasting memory in the minds of hundreds of fans. As Mississippians, we claim Archie, Peyton, and Eli as a part of our South we call home. Our sons are taught to hunt, play ball, fish, and golf—it's a skill born in our blood, handed down from our fathers and theirs. A single shot from a hunter's gun, the swing of a golf club, the arch of a fishing rod, and the roar of fans in gymnasiums, football fields, and racetracks . . . sports that await this and future generations.

They coach league teams and teach children how to swing a bat and catch a ball. They are the fathers whose hearts fill with pride when their children make their first tackle.

They are the fathers whose chests swell with love; they're patriotic, they're Southern born—filled with Mississippi pride.

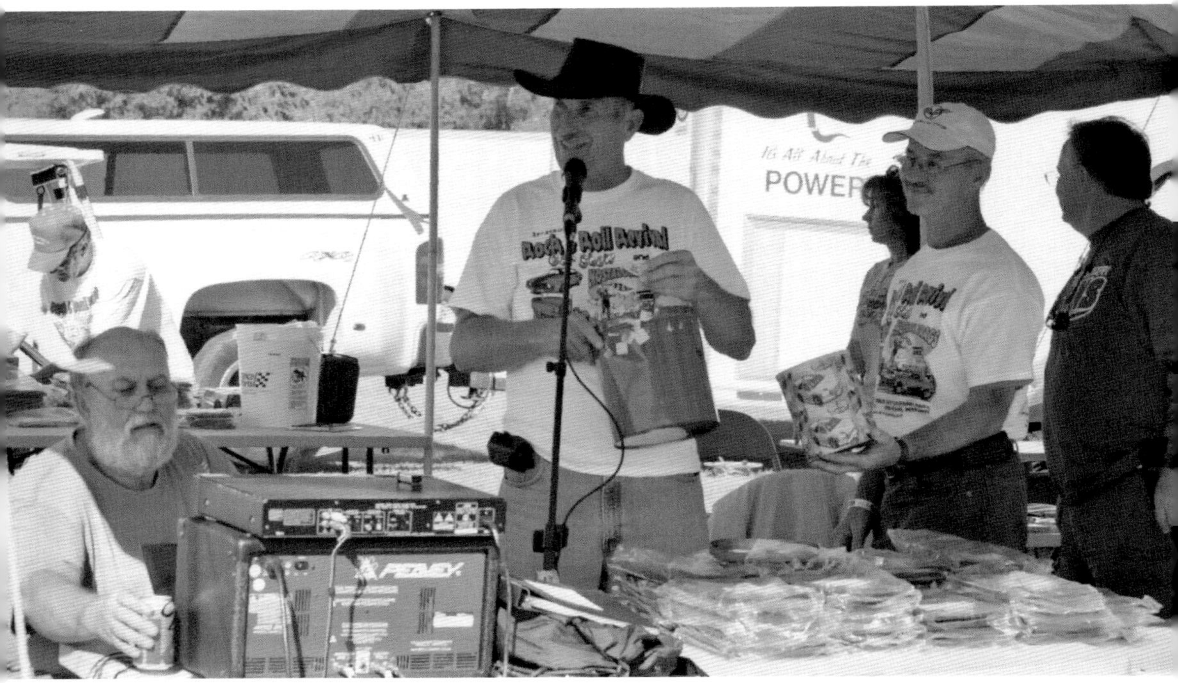

Fast Lane
His family-owned Bill Ethridge Lincoln-Mercury dealership served Meridian for over 40 years, and his Queen City Rod Classics Club formed in 1985. For 22 years, Billy Jack and his family have hosted the Rock 'n' Roll Revival car show in Meridian. Ethridge is a man passionate about racing. He and his wife, Gayle, have been drag racing for over 17 years. In 2002, 2003, and 2006, Ethridge won the national championship race in the K Prepared Class of BMW Club Racing. (Courtesy of Richelle Putnam.)

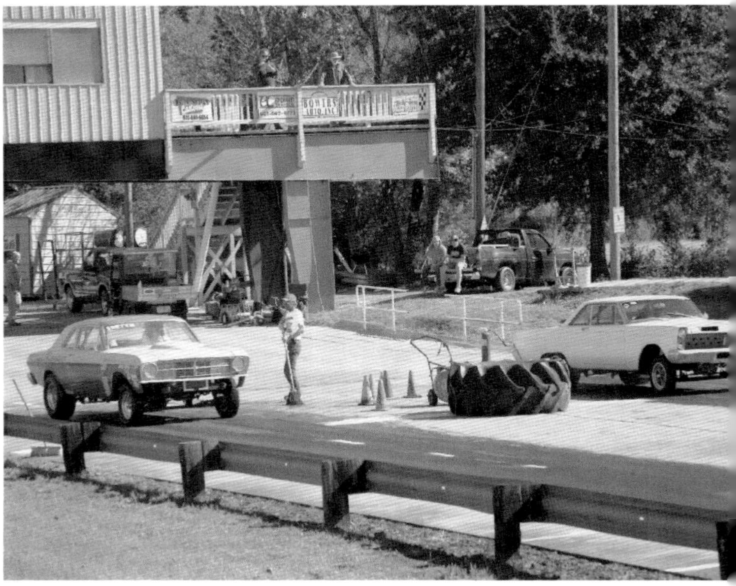

Souped-Up Oldies
Ethridge's Battlefield Motorsports Park, located on the outskirts of Meridian in the small community of Battlefield, is open on weekends from April to October. Here, spectators thrill in the screech of tires and yesteryear's nostalgic cars dragging past them in a blaze of color. The one-eighth mile track hosts motorcycles, four-wheelers, and even grandpa's souped-up car with a glass-packed muffler, modified for racing. (Courtesy of Richelle Putnam.)

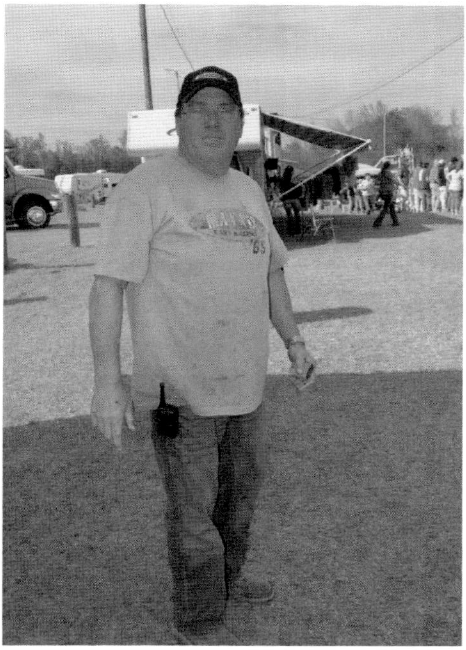

Riding Down Low

If riding down low is for you, then Randy and Trish Rawson's Causeyville Raceway has something to offer with its wheels-close-to-the-ground dirt track races. The first go-kart race of the 2013 season is Maxx Daddy's championship race, a highly anticipated event for Kart racers from across the South. A well-maintained track gives a smooth ride for drivers in colorful designed karts whose speed reaches up to 60 miles per hour. Here, Randy Rawson paused long enough at the race for a photograph. (Courtesy of June Davis Davidson.)

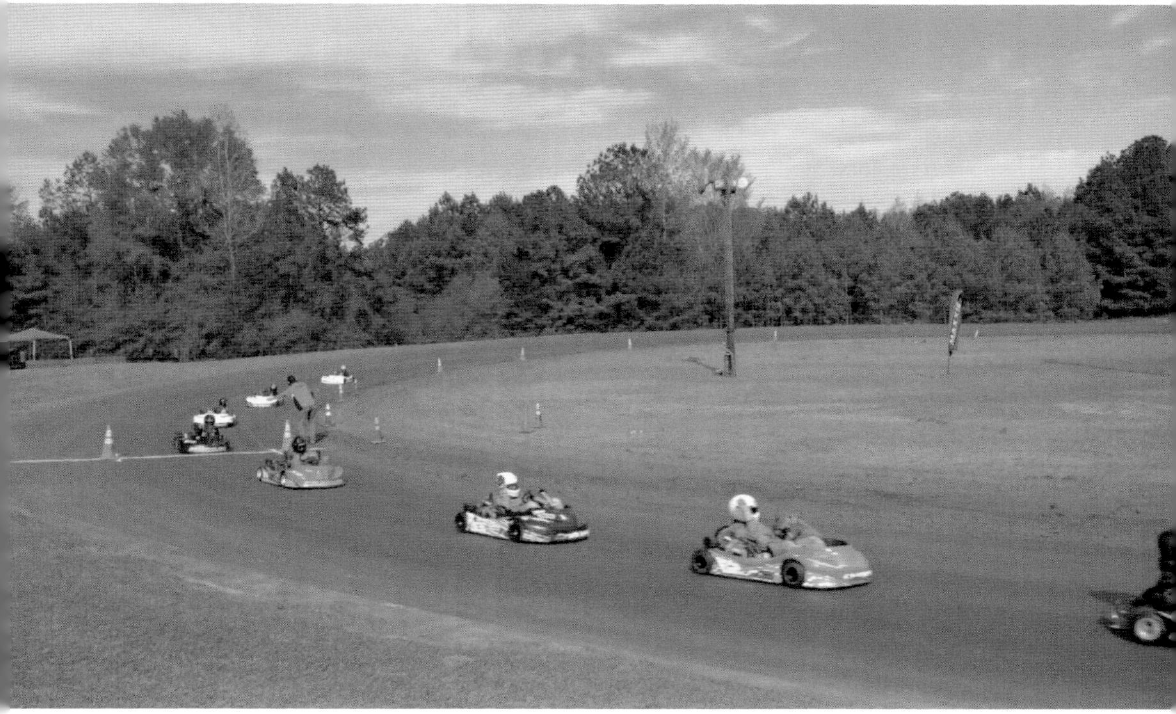

Pot of Gold

Pictured are the Senior Maxx Daddy racers on April 13, 2013. The flagman is Shane Barrett. The Maxx Daddy race is sponsored by Maxxis Tires. In 2013, four races with payouts were held at Causeyville Raceway. (Courtesy of June Davis Davidson.)

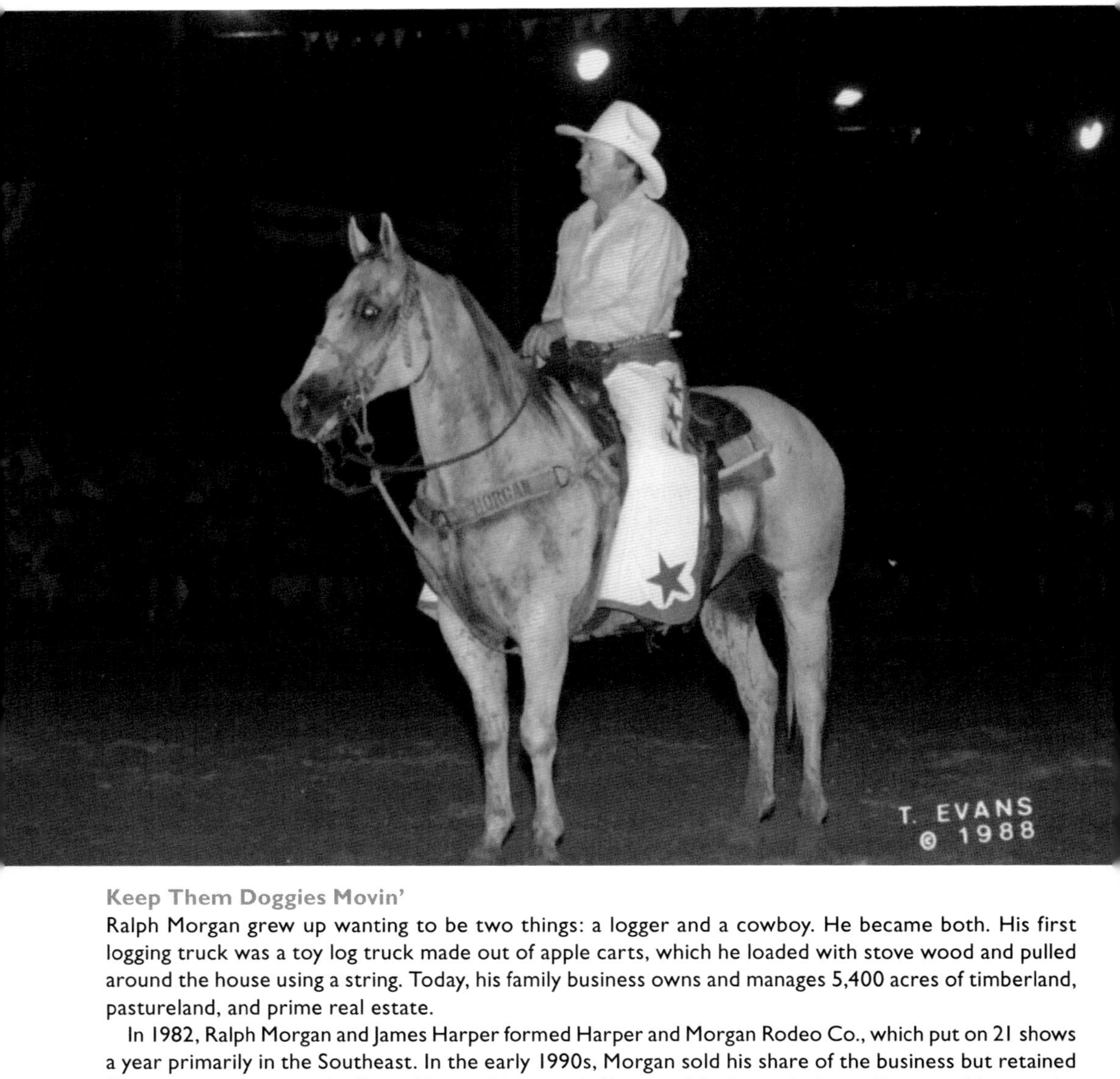

Keep Them Doggies Movin'

Ralph Morgan grew up wanting to be two things: a logger and a cowboy. He became both. His first logging truck was a toy log truck made out of apple carts, which he loaded with stove wood and pulled around the house using a string. Today, his family business owns and manages 5,400 acres of timberland, pastureland, and prime real estate.

In 1982, Ralph Morgan and James Harper formed Harper and Morgan Rodeo Co., which put on 21 shows a year primarily in the Southeast. In the early 1990s, Morgan sold his share of the business but retained 50 percent interest in the Dixie National Livestock Show and Rodeo in Jackson. For over 30 years, he has held two rodeos a year at the Ralph Morgan Arena in Lauderdale. In fact, before retiring from rodeo competition himself in 1982, Morgan won the Tri-State Rodeo Championship for calf-roping three times, for steer-wrestling, and also won numerous buckles and seven saddles. Many of his award-winning rodeo livestock made it to the National Finals Rodeo and have won numerous Southeastern circuit livestock awards. The Ralph Morgan Rodeo, which is affiliated with the Professional Rodeo Cowboys Association (PRCA), remains one of the most popular and well-attended rodeos in the state and is a 35-year tradition in Lauderdale held every April and August. (Courtesy of Ralph Morgan.)

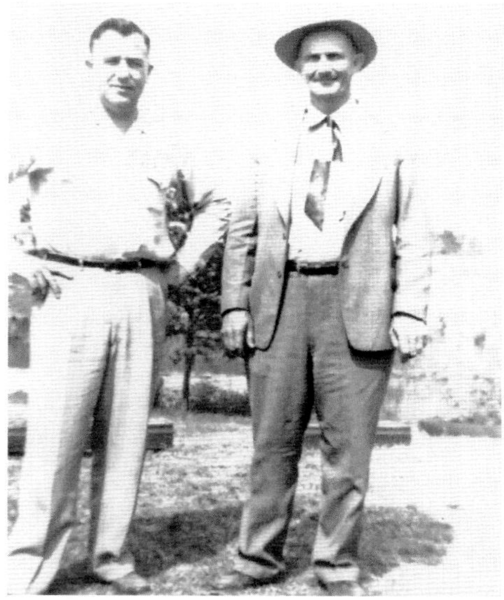

It Takes a Dream

Causeyville Race Track owner Johnny E. Robinson lived in the Shiloh community with his wife, Marjorie, and two daughters Johnnie Sue and Rose Mary. Robinson joined with his stepfather-in-law, Ben Enzor, and opened Causeyville Raceway in 1964 on Robinson's property located along Causeyville Road. Pictured on left is Johnny E. Robinson with Ben Enzor. (Courtesy of Rose Mary Robinson Onishi.)

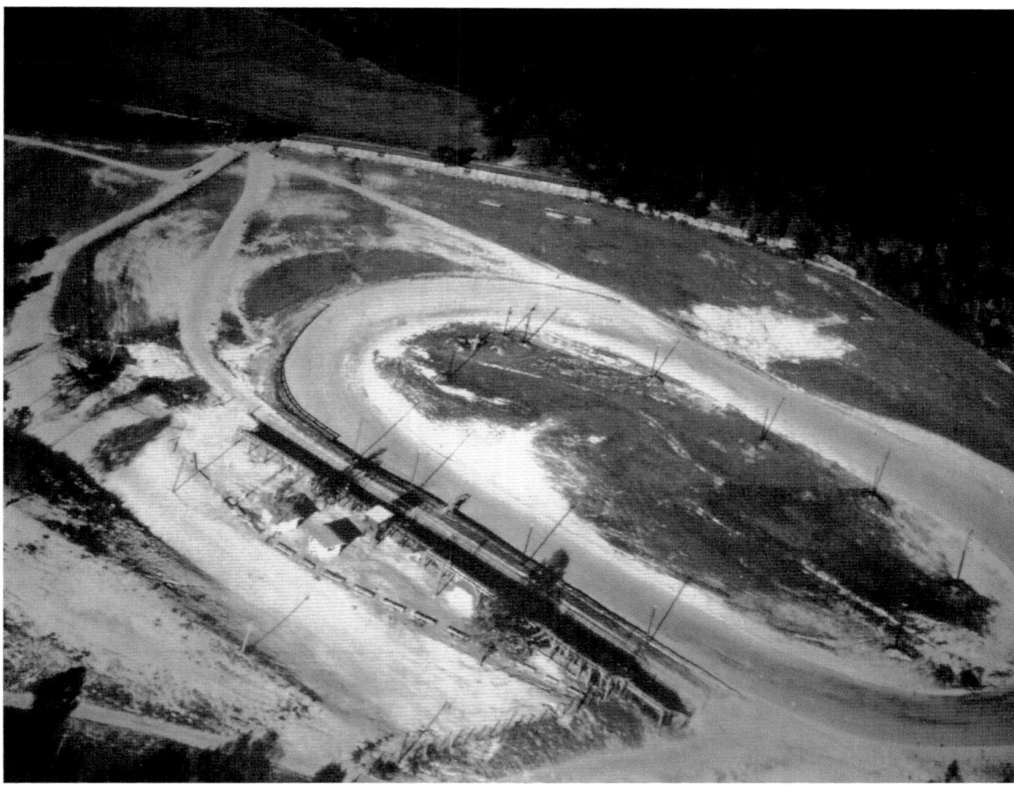

Cranking Out Speed

Causeyville Raceway thrived in the 1960s until Whynot Raceway drew its drivers away with larger pots. Johnny Robinson was a soft-spoken Southern gentleman who was held in high regard in his community. The raceway, now long silent, leaves behind fond memories of local racing legends. The racetrack was located on Causeyville Road in the Shiloh community. (Courtesy of Rosemary Robinson Onishi.)

Beard Hunter

Gene Nunnery, it is said, was a man who once talked turkey with anyone willing to listen. The former professional turkey hunter's passion for the hunt led to the invention of a pliable oral caller that mimics the sound of mating turkeys. His discovery of an archaeological quartzite site near Tallahatta sheds light on the movement of Native Americans. Nunnery is the author of *Old Pro Turkey Hunter* and *I Will Lift Up Mine Eyes Unto the Hills*. (Courtesy of Jeff Davis.)

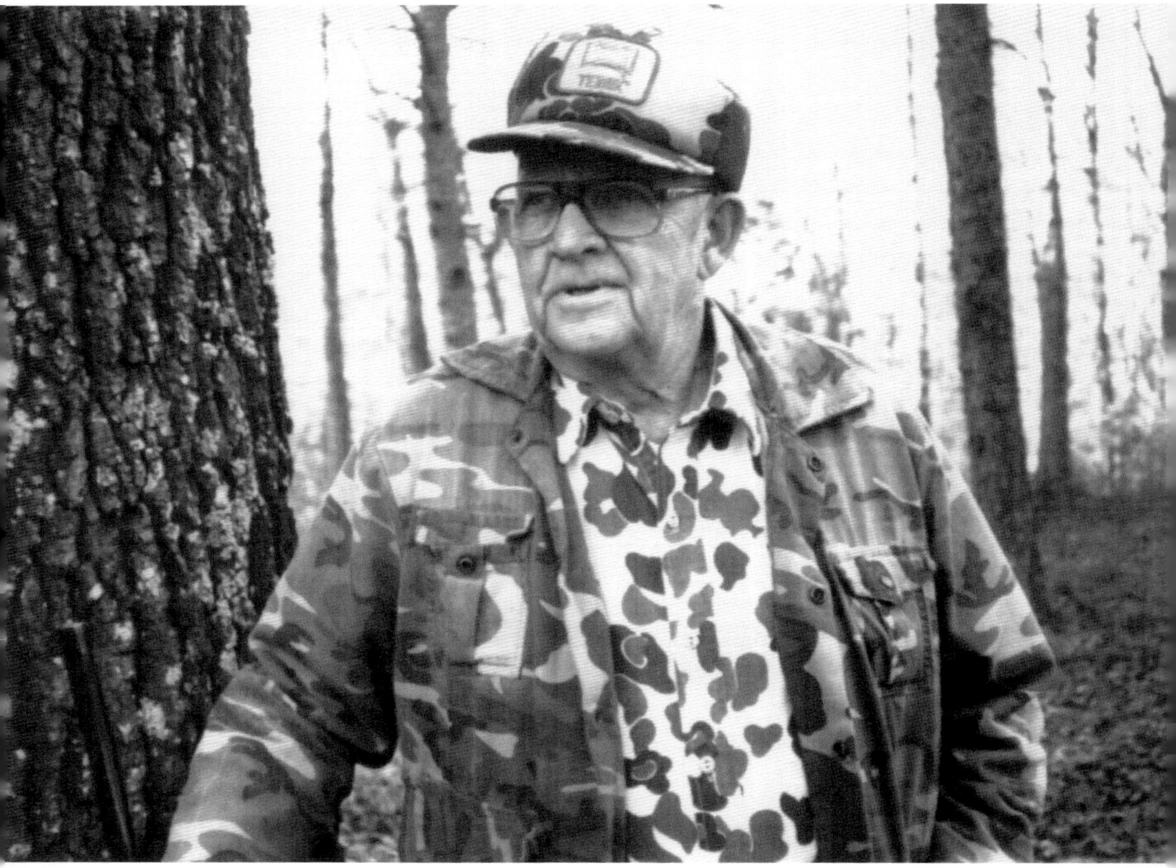

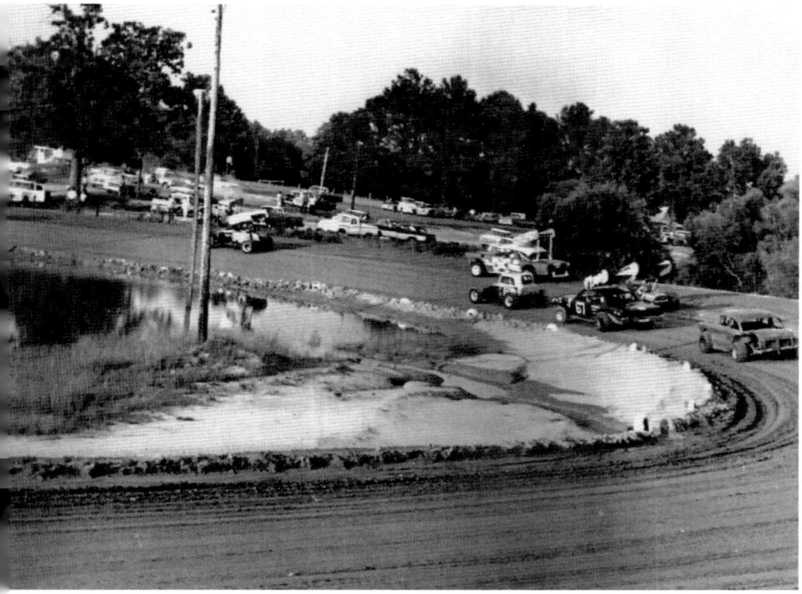

In the Fast Lane
On a Saturday night in 1966, Clyde Rutledge opened the gates of Whynot Raceway for the first time. The dirt track remained open under his supervision until 1998. The stands were filled with spectators who waited for the roar of engines to rise over the skies of Whynot. Fans cheered as cars streaked along the quarter-mile dirt track to the checkered flag. (Courtesy of Stacy Barr.)

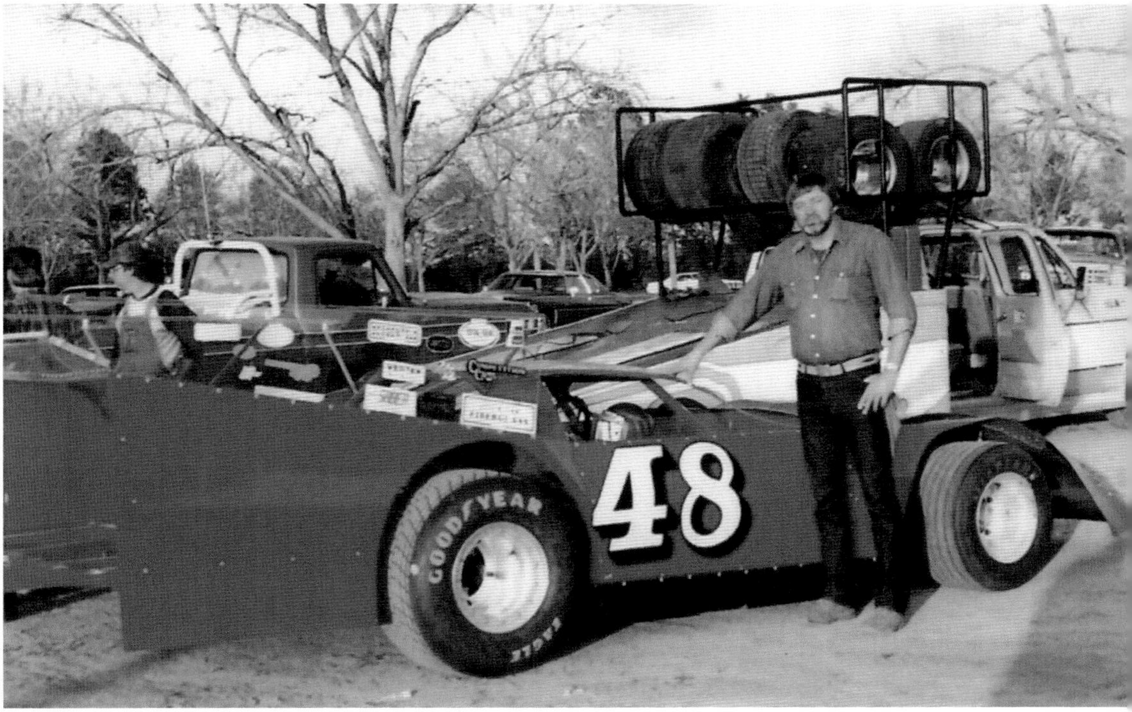

Rebel Rouser
During the late 1960s and 1970s, local racing greats Johnny Barr, Tommy Noblin, Travis Grant, and Mike Johnson were known for their dead-heat sprints to the finish line. Barr is pictured here with No. 48, *The Rebel*, owned by Tommy Shannon. Shannon once told Barr, "If you can't outrun it, buy it." Speed and ability are two common bonds between racecar drivers, but there is also camaraderie too—not only among the drivers, but with fans also. (Courtesy of Stacy Barr.)

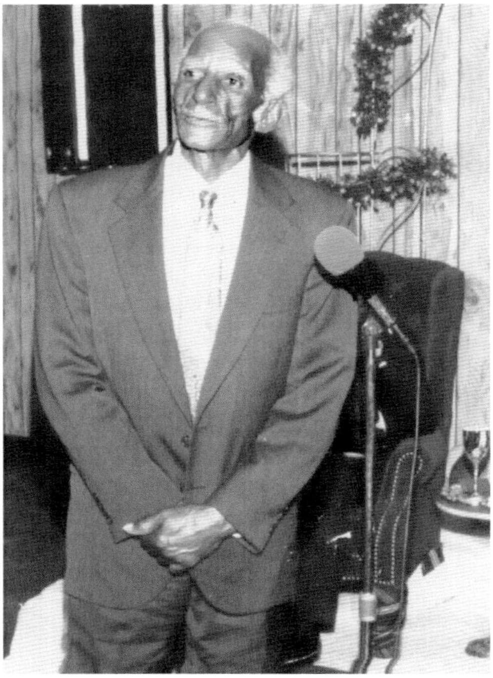

Batter Up!

Willie Boyd would probably tell you that hard work and parental guidance offer dividends. Boyd, who was born on March 22, 1928, managed and pitched for the Meridian White Sox. He played for the Acme Billings at Lloyd Royal's fairground, until he threw his arm away pitching wet balls in 1955. His son Donald said, "Lake Erie Ball Field was located on Tenth Avenue between Twenty-sixth Street and Twenty-eighth Street in Meridian. Willie Hayes, Satchel Paige, and Hank Aaron played on that field. We had it looking like a pro ball park; we even had bleachers on one side of the field." (Courtesy of Donald Boyd.)

The Swinger

"My mother was Gurthrie 'Sweetie' Boyd. Now, she was the ballplayer in the family," Donald Boyd (pictured) said. "She never missed anything we threw at her. Sweetie's swing was powerful; it looked like the bat bent. She could throw a softball 300 yards, and her knowledge and skill brought neighborhood children to her door. She helped Dad [Willie Boyd Sr.] with his sodding business. All those stones my brothers and I picked up and grass we shoveled was good exercise," he said. "As kids, we looked like pros against some of the local teams."

Willie Boyd Sr.'s son Michael played for the Los Angeles Dodgers, and Dennis "Oil Can" played for the Boston Red Sox. Donald, the youngest, played for the St. Louis Cardinals. Against the advice of his coach, their brother Neil missed the draft—and lost his opportunity to play with the Philadelphia Phillies.

One only has to look at the stats to know that the Boyds are a family of pros. (Courtesy of June Davis Davidson.)

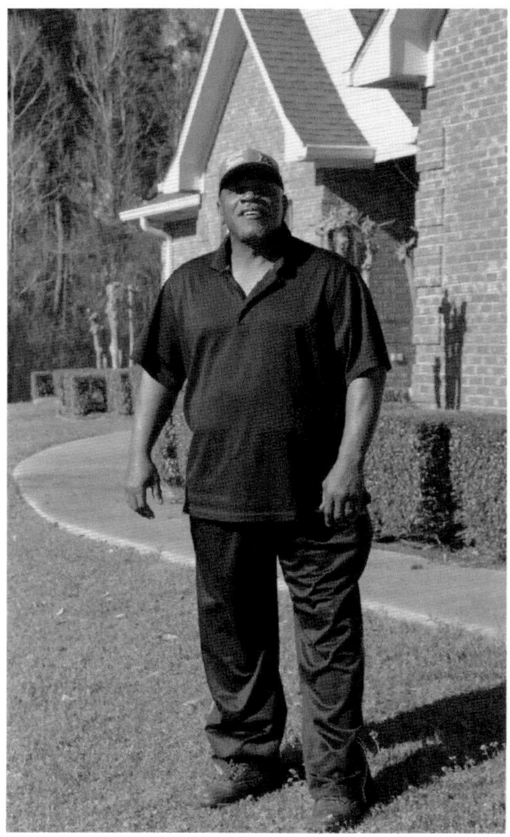

CHAPTER FIVE

Government and Military

A city depends on its successful mayors. Men like Henry Burns, who hired Meridian's first black policeman; Al Rosenbaum; who brought jobs to Meridian; and John Robert Smith, who spurred the city's growth—men with a vision that possess the desire and dedication to serve.

Lauderdale County heroes have served in our military and have fought and shed blood on foreign shores—men like Alex Loeb, Paul Irby, Sammie Wayne Davidson, Al Rosenbaum, John Aycock, and the many others who have felt the pain of war. We walk by our unsung heroes in malls, worship with them in church, cheer with them at ballgames, and cry with them at funerals. Brave men who have trudged through jungles in the Philippines, who have been held captive in subhuman conditions and tortured in prison camps.

They are our teachers, nurses, physicians, journalists, businessmen, and tradesmen; they are our patriotic men and women who answer the call for freedom on foreign shores. They are our disabled whose arms and legs were lost during battle. They carry the memory of lost friends who fought beside them. They are our heroes.

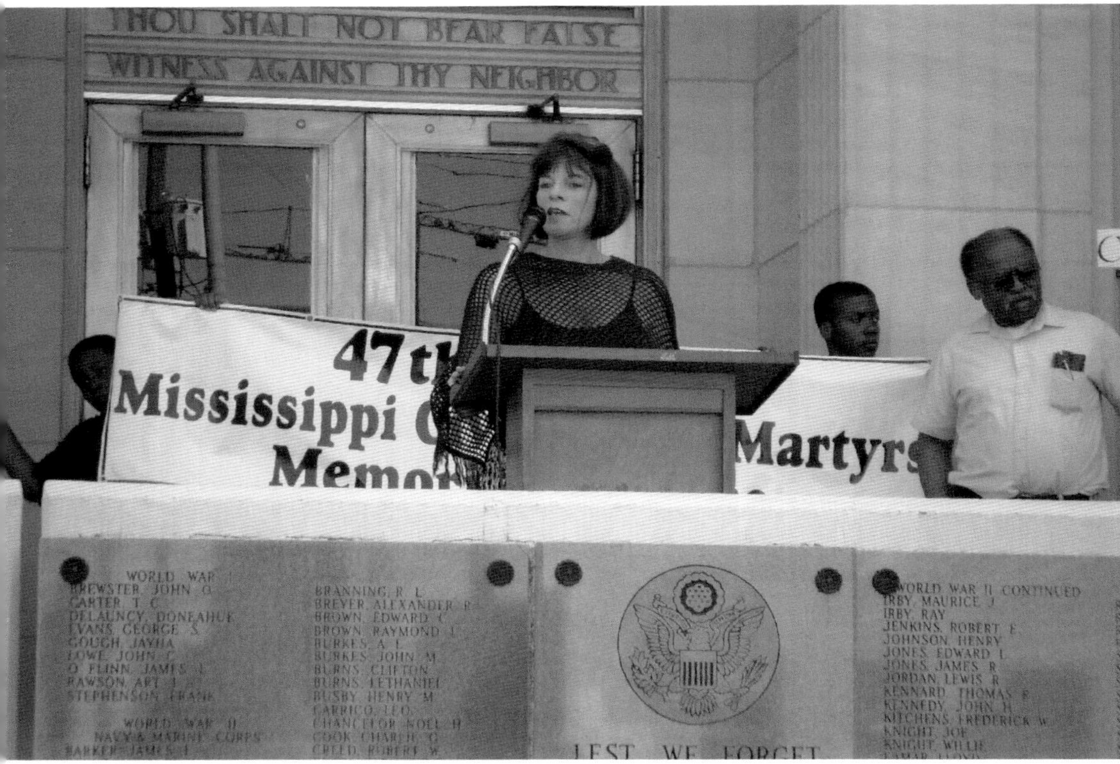

First Woman Mayor
Born in 1955 to Jean and George Merritt, Mayor Cheri Barry loves the Meridian community. Her grandmother Bonnie and her mother Jean started Bonnie Jean's, an upscale children's boutique, which lasted 20 years.

Working as a social worker for five years, Cheri became addicted to working with the less fortunate. Three days after Cheri took the Red Cross executive director position, 9/11 hit. She helped raise over $4.35 million for the 9/11 effort, something that had never been done in Meridian. Eight months later, the American Red Cross Key Chapter moved from a 1,700-square-foot building into a 5,000-square-foot building. Her efforts at the Red Cross helped carry Meridian and Lauderdale County through many disasters, including Katrina. The Meridian Chapter fed over 35,000 people every day and worked over 3,000 volunteers 24 hours a day.

"That gave me the strength I needed to do anything. I had to face individuals being without food and water and shelter and that had lost loved ones. I was going into homes that hadn't had water or food for several days. I did that for nine years. We have the most giving community that I have ever been a part of. Our citizens are the asset of the City of Meridian," said Mayor Barry.

After a serious discussion with her family, Cheri decided to run for mayor—and won! Since then, her goal has been to bring everyone around the table, get everyone's advice and suggestions, and to find a solution. "I am a problem solver," she said.

Mayor Barry expects the downtown district explode within the next few years. "Many are coming back to live." Now that the business division of MSU is here, more life is coming to downtown Meridian than in years past.

Mayor Barry champions diversity, because it reveals the character, charisma, and heritage of the various cultures. She believes that when people of different cultures and backgrounds work together, a community grows. "I see our races coming together and making Meridian whole," said Barry. "Bringing Meridian together has been one of the most enjoyable parts of being mayor." (Author's collection.)

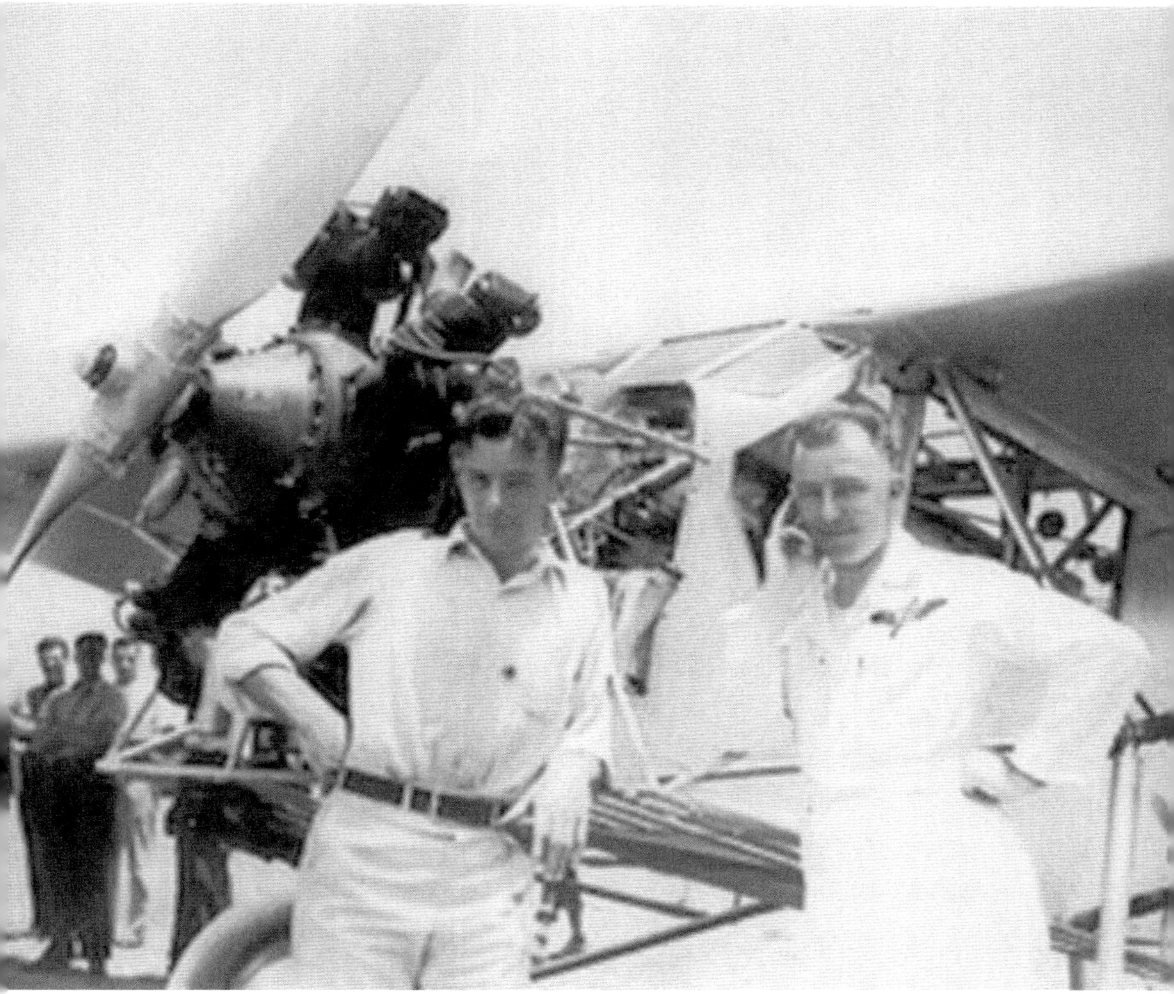

Buzzing Duo

Born in Kemper County, Algene "Al" Key and his brother Fred managed the Meridian Municipal Airport, which opened in the 1930s. Key Field, as it is known today, also included a flight school. On June 4, 1935, Fred and Al Key's borrowed plane, the *Ole Miss*, broke the world record for sustained flight. Al Key became mayor of Meridian in 1956 after defeating incumbent Henry Burns. Key served as the mayor until 1973. (Courtesy of Lauderdale County Department of Archives and History.)

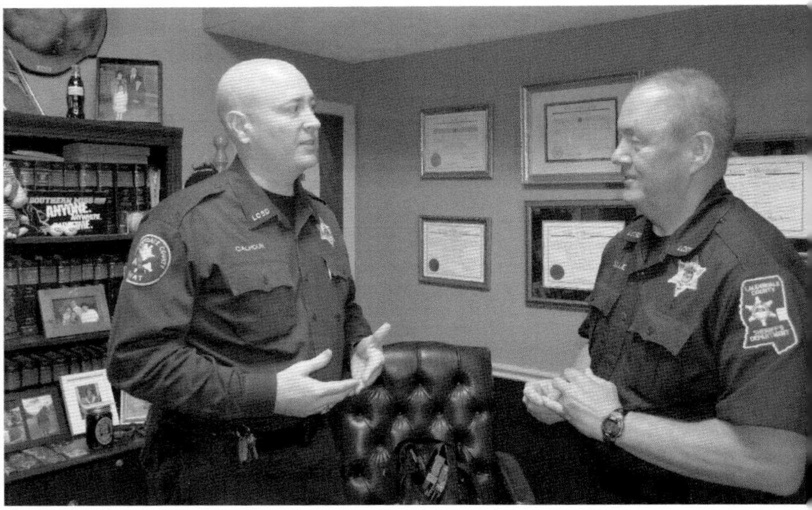

Answering the Call of Duty

Billy Sollie won the office of Lauderdale County sheriff in January 1996. In April, Ward Calhoun came on board as chief deputy. On July 8, 2003, the Lauderdale County Sheriff's Department faced their most difficult task: the Lockheed Martin plant shooting. Sheriff Sollie participated in national media interviews while also handling the criminal investigation. The sheriff's department was the first on the scene. In an interview, Sollie said, "This is something that's just not supposed to happen in Lauderdale County, Mississippi." The shooter killed five workers, wounded eight, and then killed himself. Sollie and his staff continue to serve Lauderdale County. (Author's collection.)

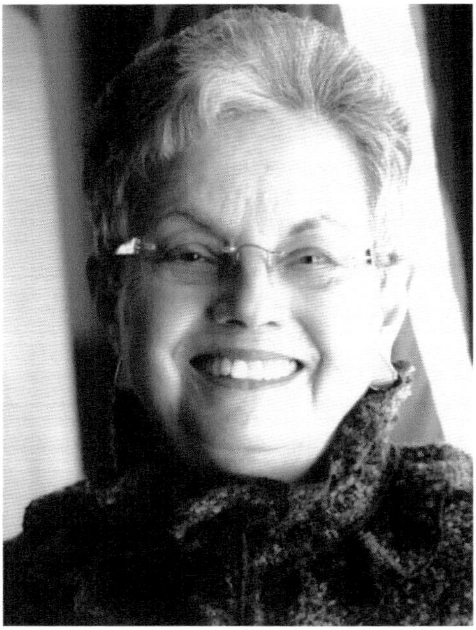

His Grace Is Sufficient for Me

Barbara Henson, whose roots date back to Meridian since 1880, has been a day care guardian for children since 1958, the year she began to keep children in her home. In 1968, she moved to her current location on State Boulevard where she began to "major in minors." This included teaching children about the love of God.

In 1976, she opened Barbara Henson's Swim Gym, adjoining the center, expanding the facility from one acre and an old house to a five-acre, state-of-the-art day care center with three pools The Barbara Henson Day Care Center and Swim Gym is licensed to care for 237 children. The center has a staff of 33 full-time employees in addition to part-time students who aid in the weekday care of children of working parents in Meridian and Lauderdale County. Area students who attend Barbara Henson's Daycare and Swim Gym are shuttled by bus from Meridian's schools to the center. In the past 47 years, three generations have passed through her doors with swimsuits, schoolbooks, and homework.

Barbara is a former coach of the Meridian Swim Association and serves on the board for the National Child Care Association. She is president of the Mississippi Child Care Association. Her achievements and awards are numerous and speak of her dedication to Meridian.

In 1993, she was elected by the Meridian City Council as its first woman president. She has served six consecutive terms on the council. Barbara and her husband, Ralph, are the parents of three children, Beverly, Ralph, and Rick; and have four grandchildren.

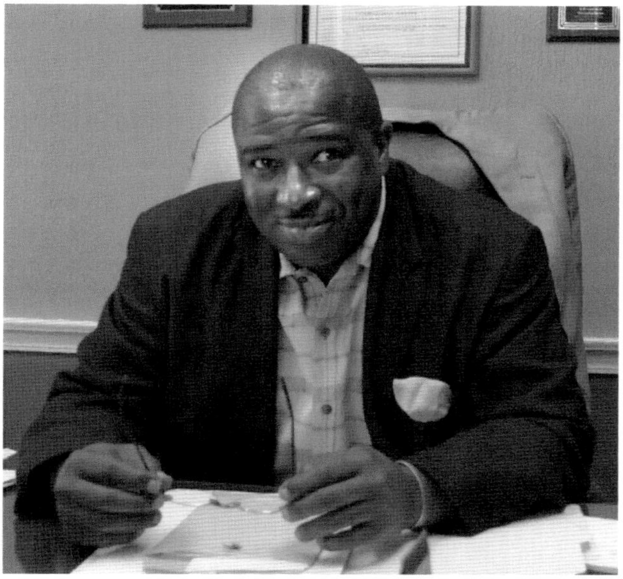

Planning Ahead
For four terms, the citizens of District 4 have elected Joe Norwood as a supervisor. The board of supervisors have elected him three times as its president. "When I leave and drive through my neighborhood, I can see a difference," said Norwood. "It's a lot better than when I found it." You have to be strategically planned, he said. "I am thinking about the kids that haven't been born." (Author's collection.)

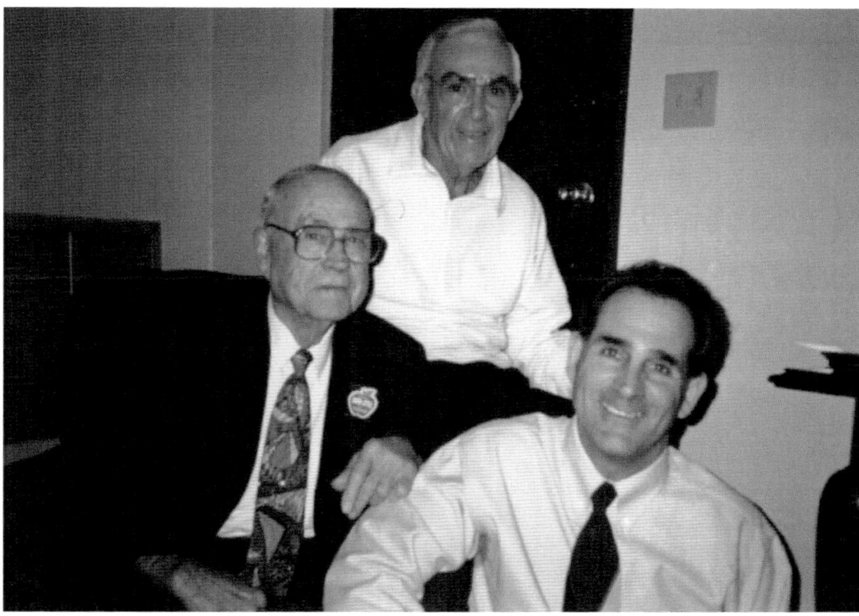

A Family Tradition
Douglas Little was born on January 4, 1917. His career as an educator began in Lauderdale County's school system. The former Southeast Lauderdale School basketball coach and principal became superintendent of education from 1972 to 1984. His wife, math teacher Tommie Lou Little, taught at Dixie High School early in her career before teaching school at Meehan and Martin. She was school principal at Vimville and taught at Southeast before she joined the faculty at Meridian Community College. On the left is Douglas Little, and his son David is on the right. In the center is Jackie Roberson. They are pictured just after the news David had won his first election as superintendent of education. (Courtesy of David Little.)

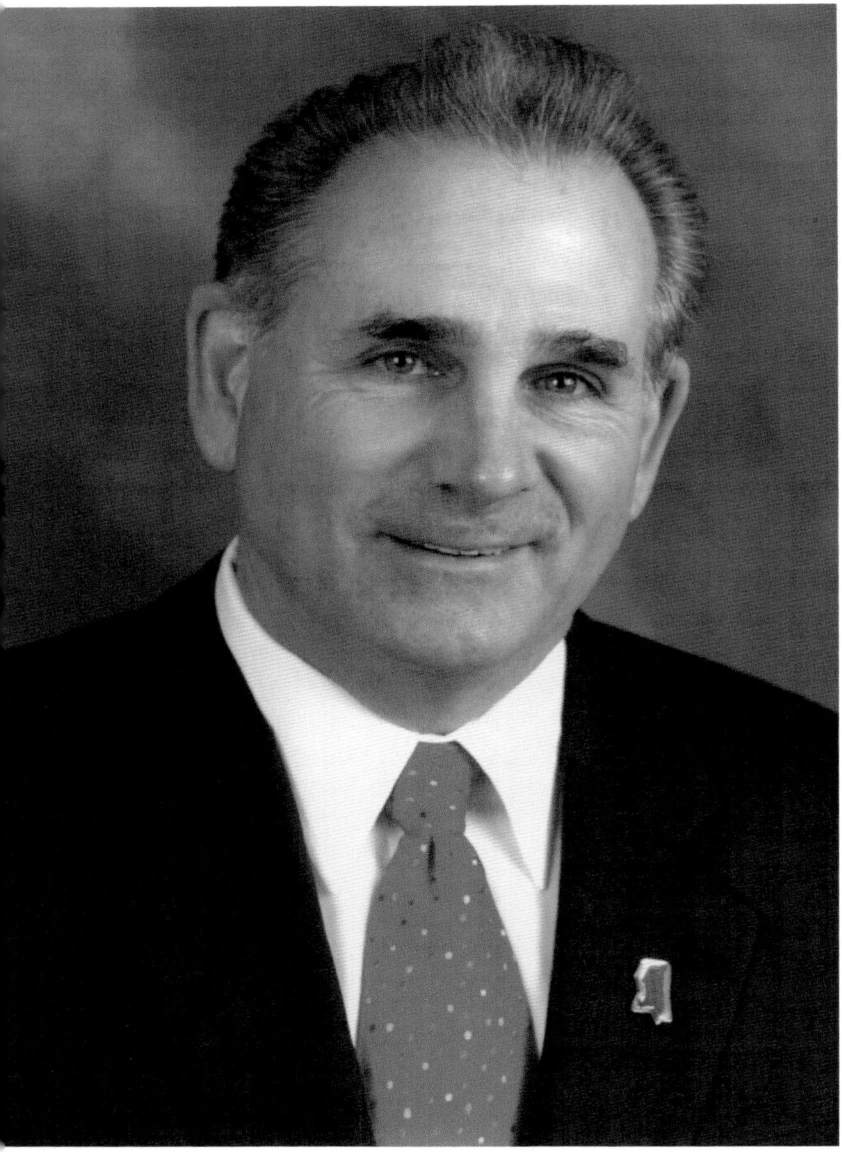

Dedication to Education

For three consecutive terms, David Little served as the superintendent of education of the Lauderdale County School Districts, overseeing Clarkdale Attendance Center, Southeast Lauderdale, Northeast Lauderdale, and West Lauderdale.

He taught chemistry and biology at Southeast Lauderdale School. David comes from a family of educators; his mother, Tommie Lou, was the principal at Whynot School, and his father, Douglas, was the principal at Southeast Lauderdale School.

David Little's parents instilled the values he has tried to live by. One of those is to honor his parents, who often told him to "leave things better than when you got here."

David Little worked for A.J. Lyon as a salesman in the early 1970s before he felt the call to teach. "One day as I was leaving Desoto, I pulled off the road and prayed for God's guidance; this is when I surrendered to teaching and returned to college."

"As superintendent of education, I tried to make a significant difference in the lives of children," Little said. David and his father, Douglas, held the office longer than any superintendent in Lauderdale County history.

"We need teachers in the classroom that provide quality education; we simply can't afford to miss a year of educating our children," Little said. His passion for teaching is shared by those who are dedicated to educating our youth. Our youth deserve the opportunity to "make this world a better place."

Portraits of Douglas and David Little are on display at the Meridian Community College Hall of Fame in recognition for their contributions to education and the community. David is married to Sandra Gibson Little. They have one son, Davey. (Courtesy of David Little.)

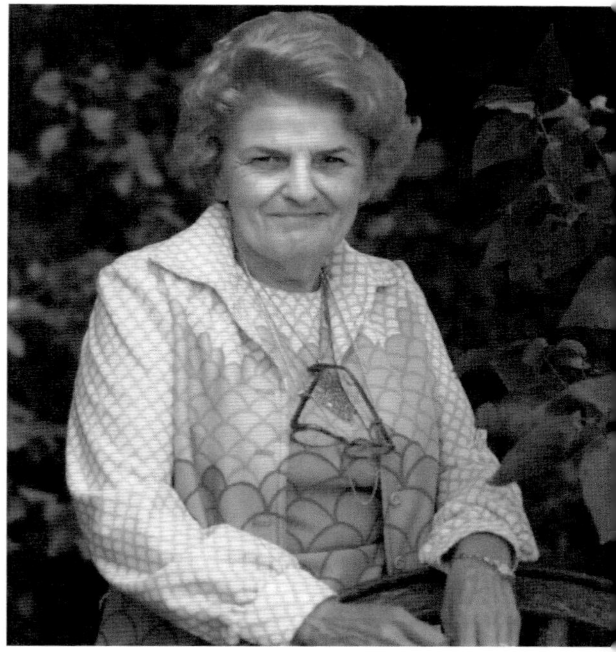

Apples to Apples

Douglas and Tommie Lou had two children who were also educators. David Little and Cecilia Harper both taught at Southeast Lauderdale School. During Tommie Lou's early career in education, she taught at Dixie High School before she became principal at Whynot School. She later taught at Meridian Community College. (Courtesy of David Little.)

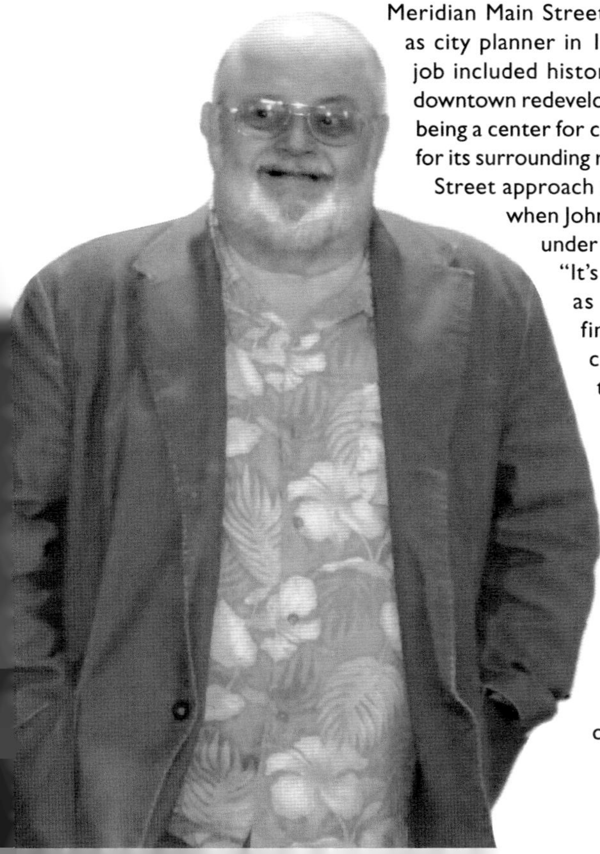

Downtown, Where All the Lights Are Bright!

Meridian Main Street executive director John McClure was hired as city planner in 1983 when Alfred Rosenbaum was mayor. His job included historic preservation, economic development, and downtown redevelopment/revitalization. "Meridian has a tradition of being a center for commerce, for food, beverage and entertainment for its surrounding regions and an even bigger market area." The Main Street approach to downtown was first developed in the 1970s when John pitched the idea of a Main Street program to be under the City of Meridian's Redevelopment Authority. "It's my hope and expectation that we can reemerge as the center for outstanding entertainment, fine dining, and great regional ethnic and home cooking," John said, adding that he would like to see downtown continue to build its strong presence of residential downtown living. "There is an exciting, vibrant atmosphere downtown, so the more people we have living downtown, the more demand and the easier it becomes to invest in downtown." Meridian Main Street has received state, regional, and national recognition for his downtown revitalization efforts and has presented papers on the subject to international forums. In 2013, McClure joined Mayor Percy Bland's administration as Meridian's Community Development director. (Courtesy of Clay Hamilton.)

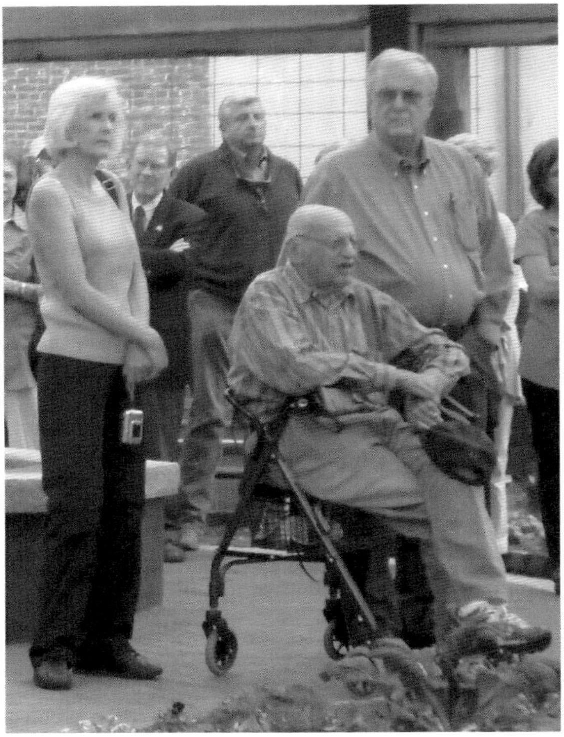

Flying High

Ike Alfred "Al" Rosenbaum, a Marine Corps pilot, served in World War II and landed the second plane during the invasion of Iwo Jima. He was awarded the Air Medal for heroism. Born on March 21, 1920, from 1977 to 1985 Rosenbaum was one of the city's most progressive mayors. He graduated Vanderbilt University with a bachelor's degree. Active in community affairs. Rosenbaum, along with Sen. John C. Stennis were instrumental in acquiring the Naval Air Station in 1957. He is credited for securing Lockheed Aircraft for Meridian. Seated, Al Rosenbaum is pictured with his daughter Ann and her husband, Allan Stewart. (Courtesy of Richelle Putnam.)

East End Dreams

James Samuel Edwards graduated from Meridian High. After serving in the US Marines, he joined the Meridian Police Department, where he later became a detective. Edwards continued his education in forensics, homicide investigation, and criminal justice courses at the University of Alabama, Ole Miss, and Mississippi State University. In 1960, Edwards received an invitation from J. Edgar Hoover to attend the FBI Academy in Washington, DC. His career includes positions at the UN for Ambassador Adlai Stevenson, as assistant chief of police, coroner, constable, justice court judge, and municipal court judge pro tem for Meridian. From left to right are Luke Scarborough, Dizzy Dean, and James (Jim) Edwards. (Courtesy of Jim Beau Edwards.)

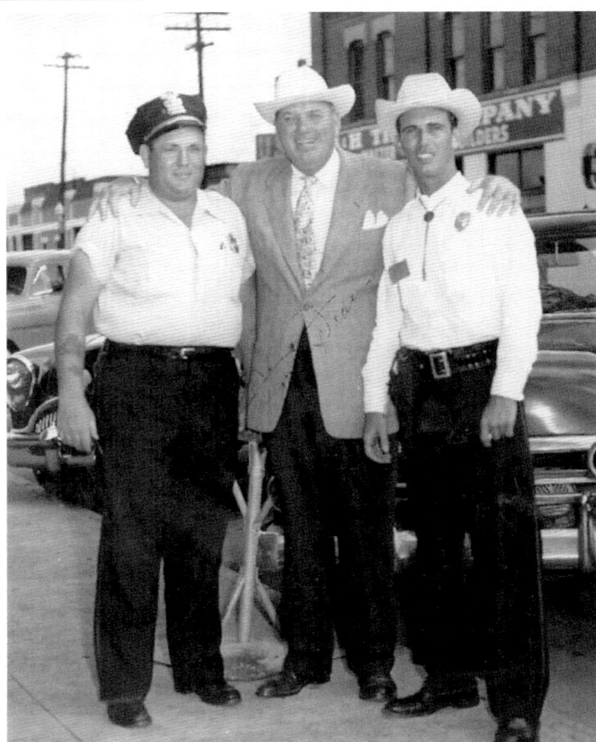

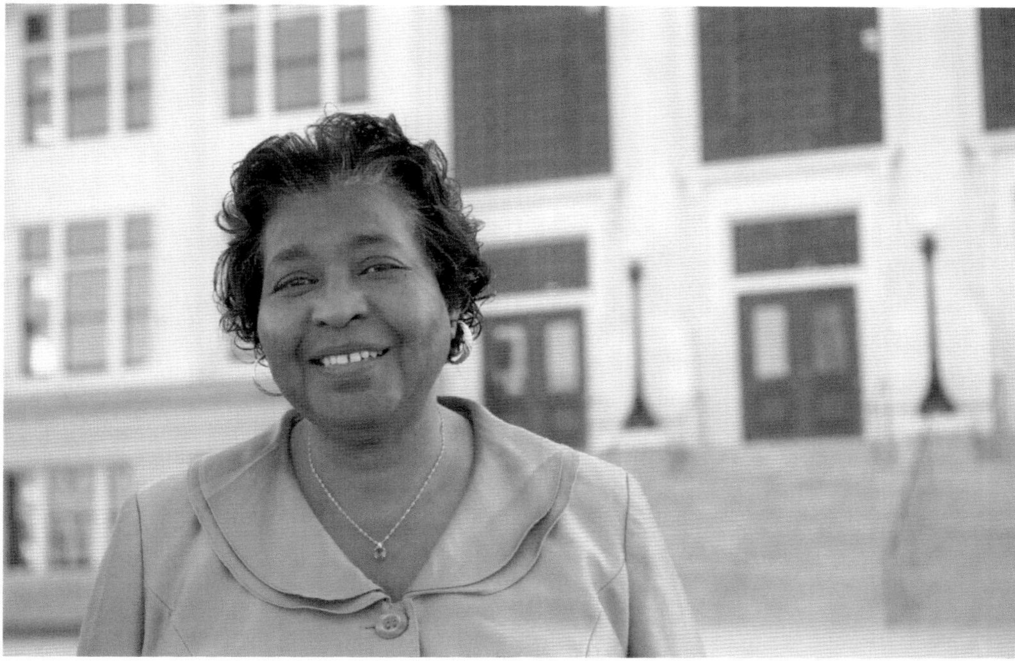

Serving through Leadership

A council member since December 1999 and a retired teacher with Meridian Public Schools, Mary Perry continues to serve her community as a concerned citizen and as a member of St. John's Missionary Baptist Church. Mary was reelected three times. Her desire as a representative was to see crime diminish in the city. She has been married to William H. Perry Sr. for over 50 years. (Above, courtesy of Mary Perry; below, author's collection.)

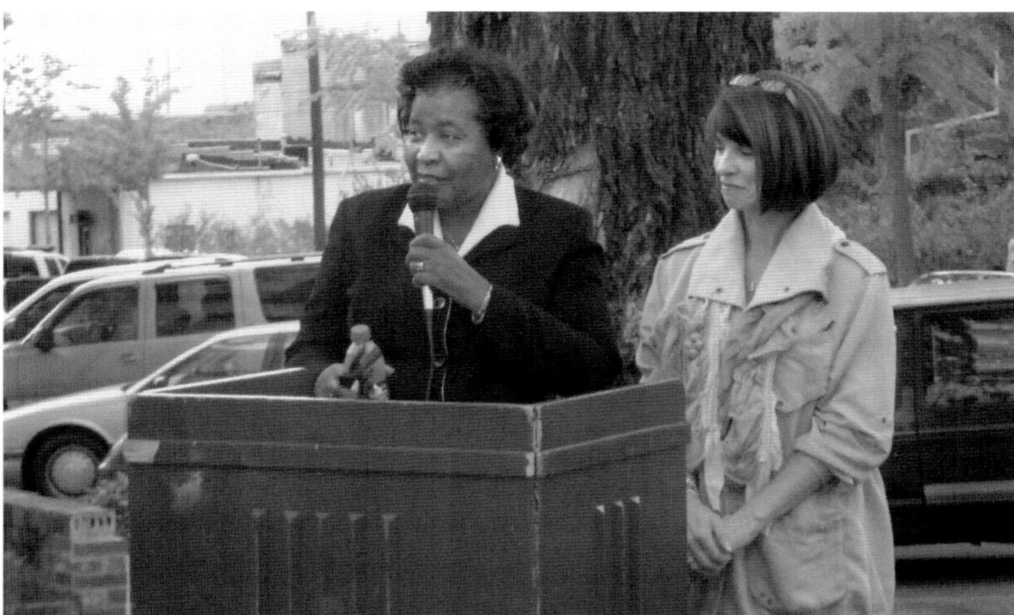

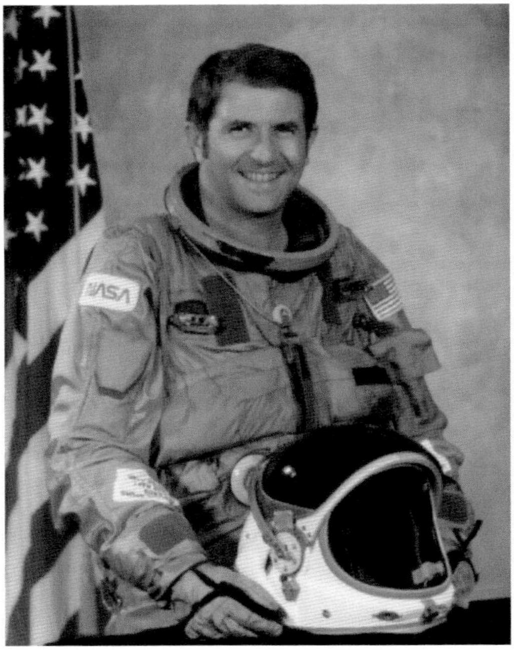

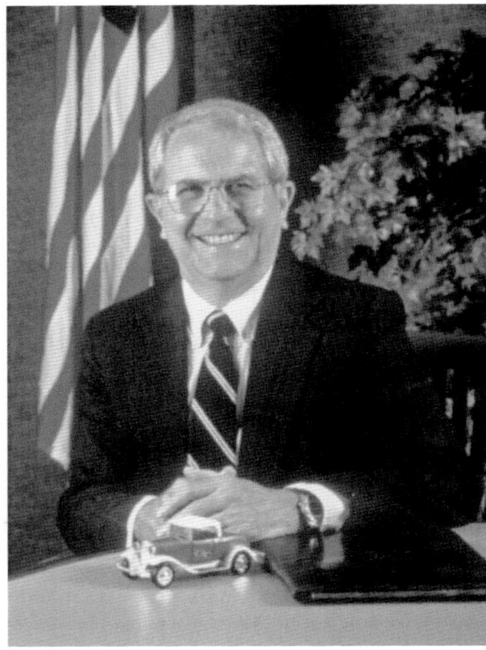

Reaching for the Stars
Astronaut and retired vice admiral Richard H. Truly, a former Boy Scout of Troop No. 2 (led by Frank Williams), made his dream into reality when his spacecraft became the first winged spacecraft to land without a parachute. "My first orbital flight was aboard *Columbia*. It was the second flight of the shuttle, and I lifted off on my birthday, November 12, 1981. This event remains vivid in my memory. The colors of the Earth are magnificent, and I never saw so many stars in my life. Floating around the cabin makes you into an eight-year-old kid again!" Truly was instrumental in rebuilding the space program as associate administrator for space flight at NASA. (Images courtesy of NASA and Richard H. Truly.)

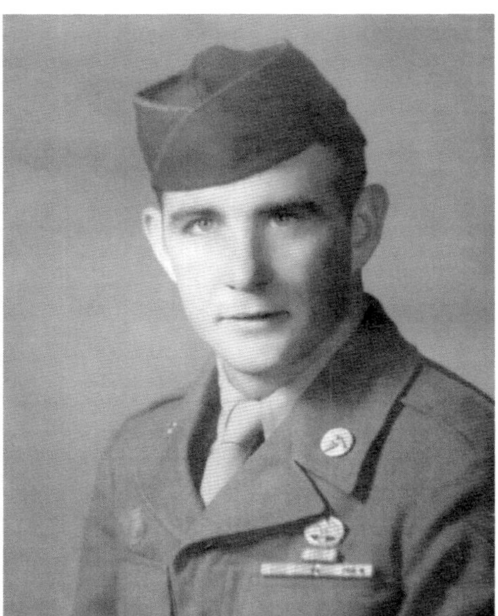

Paradise Is Called Home
Paul D. Irby was drafted into the military on February 13, 1942. He served in the Medical Corps of the 40th Infantry Division under Gen. Douglas MacArthur, commander of US forces in the Pacific. Irby left Oahu, Hawaii, with the first unit, 40th Division, to Guadalcanal and underwent jungle warfare training. He fought in battles in New Britain, North Luzon, Formosa, Leyte Island. Intense fighting prevented Irby from removing his combat boots for three months. "He received eight battle stars for his service. (Courtesy of Virginia Culpepper Irby.)

The Decoder

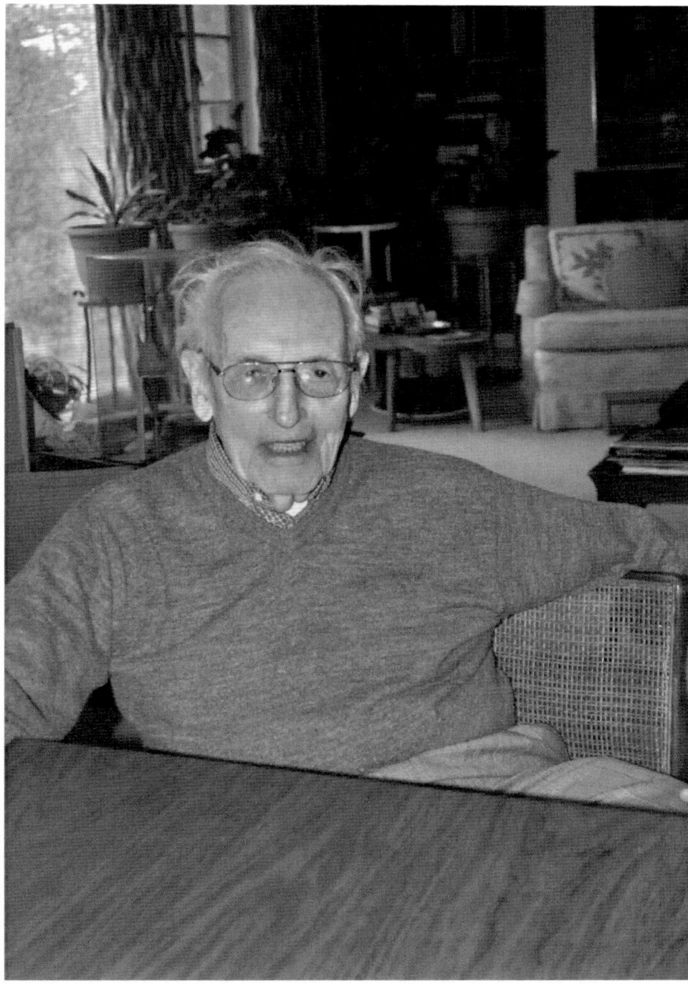

When journalist, merchandiser, and World War II veteran Alex Loeb was young, "Meridian was a much larger town that it is today." The 96-year-old Loeb said, "When I was young, I wanted to be a writer." He acquired a position at the *Meridian Star* and arrived at the paper at 6:00 a.m. "I worked as a reporter until noon, then went to the cotton exchange to get the price of cotton." Loeb graduated from college with a degree in journalism.

Loeb's grandfather Alexander Loeb opened Alex Loeb Men's Store in 1887 in the Rosenbaum Building. On June 15, 1926, Alex moved into his new building on Fifth Street. The store carried men's, ladies', and children's clothes, as well as cosmetics, shoes, sporting goods, and Boy Scout and Girl Scout merchandise. "Basically, it was a department store," said Robert Loeb, great-grandson of Alex. "Alex built the building, and Judge Little ran sporting goods department." Loeb's had locations in Starkville, Oxford, and Laurel.

Loeb was an aide to Adm. Chester W. Nimitz during World War II. "My boss was a real nice guy, but tough. "Admiral," I asked, "I know you've got waterproof shoulders, but maybe there is a crack because I've got something to cry about. For three years, I've put in to go overseas but my request is torn up." Nimitz said, "Loeb, you find a ship that's going back to the naval yard for repairs and I'll put you on that ship for training." Admiral Nimitz had written a personal letter to the skipper of the ship: "This is my aide, and I want him trained and to have a couple of weeks leave." Loeb later sent a message to the admiral, joking, "Come get me; I've been kidnapped." The admiral sent a five-star boat to pick him up.

While serving in the Navy during wartime, Loeb decoded messages sent from President Roosevelt to his commander in chief of the Pacific Fleet, Adm. Chester W. Nimitz. Lt. Alex Loeb mustered out of service in 1945.

"When I came home, my mother's brothers took me on a moonlight walk and said, 'We want to talk to you. Everything your mother's got is in that business, and it's not doing well. You and your brother need to get in there and protect her interest.' My wife and I had been married for 65 years when she died." (Courtesy of June Davis Davidson.)

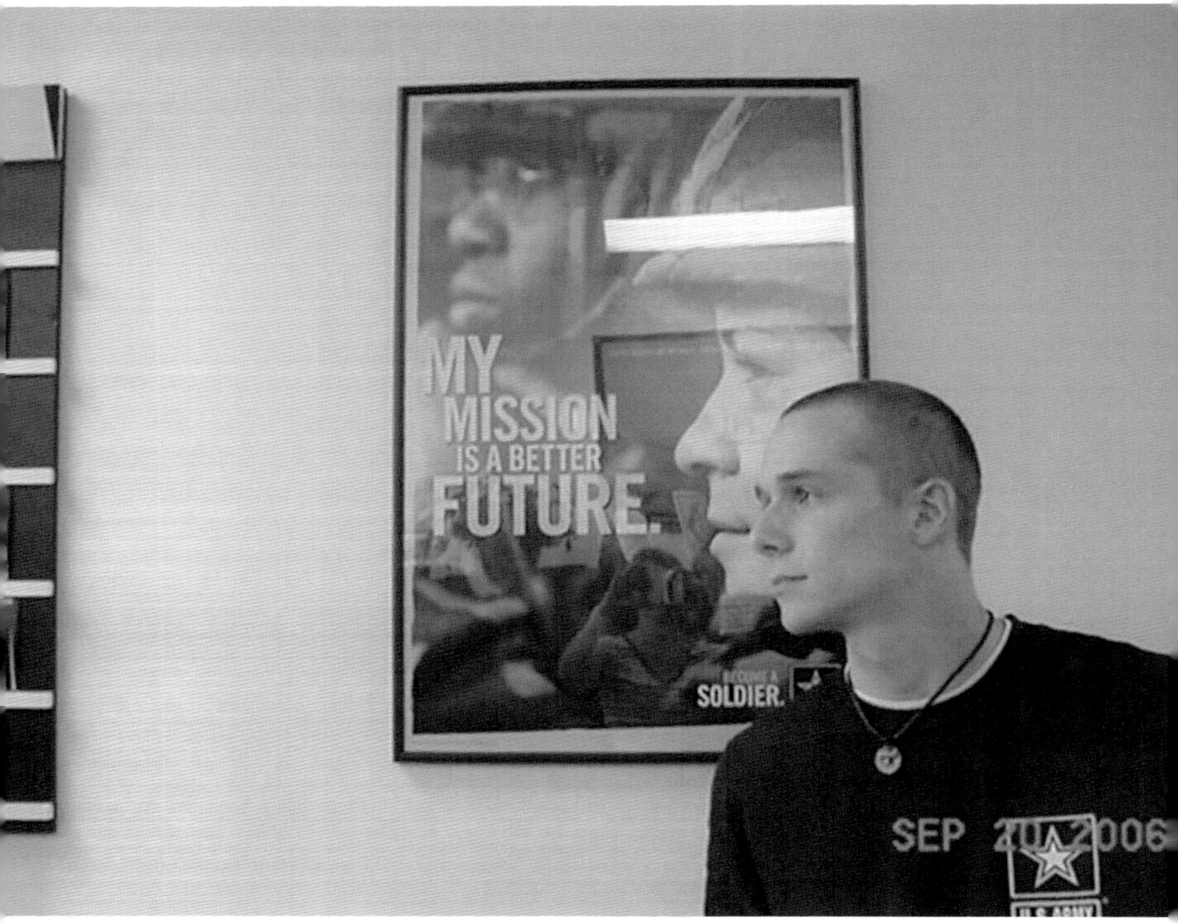

Living on a Miracle

John Aycock was serving as a corporal in the US Army, 41st Infantry Division, in Kandahar, Afghanistan, when his vehicle, complete with machine gun, radio equipment, and supplies, struck an improvised explosive device (IED). The blast hurled their vehicle into the air, and it landed upside-down in a deep hole in the sand. Knocked unconscious from the blast, John, who was team leader of the patrol, awoke to his battle buddy Jacob Southern yelling for a medic. John realized he was hanging upside-down in the burning vehicle and could not pull himself out or call for help because his hand-mic was broken. Nicholaus Ganey, the gunner on top of the vehicle, was trapped beneath the engine block and surrounded by flames. Buried underground from the blast, John was finally able to release himself from his safety belt. However, his huge backpack was a hindrance, and he could not exit the vehicle. Finally detaching his backpack, John used his helmet to dig out from under the vehicle. Once out, he and Southern threw dirt on the flames. Assistance arrived, and Southern was flown by chopper to the hospital. John, however, refused to leave Ganey underground and screaming in pain. With the aid of a Blackhawk helicopter, they were able to free Ganey, who had suffered serious burns. Though John's nose was broken and he had a concussion, he helped get Ganey to the chopper, and both were flown to Kandahar Airfield hospital for treatment. It is a miracle they survived. Each soldier received the Purple Heart. (Courtesy of John Aycock.)

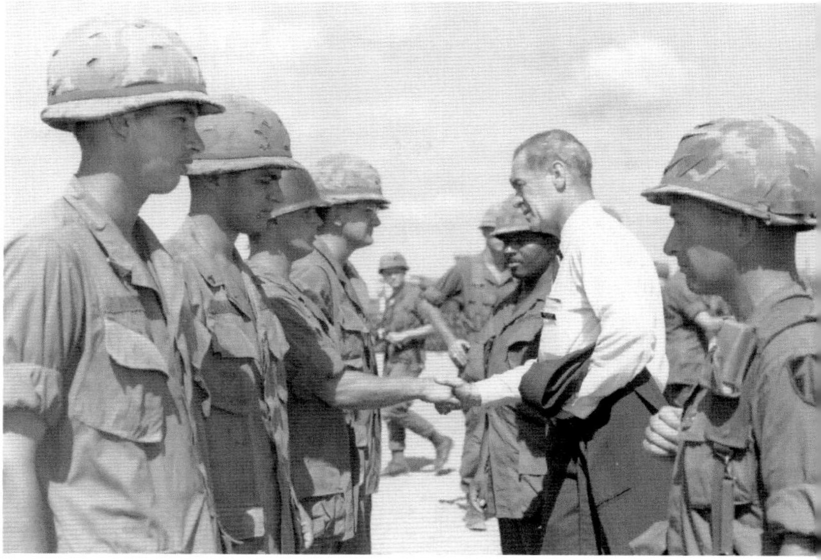

G.V. Sonny Montgomery
Beween 1956 and 1966, conservative Democrat and US Representative Gillespie V. "Sonny" Montgomery represented Mississippi's 3rd District in Congress. From 1967 to 1997, he served as US representative from Mississippi. His greatest legislative victory was the enactment of the bill that bears his name: the Montgomery GI Bill. As a World War II veteran, he believed the country should provide educational benefits to its service members. Montgomery helped make sure that veterans received health care, low-income home loans, and educational opportunities. His efforts aided greatly in keeping Mississippi military bases open. Named in his honor are the Veterans Affairs Medical Center in Jackson, the National Guard complex in Meridian, the Navy Reserve Center at Naval Air Station Meridian, a Lauderdale County Industrial park, and the Montgomery Institute, which operates in East Mississippi and West Alabama. (Courtesy of the Montgomery Institute.)

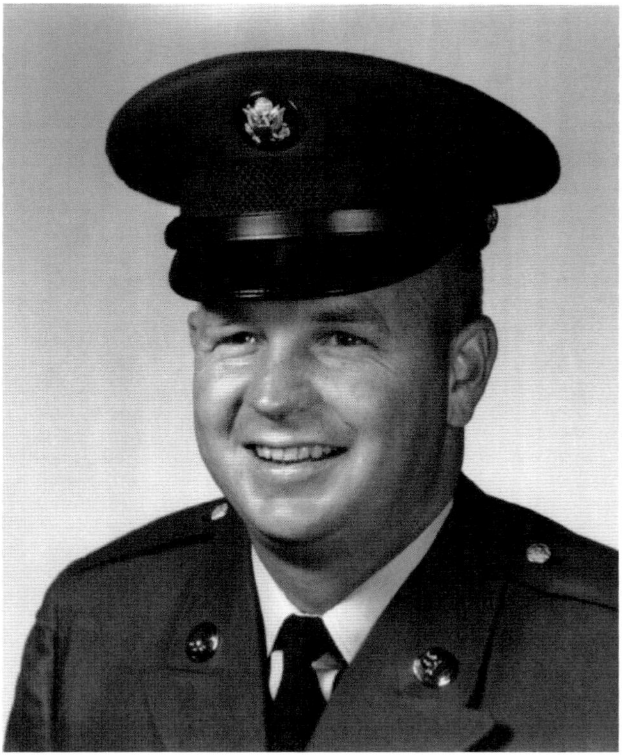

An Act of Bravery
Sammie Wayne Davidson resided in Lauderdale County when he was drafted in 1968. While fighting opposing forces in Vietnam, Davidson volunteered for a hazardous mission, one that would take him by river into enemy territory where he, alone, exchanged fire with the Vietcong. The enemy retreated into a cave under Davidson's hail of fire. Davidson held them until his unit arrived. For his courage, he received two bronze medals. Davidson's brother Alton Ray "Cecil" served on the USS *California* in World War II, and his brother Walter "Earl" served during the Korean conflict. (Courtesy of Sammie Wayne Davidson.)

INDEX